BINGHAM GENEALOGICAL TREE

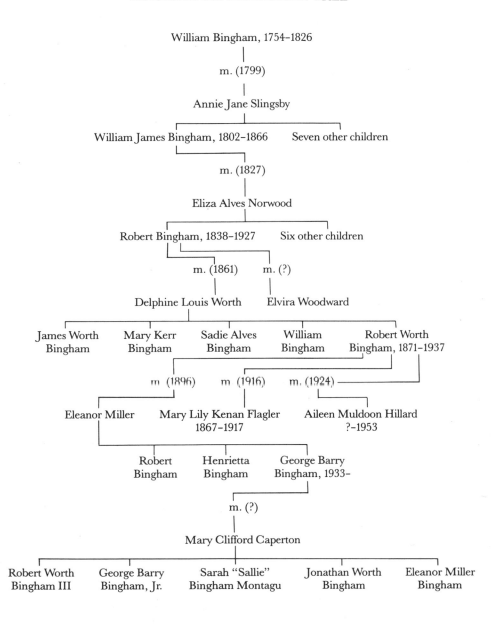

William Bingham, 1754–1826

m. (1799)

Annie Jane Slingsby

William James Bingham, 1802–1866 — Seven other children

m. (1827)

Eliza Alves Norwood

Robert Bingham, 1838–1927 — Six other children

m. (1861) — m. (?)

Delphine Louis Worth — Elvira Woodward

James Worth Bingham — Mary Kerr Bingham — Sadie Alves Bingham — William Bingham — Robert Worth Bingham, 1871–1937

m. (1896) — m. (1916) — m. (1924)

Eleanor Miller — Mary Lily Kenan Flagler 1867–1917 — Aileen Muldoon Hillard ?–1953

Robert Bingham — Henrietta Bingham — George Barry Bingham, 1933–

m. (?)

Mary Clifford Caperton

Robert Worth Bingham III — George Barry Bingham, Jr. — Sarah "Sallie" Bingham Montagu — Jonathan Worth Bingham — Eleanor Miller Bingham

THE
BINGHAMS
OF
LOUISVILLE

THE BINGHAMS OF LOUISVILLE

The Dark History Behind One of America's Great Fortunes

DAVID LEON CHANDLER
WITH MARY VOELZ CHANDLER

Crown Publishers, Inc.

NEW YORK

OTHER BOOKS BY DAVID LEON CHANDLER

Henry Flagler
100 Tons of Gold
Criminal Brotherhood

Portions of this book have previously appeared in *Southern Magazine*.

Published by Crown Publishers, Inc., 225 Park Avenue South, New York, New York, 10003 and simultaneously in Canada by the Canadian MANDA Group.

CROWN is a trademark of Crown Publishers, Inc.

Manufactured in the United States of America

Library of Congress Cataloging-in-Publication Data
Chandler, David Leon.
The Binghams of Louisville.
Includes index.
1. Bingham family.   2. Louisville (Ky.)–Biography.
I. Title.
CT274.B52C48   1987   976.9′44   86-31131

ISBN 0-517-56895-0

10 9 8 7 6 5 4 3 2 1

First Edition

CONTENTS

Preface

HIS BOOK IS A resurrection, sprung back to life after being pronounced dead by the original contractor, Macmillan Publishing Company. In the spring of 1987, barely three weeks before *The Binghams of Louisville* was scheduled to be shipped to retail stores with the book endorsed by favorable prepublication reviews, Macmillan halted the press run. Three months later, on July 21, 1987, with thousands of unbound copies in the warehouse, Macmillan officially announced cancellation.

Why?

"Serious substantive disagreements" over the author's interpretation of his research, said Macmillan in a four-paragraph news release, adding that the cancellation was "not based upon legal considerations and is, in fact, contrary to Macmillan's own commercial interests."

The cancellation was a surprise to us. Until that day, we had never been told by Macmillan that we had disagreements, interpretive or research, substantive or otherwise. Our reactions were mixed. Mary was furious. David was more laid back and laconic. "Good riddance," however, more or less summed it up for both of us.

□

The rarity of the act and the brevity of the explanation triggered immediate interest from the national media and First Amendment specialists. Some stories suggest that Macmillan had been cowed by the book's main foe, Barry Bingham, Sr., eighty-one-year-old patriarch of the Louisville Bingham clan.

Reporters sought answers and details to no avail. No further explanation was or would be forthcoming—not from Macmillan, nor from us. We flat didn't know anything beyond what Macmillan had said publicly: there were no legal or commercial problems.

Thus, a book that attempts to answer a seventy-year-old mystery itself became the centerpiece of a modern mystery. Why *was* it cancelled?

Intimidation is a reasonable hypothesis. Macmillan made its decision after Barry Bingham became alarmed by our conclusions that Barry's father, Judge Robert Worth Bingham, had caused the death of his second wife, Mary Lily Kenan Flagler, in 1917 by having her drugged with morphine. (With the money he inherited, the Judge bought the *Louisville Courier-Journal,* established a communications dynasty, became a national political power, and ultimately was appointed by President Franklin Roosevelt as ambassador to Great Britain.)

☐

Our book was based in small part on documents written by the Judge and donated by his son Barry to the Filson Club, a private museum in Louisville which is partly supported by Bingham philanthropies and which had given us written permission to use the documents.

After seeing *The Binghams of Louisville* in manuscript, however, Barry Sr. began his assault by copyrighting those documents approximately one year after we had used them and just prior to book publication. He claimed the copyrights were his by right of inheritance.

"In an even more unusual step," reported the *Los Angeles Times,* "he also copyrighted the written answers through which he previously had replied to [author David] Chandler's questions." Barry Sr. then personally delivered to Macmillian's New York headquarters eight pounds of documents challenging the book's accuracy.

The *Washington Post* reported:

Bingham says the author's theory about his stepmother's death has been "completely repudiated" by his lawyers and researchers. But he said he has made no effort to suppress Chandler's book. "How could I?" Bingham asked.

Macmillan officers were stunned.

"The sheer weight and mass of the challenge impressed us so that we immediately halted the presses before we even looked at the validity of Bingham's material," a Macmillan representative later told David.

Although halting production, Macmillan did not immediately fold its tent. It launched a month-long legal review which concluded with David being told there were no legal problems but that some text changes might be required, mostly in the footnotes section.

We heard nothing for the next two months. Our literary agent's phone calls went unanswered. Eventually we learned through press accounts that Macmillan staff was engaged in two months of "difficult internal debate." Meanwhile, the stonewalling continued. Reported the *Washington Post:*

Ned Chase, the Macmillan editor of Chandler's book, would say only that "We're studying the situation," and referred questions to the publishing company's legal department, which refused comment. . . .

The cancellation disturbed media and constitutional experts, including attorney Floyd Abrams who told the *Los Angeles Times:*

What the Binghams seem to be doing is using copyright to suppress speech of which they disapprove, which is especially troubling. That is not what the copyright laws were supposed to be about.

Said the *Times:*

Abrams' concerns were first voiced by Barry Sr.'s estranged daughter, author Sallie Bingham, who recently wrote letters to book editors and newspaper executives around the country, charging her father with using "legal intimidation . . . to chill" publication of Chandler's book.

Barry Sr.'s attempt to copyright his written answers to Chandler, Sallie Bingham argued, threatens "all authors who depend on interviews for information . . . when the conclusions they draw from interviews are unflattering."

Upon detailed examination, it turned out that many of Bingham's documents were barely relevant. For example, he enclosed copies of the Kentucky Constitution, the will left by his father (which didn't specifically mention any inheritance of documents), and entire front-to-back copies of old *Courier-Journals*. The result was a bulked-up presentation which was hollow like a bell.

Sallie Bingham, while preparing a memoir on the family for another publishing house, studied the presentation and denounced it. She wrote Macmillan's editors a three-page, thousand-word letter analyzing her father's documents from the unique perspective of a scholar, author, and family insider:

It seems to me, that this enormous pile of legal documents contains very little which pertains to the accuracy of Chandler's book. . . . Although the sheer bulk of these legal documents is intimidating, as it is surely meant to be, you will note on close examination that most of this bulk is made up of meaningless Xeroxes of meaningless documents . . . there are gross inaccuracies involving the attempt to discredit Chandler's book.

Ms. Bingham described to Macmillan several detailed examples of what she considered an inaccurate presentation, then concluded:

I cite [the above] as only one of several examples of partial or distorted use of material from the Filson Club—ironically, the very misuse of which Chandler himself is accused.

. . . In sum, it represents an attempt to intimidate You, David Chandler, and other writers about the Bingham family. . . .

I have gone into this in such detail because I believe this is an issue of enormous importance to all writers, and especially perhaps to scholars, since it also involves an attempt to suppress a writer's use of papers given to a historical archive.

One can understand publishers' wariness of Barry Bingham. His personal resources are vast. He is a competent, battle-tested newspaperman who retired from publishing in the midst of management and personal disputes involving him and his wife, his son, Barry Jr., and his two daughters, Sallie and Eleanor.

Leaving the business in 1986 after selling his newspaper, printing, and broadcasting companies, Barry received hundreds of millions of dollars which he could spend as he saw fit. Then aged eighty, he was unlikely to invest the money in new companies. He needn't save it for his children, who were not only warring with him but had large fortunes of their own. He was free to do what he had spent much of his adult life doing—protecting his father and the Bingham family from the Scandal.

That scandal, or the money which triggered it, began with Henry Flagler, John D. Rockefeller's partner in Standard Oil, owner of the powerful Florida East Coast Railway and founder of the Florida east coast, including both Miami and Palm Beach. In 1985, David completed a biography on Flagler, who died in 1913 at the age of eighty-three leaving a widow, Mary Lily Kenan Flagler, who was still young and attractive. After finishing the Flagler book, David moved on to the Binghams, using what he had learned of Mary Flagler's last years as a starting point.

□

Ironically, we began this book's research thinking that the Judge might be the victim rather than the villain. Based on our earliest information, it seemed plausible that to forestall the Judge's inheritance, and a possible seat on the board of Standard Oil, Mary Lily's heirs and business colleagues had deliberately floated rumors of drugging and murder. The Judge, out of loyalty to his wife, had remained silent and endured the abuse.

As the research proceeded, however, it became persuasive that the Judge had conspired with the dermatologist to drug Mary Lily, resulting in her changing her will.

In our interviews—personal, by phone and by mail—with Barry Sr., we found that he calmly and professionally disagreed on that central theme. Barry Sr. took the position that his stepmother had "died of natural causes. She had a heart condition. There was an autopsy. There was no question of foul play whatever."

In response to our questions, Barry Sr. said that he had never seen the autopsy report.

We learned that the original report was held in a locked box by the Kenan family in Chapel Hill, North Carolina. In an interview at Chapel Hill in August 1984, Kenan family historian Thomas S. Kenan III, confirmed that he had the box. It contained not only "the autopsy report from [New York City's] Bellevue hospital, but a detective report investigating her death and other matters relating to the death." However, said Tom, he couldn't release the contents. "It wouldn't be fair to the Bingham family . . . it would renew the problem between the families."

He suggested instead an arrangement, later confirmed in writing, that allowed us to ask specific questions which Tom would answer by going to the locked box and reviewing the material. This arrangement worked well and over a two-year period, we exchanged nearly a dozen letters and twice that many telephone interviews.

□

As the book research was nearing an end, it became apparent that there was only one way of obtaining a definitive answer to whether Mary Lily had been poisoned or drugged.

David was doing most of our detective work and he needed the actual autopsy report to show copies to doctors for analysis and prove or disprove the circumstantial evidence of poisoning and morphine addiction.

David detailed the situation to Tom Kenan who declined to produce the document, saying he was unable to overcome his family's objections. David repeated the request to Barry Sr., explaining that rumors persisted in Louisville that he still had a copy. Barry said he couldn't help. In a list of questions submitted in writing, we also asked him about rumors that he had documentation that Mary Lily had died of alcoholism. He said he didn't.

Proceeding on the best available information, we finished the book and drew the hypotheses presented in chapter 16.

□

Paradoxically, in his efforts to kill *The Binghams of Louisville,* Barry Bingham has impeded our efforts to more fully portray his side of the story. Not only did he introduce the copyright problem, but he has finally released documents from a Baltimore doctor concerning his theory that his stepmother died from alcoholism. (Which, he says, his father discovered only after their marriage and kept secret to shield her.) Although the documents do not prove Barry's theory, they do provide a basis for his argument. The documents are more fully described in footnote 30 of chapter 16.

Copyright expert and Stanford University law professor Paul Goldstein told the *Los Angeles Times* that while Barry Bingham and his lawyers might have every right to copyright material "if the Binghams are saying on the record that their motive is to stop an interpretation of history they disagree with," Goldstein said, "that might raise questions in a court's mind."

Bingham's gambit—the use of money and copyright to stifle unwanted research and publication—remains untested as law. But as a technique it has been somewhat effective. Following the cancellation, we learned that Bingham's resources had indeed disheartened other publishers who were either considering books about the Bingham family, or were interested in publishing this book. Crown Publishers, bless them, was not intimidated and the result is the book you see before you.

David and Mary Chandler
November 1987

The Knave of Hearts

I F YOU LIVED in Louisville, conservative and Southern, if you grew up in a place which prided itself on mansions, and juleps and the Kentucky Derby, then you knew about the Binghams, and it came like an act of public blasphemy, an outrage to some but fresh air to others, when the Judge's dissident granddaughter cried foul. Yes, Sallie Bingham set the town on its ear with her feminist revolt. Binghams didn't do that. Binghams, as Sallie herself has said, always set a good example. They do their duties without complaint.[1] Bingham children go to private schools and the best colleges, and while the men return to run the newspaper and broadcast companies, the women marry and keep house and bear children. And the big thing, maybe the most important item of style, is that the Binghams never, never make themselves conspicuous.

Yet there she was, Sallie Bingham, making a spectacle of herself, or worse yet of the family, across front pages of nearly every newspaper in the country. Sallie and the Binghams on network television, Sallie and the family on magazine covers. Yes, this was the same Sallie whom we only had seen before in pictures on the society pages, a little blond girl in properly starched dresses sitting on her mother's knee at social teas; or the young author whose stories and plays were sometimes reviewed in *The New York Times*. She was always discreet, mannerly Sallie who, when at the age of forty she moved in with her lover, sent her father a polite memo informing him of the fact so that there would be no unwelcome surprises. Ultimately we knew her as a matron with children, multiple marriages, and a stalled career who nevertheless throughout her life had dutifully obeyed the family code.

It was quite a scene when she spoke out. For nearly seventy years, the Binghams had presided as the mandarins of Kentucky, reigning from a huge red-brick Georgian mansion on a hilltop a few miles outside of Louisville, the mansion where Sallie was raised. Then, angry because her father and brother refused to share family power, soft-spoken Sallie simply destroyed the dominion. Tumbling down came the Bingham communications dynasty, characterized by a strong tradition of public service and liberal causes, bludgeoned to its knees by a blonde, blue-eyed, Athena.

Warring against perceived sexism, wielding her blade with deft precision, she felled the dynasty controlled by the family males. But it was not enough. No, she needed to tell them and Louisville why. As she saw it, the injustice, the outrage, went beyond the fight with her family. It went back seventy years, to the death of a woman named Mary Lily Kenan, her grandfather's second wife.

In Louisville, you would grow up with dark whispers of that scandal, and to this day the circumstances of Mary Lily's death taint the Bingham fortune and are a topic of regular conversation among the old families.

But the history of Bingham revenges and mysteries, of female victims and male sexism, goes back much further than even Sallie's rage—it traces to the American Revolution and a continuing series of conflicts between the Binghams and the Kenans competing for power in the new state of North Carolina.

There are many Kenans and many Binghams in the tale—Irishmen who came to America in strange ways, one hidden in a barrel aboard a sailing ship. There is James Kenan, an American hero of the Revolutionary War, fighting Whig Binghams who sided with the British in the battle of Wilmington. There are Kenans and Binghams commanding Confederate units in the Civil War and standing beside Lee in his final battle at Appomattox. And there are the contemporary Binghams, such as Sallie's father, Barry Sr., a handsome and charming man with a musical, baritone voice and storytelling manner who, in 1931, married Sallie's mother, Mary Clifford Caperton, a Richmond girl whom he had met while he was at Harvard and she at Radcliffe; Barry, scarred survivor of many tragedies, who, when Sallie split the family asunder, said he could not have endured without the support of his wife: "It would have been almost impossible alone." [2]

Ultimately, however, the story revolves around Sallie's grandfather, Robert Worth Bingham, popularly called "the Judge."

An impoverished North Carolina law student, he came to Louisville at age twenty-five in 1896 on borrowed money and immersed himself in Democratic party politics, a toady who kicked back 10 percent of his salary to win a series of political appointments including county attorney, mayor, and circuit judge. Along the way, he parlayed his undeniable charm into successive marriages with three rich wives—a sort of a lady killer, you might say.

We find him not at the beginning of his life, but at the end of it.

□

December 1937

Robert Worth Bingham, the American ambassador to Great Britain, crippled with the little-known cancer called Hodgkin's disease, has returned to the States to die in a Baltimore hospital. The room is crowded with his family. Scattered about in various postures and positions are his son and daughter, his wife and his stepson. In the center of the room is his doctor, flanked by two nurses.

He has been in many such rooms in the last years of his life and they are all the same—beige walls, beige ceilings, and beige linoleum floors. On this snowy December day, attempts have been made to spot the room with color; his family, friends, and even the President of the United States have sent all shades and hues of flowers—red, yellow, violet, ivory, blue, pink, and orange. There are by actual count several hundred roses, mums, carnations, violets, and lilacs arranged around in sprays, vases, and potted plants. But it doesn't work. The immediate effect is only to emphasize depression. The attempt to cheer is an unnecessary irony because death, and birth, are the least cheerful moments in life.

□

The physician is Hugh Young, a close friend since college days. He stands helplessly watching the disintegration of his boyhood idol who was once a tall, slender, and athletic prince. Now Bingham is falling apart, his precisely barbered white hair is falling off in thatches. His fingers beneath the manicure are splayed and split. His groin is grotesquely swollen with cancer. He itches to the point of agony. His eyes bulge and water with pain. Yet despite the torment, he remains stoical, heeding the rules of his class. Inwardly, his mind is alive and sharp and he rages at the injustice of his death. His body is killing him before his time.

□

The medical team has finished its prodding and probing and taking of temperature. Bingham's eyes are fixed on Young, now at the foot of the bed, pondering meaningful scribbles on a medical chart. Young's brows furrow, then he looks up at Bingham. Their eyes lock.

They have known each other for nearly half a century, from when they were students at the University of Virginia. Bingham, handsome and tan as a polo champion, was then a worshipped football star—a lad who had a way with the professors, success with the ladies, and a stylish fashion which set the pace for the campus.

Following college, their friendship held despite the splitting of their career paths. Both eventually became highly successful, the friends of presidents, princes, and men and women of world renown. Young was to be one of the world's leading urologists, the deviser of breakthrough surgical techniques, and the developer of Mercurochrome, an antiseptic which, prior to the development of antibiotics, was the primary protection against blood poisoning.[3] Bingham, in addition to his ambassadorial post, was to become one of the most powerful newspaper publishers in America and an important figure in the Franklin Roosevelt political machine, being a supporter, friend, and financial backer of the president since the early 1920s. He was also to found a dynasty, the foundation of his power being his newspapers, the *Louisville Courier-Journal* and the *Louisville Times*.

□

When Hugh Young arrived at the hospital room earlier in the day, Bingham had been unconscious. Young had bent over him, saying, "Bob, this is Hugh." Bingham's eyes fluttered open, a faint smile crossed his face, and he gurgled some reply.

As the two old friends stared at each other, Young was again struck by the strong physical resemblance between Bingham and another patient of years before, Woodrow Wilson. Young had been Wilson's physician and he found the likenesses to be uncanny, even now with Bingham bedridden and the spectacles put aside. Young had been with Wilson in his final hours, as he was now with Bingham in his. Wilson had been sixty-eight years of age at his death. Bingham was sixty-six.

□

There was little more to do. Bingham had been operated upon four days earlier. The surgeons had found an "extensive infiltrating mass," the cancer, spreading up and down the abdominal cavity. It had gradually strangled the vessels that went to Bob Bingham's liver, kidneys, spleen, and other vital organs. The final stages had been rapid. Severe pain came only at the last and could be kept endurable only by opiates.[4]

Weakly, Bingham held up his arm, his eyes beseeching his friend for relief.

"Okay, Bob," said Young, his voice halting and shaken.

He nodded to the nurse who came forward with a tray. Bingham extended his arm. She dabbed it with alcohol, then injected the morphine.

He relaxed into his pillow and closed his eyes. Minutes passed. The people in the room began to stir restlessly. Suddenly, Bob Bingham's eyes snapped open again. The whites remained crosshatched with red, but the irises were hazel and the watery look of pain was gone.

He muttered something.

Young leaned closer to hear him.

"I want my wife," Bingham seemed to be saying.

His wife, Aleen Bingham, and the doctor exchange sad glances.

"She's right beside you," said the surprised Young. Aleen and Bob had been husband and wife for thirteen years, since 1924 when they had taken vows in London in a special ceremony before the Archbishop of Canterbury.

"No," says Bingham fretfully. "Not her. The other one."[5]

The "other one" was Mary Lily Kenan. Hugh Young had been best man at that wedding in 1916. Less than a year later, Bob Bingham was the main suspect in Mary Lily's death.

□

Perhaps it was the morphine that spun Bingham back twenty years in time. Mary Lily had taken a lot of morphine, much of it supplied by Bob Bingham. Indeed, she had died saturated with morphine on a hot July day in 1917.

If you had known Mary Lily you would have found her charming, a voluptuous little beauty, a bit over 5 feet tall, with thick, dark hair and blue eyes. She was generous, humorous, intelligent, said her intimates, and her voice was pure and clear as the bells of angels. It was a pleasure, they said, to be in her company.

Like Bingham and Young, even before they had gained their respective reputations, Mary Lily was a power in her own right. She owned more and controlled more than they ever did or would. Her properties included railroads, hotels, newspapers, and much of Florida. That's not just tracts of land in Florida but *much* of Florida—hundreds of square miles of beach and waterfront land and thousands more square miles of inland groves, farms, and residential tracts. She owned them completely and totally, in the same way she owned shoes in her closet. And yes, princes and presidents, including Woodrow Wilson, dined at her table.[6]

She was the oldest of four children of a highly prominent and wealthy North Carolina family which originally came to America in the 1730s and established a tradition of leadership, heroism, and philanthropy that included the founding of plantations, towns, cities, and the University of North Carolina. Like most of the Southern patriciate, the Kenans fell onto hard times following the Civil War. Land, plantations, and mansions were lost, but the Kenans survived, reputation and honor intact.

Bob Bingham came from almost identical Scotch-Irish stock. His forebears, the Worths and the Binghams, likewise came to America in the eighteenth century.[7] The Binghams had founded important and prominent schools and, like the Kenans, had made substantial philanthropies to the University of North Carolina. The Worths and the Binghams included powerful cotton merchants, a governor of North Carolina, and several Confederate war heroes.

Obviously, Mary Lily and Bob Bingham were well matched for each other. And indeed, in the early 1890s, in the full bloom of their youth, they came together as lovers in a series of interludes during college vacations and romantic summers. They danced, went to parties and picnics, strolled, boated, and rode—often in the company of Bingham's close friend Hugh Young.

"We had what you might call an affair then," Mary Lily recalled. "But our paths took us in opposite directions."[8]

Something had happened.

Friends speculated it was more than a lovers' quarrel, blaming financial pressures from the respective families. In fact, it was something else which caused their paths to diverge, and that something will be explored later. In the meantime, in the late 1890s, both went to other romances, other mates.

Bob Bingham wooed and wed a lovely and rich Louisville heiress named Eleanor Miller. Mary Lily became the mistress and later the wife of Henry Flagler, a near-mythical robber baron who, with John D. Rockefeller, was the co-founder of Standard Oil.

Then, in 1913, both Eleanor Miller and Henry Flagler had fatal accidents, accidents which occurred more than 600 miles apart but within ten days' time of each other; happenings a Westerner might see as a coincidence of timing but which a Hindu would call "karma."

Like comets locked in doomed orbit, Mary Lily and Bob Bingham came together again and from that day forward their fate unfolded like *Rebecca,* Mary Lily being a woman who stepped from the sunlight into a dark marriage and a house of shadows.

□

She was the richest woman in America, and she bought handsome, proud Robert Worth Bingham like a lap poodle.[9]

It was done on her initiative.

She gave him nearly $1 million in wedding gifts, and she was sure that with generosity and time she would domesticate him and win his affection and attention.

She acted on the commands of her heart, not her mind, and therein was her doom.

Bingham was cynically ambitious. Ambitious for his good name. Ambitious for money. And ruthlessly ambitious for power. He had somewhere along the line become totally attracted to power and he served it without question, demeaning and whoring himself in the process. He adapted to power by molding himself to his environment's demands. We might say he was worse off for it, having forfeited his value and integrity. But he would say nay, that he was better off. He was well rewarded for making the forfeit.

To obtain his goals, he sold himself, pure and simple, to Mary Lily. But not in good faith. He gave her not love nor intimacy nor even simple friendship. Throughout their brief marriage, he showed not the least sign of affection or protection.

They married, and nine months later, a captive in her own rented mansion, she died. The ink was barely dry on a change in her will. He took her money, then revenged himself by coolly watching her go. The sole beneficiary of that change in the will was Robert Worth Bingham.

□

What exactly happened?

The undisputed facts were that Mary Lily died in her home on July 27, 1917. An autopsy showed she was heavily dosed with morphine and her chief physician, a close friend of Robert Worth Bingham, attributed death to "oedema of the brain," a swelling of the brain triggered by failure of the heart.

Since that day, the various factions have put forth two opposing scenarios.

In the first hypothesis, supported by some of the Kenans, Robert Worth Bingham is a villain who sought out Mary Lily to pay off his debts and kept her drugged so she would change her will, a drugging which ultimately led to her death.

In the second theory, that of some of the Binghams, Robert Worth Bingham was an innocent victim, having been accused of the above crimes but unable to fully defend himself for various reasons including a desire to shield Mary Lily from a scandal horrible beyond imagination.

A third speculation, held by neither of the factions but nonetheless tenable, is that Mary Lily caused her own death by overdosing herself with morphine and bourbon, either accidentally or deliberately.

To this day, Louisvillians not only talk about the Bingham history, but also about a coverup.

Virtually all letters, correspondence, newspaper files, photographs, and other documents concerning Mary Lily and the period of her marriage to Bingham have been lost, removed, or withheld from the public archives, including the public library, the newspaper morgue, the Library of Congress, and the Bingham Collection of the Filson Club, the latter two agencies being the official repositories of the family archives.

This gap in the evidence was made dramatically clear in the fall of 1985 when archivists at the Filson Club received dozens of crates of the long-awaited "Bingham Papers," which was supposed to be the documented history of four generations of the family—a history compiled by the Judge and maintained by his son, Barry.

Upon opening the crates, the archivists were surprised to find no correspondence, photos, financial papers, court records, diaries, or newspaper clippings from July 1915 through July 1918. The missing records were particularly crucial because, unlike many cities, there were few alternative sources for historians. The

Great Ohio River flood of 1937 had destroyed virtually all private and family records in Louisville prior to that date.

But the Judge's records hadn't been destroyed by the flood. They had simply vanished. And not only was there a three-year gap in the Filson Club papers, but there was a comparable gap in the newspaper files at the *Courier-Journal* and the *Times*.

Museum officials looked into the mystery and wondered whether the records had been removed personally by Barry, the Judge's son. The logic was there. He had motive, in that he would obviously prefer to shield his father's reputation from scandal, and he had unique opportunity, being not only the sole caretaker of the archival papers but he was also one of the few people with the opportunity and authority to remove the newspaper files. Museum officials concluded that Barry arbitrarily removed three years of Louisville history and, they said, "There is no appeal."

But Barry has denied any such tampering with history. He says that after his father's death, he made all of the papers available to the public. Documents from the early years through 1917 were sent to the Filson Club, said Barry. Documents from the later years went to the Library of Congress.[10]

Taking the man at his word, the tampering must have been done before he received his father's papers. And the only person with motive and opportunity to do it then was the Judge himself.

□

In any event, one thing is clear. The missing papers only seem to enhance the smell of murder surrounding Mary Lily's death.

The rumor was and is widespread in Louisville.

"He killed her, didn't he?" says Sallie, feminist granddaughter.[11]

"It was her money that started his loot, wasn't it?" we were told by a court records archivist when seeking a copy of Mary Lily's will.[12]

"*Prominent?* Prominent for murdering his second wife!" exclaimed a senior staffer of the Louisville Free Public Library when asked if there were a special file on Robert Bingham because of his prominence.[13]

Barry Bingham believes that not only was his father innocent, but that Bob Bingham behaved nobly in the matter of Mary Lily's death, and Barry wants his own perception to prevail as history. Some forty years after the Judge died, Barry explained this perception to his children, the Judge's grandchildren, when he sent them each a scrapbook of testimonials and other memorabilia about the Judge.

Barry Sr. made an effort to acquaint his children with their grandfather, noting that during his four and a half years as ambassador the Judge had directed and participated in several important international conferences and negotiations. The Judge's career, according to Barry Sr., was constantly focused on public service—a goal which included his purchase of the *Courier-Journal* and the *Louisville Times* and a pioneer effort in radio broadcasting which began in 1923. The Judge's courage was tested repeatedly, including his time as ambassador when he was afflicted by repeated illness, the cause of which was unknown at the time. Despite the remissions, the Judge remained active. It was a time when the Judge enjoyed shooting birds on the moors of northern England and Scotland. In an ominous note, in what appears to be an oblique reference to the Mary Lily scandal, Barry Sr. reminded the young Binghams that the Judge's life contained dark periods as well.

In a foreword to the Bingham family genealogy, Barry also stressed the value of truthful family histories:

People . . . are apt to find unexpected turnings and doors opening into unfamiliar rooms. Not everything they discover will be pleasing. It is a truism that every family tree harbors its quota of rascals. But even if the traditional horse thief is found clinging to one of the branches, he may have had other qualities that were interesting if not admirable.[15]

Despite his faults, there was something positive and special in Judge Robert Worth Bingham. That something was style and energy. The family institutions he established survived for two-thirds of a century, remarkable in this day of speed, transiency, and impermanence. Listen to Louisville's Roger Davis, entrepreneur, film actor, and restorer of the turn-of-the-century showcase Seelbach Hotel:

The Binghams have remained for real. They, and Louisville, have hung on with a tenacity unprecedented in the United States for trying to be somebody. The Binghams have perpetuated this. They have instilled this in all of Louisville, the desire to be somebody. They are still drifting between a John Singer Sargent painting and life.

This is the story, a tale of the hunter and the hunted. It is in some ways a fable, illustrating a truth of nature that if you reach out and touch something beautiful, it may hurt you. It is also a tale of the lonely. But do not be too quick to assume which is which. That comes out only in the telling.

The Binghams

WHEN Bob Bingham's great-grandfather, William Bingham, first came to America in the summer of 1791, George Washington was midway through his first term as president and Philadelphia was the nation's capital.[1]

The country was two years old.[2] Officially, it stretched from Maine to Georgia and from the Atlantic to the Appalachians. But unofficially it ran to the Mississippi. Pioneers had already crept across the mountain passes to claim the unbelievably rich hunting and farming lands watered, fertilized, and drained by great rivers such as the Illinois, the Ohio, the Kentucky, the Tennessee, and the Mississippi.[3] It was a nation of farmers, fishermen, and craftsmen. There were few towns and fewer cities, with New York, Boston, and Philadelphia being the most prominent.

Into this mix of wilderness and opportunity came thirty-seven-year-old William Bingham, a man who, like many an immigrant before and since, was eager for fortune and anxious to escape the clutches of his native government.

Born in 1754 in County Down, Ireland, Bingham was a minister who, as a good Presbyterian churchman, had matriculated at the University of Glasgow in Scotland from 1774 to 1778.[4] However, for reasons not well defined by history, he failed to graduate and returned to Ireland where he became fascinated with the idea that the English, who had ruled Ireland since the twelfth century, should give the country back to its inhabitants.[5] To support this argument, he became involved in revolutionary activities, and by 1791 was a founding member of the "United Irishmen," a group dedicated to the overthrow of English rule in Ireland. When the English uncovered the terrorist plots of the United Irishmen, they uncooperatively began to hang them. Accordingly, the Reverend William took to cover. He was eventually advised to escape to Wilmington, North Carolina, where a job awaited him as headmaster of a private academy.

According to family tradition concerning William Bingham and his three brothers:

All belonged to the great secret society, the "United Irishmen," every member of which took a solemn oath to work and fight for the independence of Ireland. This spirit of republicanism was stimulated by the example of America and France . . . soldiers pursued one of [the Bingham] brothers to a ship lying at anchor in the harbor, where the sailors, who were in sympathy with him, headed him up in a beef barrel with the bung left out to breathe through, and after a long search, the soldiers went ashore just before the ship weighed anchor. When the ship crossed the bar, the head was knocked out of the barrel, and the temporary prisoner released. . . .[6]

William Bingham had been aiming for North Carolina, but the expedience of his unscheduled departure caused him to land more than 500 miles to the north, at New York City. By the time he reached Wilmington, he found the post filled and himself broke.

A stranger stranded in a strange land, he may have used Masonic connections to gain positions as a private tutor and, later, as headmaster of a local academy. By 1794, Bingham had moved to Pittsboro, North Carolina, apparently for his health, and from that point onward his career is well-documented. On January 2, 1795, he opened Chatham Academy, a private boarding school that quickly gained a national reputation. By June 22, 1795, the North Carolina Journal listed Chatham as one of four schools preparing students for admission to the upper classes at the University of North Carolina.[7] The school's curriculum included reading, writing, arithmetic, Latin, Greek, English grammar, geography, history, Euclid's elements, logic, and moral philosophy. Tuition for reading, writing, and arithmetic was $8 a year, for the other subjects, $12 a year.

By the middle of 1797, a building had been erected for ladies and a woman assistant hired. The women's curriculum included "useful and ornamental needlework."[8]

□

Despite his anti-English activities in Ireland, William Bingham seems to have embraced the Tory or pro-English factions in America, a Bingham family bias that would persist through the generations for the next 190 years or more.

One of the causes, and certainly a consequence, of William Bingham's Anglomania was his marriage in 1799 to Annie Jean Slingsby, the daughter of Colonel John Slingsby, an officer in Cornwallis' army who had been commander of the British forces in the Wilmington district of North Carolina during the Revolutionary War. Following the war, Slingsby had settled in the Cape Fear region, some 25 miles south of Wilmington.[9]

In 1801, William left Pittsboro to accept an appointment as professor of ancient languages at the nearby University of North Carolina. He remained only four years, however, resigning or being fired in 1805. His departure was partly or wholly caused by his extreme pro-British political opinions.[10]

Those opinions were particularly offensive to General James Kenan, a university trustee and Revolutionary War hero. In the war, Kenan had led American forces in their successful fight against the British troops of the very same Colonel Slingsby who was to become Bingham's father-in-law and grandfather of the Bingham children.[11]

From this early conflict onward, the paths of these families, the Kenans and the Binghams, would touch each other and intertwine for the next 112 years, culminating in the doomed relationship of Mary Lily Kenan and Robert Worth Bingham.

□

William and Annie Bingham had five children, only two of whom seem to have prospered—the eldest son, William James, born in 1802, who became headmaster in 1826 when his father died, and the youngest son, John Archibald Bingham, who became a Presbyterian minister.[12]

Robert Worth Bingham, born in November 1871, was the grandson of William James.

The Kenans

THERE ARE three families involved in this story: the Binghams, the Worths, and the Kenans, all part of the small colonial kinship groups which made up Southern society. The Kenans were perhaps the most prestigious of the three because of their lengthier presence in America and their ownership of plantations. The Worths, Bob Bingham's maternal forebears, however, had become important commercially and politically in the mid-1800s. The Bingham prestige was based on more intellectual attainments, the Bingham males being mostly occupied as professors at various colleges and universities. Individually, they were regarded as among the most learned of men, and the Bingham School, of course, was nationally recognized as one of the top college preparatory academies in the land.

They were all big frogs in the little pond of North Carolina, the location of the first English-speaking settlement in North America.[1]

Mary Lily's forebears had arrived in the Carolinas in the 1730s when the brothers Thomas, Felix, and William Kenan emigrated from northern Ireland.[2]

Originating in Argyleshire, Scotland, the Presbyterian Kenans had moved to Ireland in 1641 to escape religious persecution. They were already prominent, being described in contemporary references as "a race of gentlemen, highly esteemed, and always prominently identified with questions concerning the public welfare."[3]

The term "New World" carried a variety of meanings.

Coming to America at the time was somewhat akin to a journey to the moon. To make a new life for themselves, people voluntarily left their homes far behind with little idea or hope of ever returning. Risking life and limb, enduring hardships and incredible privations, they lived under virtually Iron Age conditions. Yet the rewards often made it worthwhile. The lands were fertile. Forests and streams teemed with game and fish. There was minimal government. And perhaps most important of all, there was little of the oppressive class structure which suppressed the people of Europe.

□

All three brothers settled near the present-day town of Kenansville, North Carolina.[4]

Mary Lily's line of descent was from Thomas Kenan, born about 1700 and therefore in his mid-thirties when he and his bride, the former Elizabeth Johnstone of Armagh, Ireland, landed at the port of Wilmington, North Carolina. The couple, Mary Lily's great-great-great-grandparents, cleared a farm from forests near Indian Graves, about 50 miles to the north.

This was a settlement of Germans and Scotch-Irish Presbyterians and was so named because they had won the land after numerous battles with the fierce Tuscarora Indians. Situated in the fertile coastal plains of southeastern North Carolina, 100 miles southeast of Chapel Hill, and well-known for its crystal-clear springs, the growing community was, in 1750, designated as the seat of newly chartered Duplin County and renamed Golden Grove.

Thomas and Elizabeth Kenan had eight children, all of them born in their North Carolina home and seven of whom survived to maturity, a remarkable health record in view of the infant mortality rate of the era.

The family prospered from the beginning, buying large tracts of farm- and timberland in the area. They built a plantation called "The Lilacs" with a Georgian-style house that included a raised basement particularly appropriate to the climate. There they laid down fields of wheat, barley, and corn; raised livestock; built fruit orchards; constructed kilns and stills; and tended dairy herds— all with the help of numerous black slaves and indentured white servants.

Indeed, the Kenans, like many Americans of the era, showed a remarkable coolness of mind toward owning people. Bequests of slaves are common in countless Kenan wills from the 1760s through the 1860s, starting with Thomas' bequest upon his death of "my Negro woman Charity" and "one Negro girl named Sidy" to his granddaughters "and their heirs forever." [5]

□

Thomas Kenan died in 1765, the year of the Stamp Act, a tax without representation, which was imposed by the King of England on the American colonies and which was a seminal event for the American Revolution. Before his death, however, Thomas saw his twenty-five-year-old son James Kenan lead a group of guerrillas to the port of Wilmington in one of the era's most famous raids against the Stamp Act.[6]

After defeating the British garrison commanded by Colonel Slingsby, James' rebels seized the harbormaster's office, took the newly appointed "stamp master" hostage, and forced him to resign. They then manned guns to prevent the landing of stamp paper from the British sloop-of-war *Diligence*. Finally, to complete the day's work, they burned the colonial governor in effigy.[7]

James Kenan went on to become a member of the Colonial Assembly in 1773 and 1774 and a strong advocate of American independence. When war broke out, he was named the commanding officer of the Duplin County militia. Engaging in numerous battles, he was noted for his skills of ambush and maneuver, which frequently carried the day against superior British and Tory forces. At the end of the war, he was promoted to brigadier general.

Returned to private life, James Kenan expanded family holdings, both in the Wilmington area and in Orange County, the latter area already being platted as the site of the nation's first state-supported college.

As a member of the North Carolina Constitutional Convention, he helped ratify the Constitution and was important in formulating and passing the first ten amendments, the Bill of Rights. Upon his mother's death in 1789, he inherited the family plantation and manor house, which he renamed "Liberty Hall" because of the numerous secret and public meetings held there before and during the Revolutionary War.[8]

In 1790, James Kenan and his wife, Catherine Love Kenan, donated 200 acres of their Orange County farmland to provide the site for the University of North Carolina. Part of that land became the center of the college and the remainder was sold off as lots to form the college town of Chapel Hill.[9]

By the time of James Kenan's death in 1810, the family owned twenty-two slaves, a medium-sized fortune in those days. James' will included awards of:

Two yellow men slaves, Blick and Moses, to my son Daniel Love Kenan . . . my Negro wench Thea and all her children, to my daughter Sarah Kenan and her heirs forever . . . my Negro wench Hagar and her children and also my Negro boy Isaac, to my daughter Jane Kenan and her heirs forever . . . to my granddaughter Sarah Norment my Negro boy, Ireland. . . .[10]

Such slave bequests, and the slave population, continued to grow and split among the heirs for the next three generations of Kenans until they reached Mary Lily's father, William Rand Kenan. Born in 1845, the son of Owen Rand and Sarah Graham Kenan, he was raised in a household of eighteen slaves. Those were house or servant slaves; agricultural slaves, field hands, added another fifty-one people to the census count.[11]

□

Prosperous and respected for more than a century, the Kenans represented the social and educational elite of North Carolina. The family especially loved music, and all the children played instruments or sang. In William Kenan's boyhood home, there was a well-stocked library of several thousand volumes and reading was encouraged at an early age.

Bolstered by this strong family background, he entered the

University of North Carolina in 1860 at the age of fifteen. Three years later, however, on his eighteenth birthday, he withdrew to enlist as a private in the 43rd North Carolina Regiment.

The unit was well-stocked with Kenans. The regimental commander was Colonel Thomas Stephen Kenan, William's older brother by seven years. Another older brother, James Graham Kenan, was a captain and a company commander.

Shortly after William's enlistment, Colonel Thomas was captured at the Battle of Gettysburg and taken to Ohio as a prisoner of war.

Following his brother's capture, William was elected to the rank of captain. While on leave at Chapel Hill in 1864, nineteen-year-old William married Mary Lily's mother, twenty-two-year-old Mary Hargrave.[12]

William returned to the war and was with Robert E. Lee (and Bingham) at Appomattox. Shortly after his parole, he and Mary Hargrave settled in Wilmington. In a short while William became one of the principal wholesale merchants in the city, which at that time, with a population of some 20,000 people, was the largest in North Carolina. Through the influence of the family, William soon afterward was appointed collector of customs at Wilmington. Along with his mercantile interests, the position made him, relative to the times, wealthy.[13]

□

Mary Lily, born June 14, 1867, was the first of William and Mary's children, being followed by sister Jessie in 1870, brother William Rand Kenan, Jr., in 1872, and sister Sarah in 1876.

Later stories about Mary Lily's background would cast her in a Cinderella role, the poor daughter of an impoverished family who found wealth and happiness in the arms of one of the world's richest lovers.

In fact, Mary Lily and her family never knew even middle-class poverty. They lived well in Wilmington and often spent holidays in the home of her grandfather at Kenansville. Her maternal grandparents, the Hargraves, lived in an equally spacious home in Chapel Hill. She and her brother and sisters were fond of ice cream and they would fill up on it until they could eat no more, then go out and run about and play until they could go back for more. Their Sunday dinner always included "iced tea, year round, with the glass nearly a quarter full of sugar, lots of pickles and salad, and at the end a hot fudge sundae." [14]

She was sent to Raleigh for her upper education, boarding with her uncle Thomas Stephen Kenan, the Confederate colonel who by the 1880s was attorney general of the state. In Raleigh, she attended St. Mary's College for a classic curriculum and then Peace Institute, a two-year liberals arts college for women, where she became an accomplished pianist and vocalist. [15]

According to those who knew and saw her, Mary Lily was a strikingly beautiful young woman. [16] It was said she was always popular with men, never without an escort, and her suitors were struck with her grace and charm and her taste for clothes. With long, thick dark hair, blue eyes, and standing at a pretty, buxom, 105-pound, 5-foot-1, she was attractive and sensuous. She had a mature intellectual development which included a broad, classical education. In personal and social matters, she had a grace of style which "awed men and excited the envy of other women." [17]

She had some beaus, including a flirtation in the summer of her seventeenth year, 1884, with Sterling Ruffin, an eighteen-year-old university freshman. Although Ruffin, who was never to marry and would become the physician of presidents, found her to be a "pretty maid," her schoolgirl manipulations annoyed him and, he claimed in a letter to his sister, he quickly gave her the "go by." [18]

□

After leaving Peace Institute in 1888, twenty-one-year-old Mary Lily entered a time of carefree drifting, alternately living at home or visiting relatives and friends in New York or such spas as Newport, Rhode Island; Hot Springs, Arkansas; and St. Augustine, Florida.

In January 1891, she was invited by family friends, Mr. and Mrs. Pembroke Jones of Wilmington, to accompany them on a yachting cruise to the Caribbean.

The Joneses also invited a house guest, a school friend of

Mary Lily's, Miss Elizabeth Ashley, who was the niece of Henry Morrison Flagler, the legendary capitalist who had created Standard Oil and in the 1880s and 1890s was molding the swamp and grasslands of Florida to his design.[19]

Flagler was also a friend of the Pembroke Joneses. Jones, a Wilmington native, had amassed his fortune in cotton and rice and had met Flagler through a common interest in railroads, shipping lines, money, and yachts.[20]

The cruise was aboard the yacht *Narada*, owned by Harry Walters, a mutual friend of Jones and Flagler, and the guests included Flagler and his wife, the former Alice Shourds.[21] Mary Lily was fascinated with Flagler, and although Civil War animosities were still strong and Henry was a Northerner, he was hardly to be considered a Yankee. During the Civil War, he and his partner, John D. Rockefeller, expressed no interest in the Union cause and had avoided military service by buying substitutes. Following the war, Flagler had financed a charity for Southern war victims.[22] And since 1884 or thereabouts, he was the South's, and the nation's, most awesome builder, converting the junglelike peninsula of Florida into a modern state of resorts, farms, groves, railroads, and cities.

□

Following the yachting party, Mary Lily and her group returned to the snows of North Carolina. Shortly afterward, to her absolute surprise and delight, Flagler sent a special train pulling his private car, the *Alicia*, to Wilmington so that the Joneses, Miss Ashley, and Mary Lily could travel in comfort directly to the door of his palatial hotel in St. Augustine, the fabled Ponce de Leon.[23]

The Ponce de Leon was the queen of Flagler hotels, a palace in strong contrast to the rest of Florida, a change from a jungle where the charms were natural to a mass of beauties that was man-made. To live in the Ponce de Leon was to stay in fairyland.

Leaving the train, which stopped in the center of the hotel gardens, the Jones' party swept by a bevy of young girls clustered before the clerk's desk. They were greeted by the manager in the center of a long, yellow-carpeted parlor. In a corner, a semicircle of musicians half enclosed a piano. There was laughter and chatter and rollicking couples. Then the party was shown to two magnificent suites, one for the Joneses and the other for Mary Lily and Elizabeth.

That first night there was a ball, and there sixty-one-year-old Henry Flagler danced with twenty-three-year-old Mary Lily Kenan.[24]

Flagler was impressed with her from the start, and his wife, too, admired Mary Lily for her pleasing personality and elegant manners.

For Mary Lily, it was a dream come true. Since girlhood, she had wanted to live in capitals, where she could see grand opera, miles of swell carriages, a distinguished society, and where something happened every night. Mary Lily was dreadfully miserable when there was nothing going on.

In St. Augustine, it seemed that nearly every such wish was gratified. Here she saw the rich and famous, the royal and the infamous. The quaint old city, with some streets too narrow for carriages and scores of ancient houses that would be notable anywhere, was a joy. On those streets she saw the same happy couples she had seen in the hotel, now keeping a slow-measured tread on the pavements, taking in the frames of staring photographs, the nickel-in-the-slot machines, the shops of gimcrack souvenirs made in Germany and New York, the peanuts and soda water, the odor of perfumes, the rustle of silks, the peeping slippers. Apart from the crowds, the driving and horseback rides were pleasant; there were country walks and orange groves. There was tennis and bathing and shopping. Concerts and dances and exhibitions were frequent. And all this attended by the best of society.[25]

To complement all this were the attentions being paid her by the awesome Flagler. Despite his years, he was a man of exceptional good looks and virility. He was described as the very glass of fashion.[26] A man with luxuriant white hair and a mustache which he groomed with scrupulous care, he was saved from being a dandy by his manly manners. His wise eyes, violet in color, his attitude of command and power, and his soft-spoken charm gave him an extraordinary success with women. He was a bold and fearless entrepreneur and the lure of adventure was always alive in his restless mind.

In the beginning, when they first met in 1891, Flagler's interest in Mary Lily seemed fatherly. He lavished attention on her and Elizabeth and frequently took them on trips in his private car, up and down the East Coast, from New York to Palm Beach. But it was all platonic. Flagler had his wife in St. Augustine, and he had a mistress in New York City.[27]

Passions

THE CIVIL WAR had enriched men like Flagler and Rockefeller, who sidestepped military and patriotic causes to build their fortunes. But the war was a disaster for nearly all white Southerners—particularly the wealthier families like the Binghams, Worths, and Kenans. Specially focused congressional legislation took away not only their slaves but their citizenship and most of their land. Overnight they were reduced from wealthy to barely surviving. Prior to the war, tax rolls show the men of the three families as doctors, lawyers, educators, plantation owners, bankers, and manufacturing chiefs. In the several years following the war, they are listed as insurance salesmen, farmers, and day laborers.

In a letter to author Margaret Mitchell, Bob Bingham described the searing effect the war and its aftermath had had on him. His earliest memory, he said, was of "clutching my mother's skirts in terror at a hooded apparition, and having my father raise his mask to relieve me. Then he went out in command of the Ku Klux in our district." [1]

The Ku Klux Klan was part of the post–Civil War experience of the South and it was that history which helped shape the characters of Bob Bingham, Mary Lily, and many others in this story.

Bingham told Mitchell that, raised by a black woman, he had come to hate Yankees.

My Mammy had been my father's before me. I loved her next to my own Mother. She was a noble character by any standard of measurement. My Mother was Melanie to the last emotion, but very beautiful, outside as well as within. Melanie was beautiful, too. Even you must not deny me that. They were saints, both of them, my mother and Melanie. They were great ladies, as my grandmothers were, and they both glowed with an inner fire, a spiritual fervor, which illuminated them and all around them. My elder brother, my mother's first child, died in infancy, because no doctor could come, no medicine could be obtained. "God damn the Yankees," all of my blood who survived, said, too.[2]

Mitchell, although some thirty years younger than Bingham, replied that her family had endured kindred horrors and noted it was an experience common to Southerners of their class.

You wrote of your father's imprisonment on Johnson's Island. I, too, was raised on stories of that dreadful place, for some of my relatives had the bad fortune to be imprisoned there. I am still haunted by the stories of the freezing weather, the insufficient blankets and the smallpox epidemics. My relatives told how the only way they kept themselves from freezing to death was by rolling themselves in the filthy blankets of men who had died of the disease. There was so much in your letter about your family that paralleled experiences of my own kinfolks and made me feel almost as if I had had a message from a distant relative. But perhaps the experiences of all of our ancestors were somewhat similar, and so we Southerners can share in a common tradition that binds us closely together.[3]

The common tradition that bound the Southerners and so traumatized Bob Bingham's generation was Reconstruction, that period from 1867 to 1876 during which multitudes of ex-Confederates were robbed of their land, homes, businesses, and citizenship. Martial law prevailed everywhere and Union army troops dispensed what passed for local justice and administration. They were assisted by local blacks and Northern administrators, the latter also controlling the governors and legislatures of the Southern states. Southerners correctly regarded themselves as ruled by Yankee bayonets, carpetbaggers, and scalawags—carpetbaggers being Yankees who came South to exploit the Southern condition and scalawags being renegade Southerners who helped them.

Propertied white Southerners, suppressed by Union troops, were particularly picked clean. The sufferings of the Civil War and the injustices of Reconstruction set fires of outrage burning in the propertied families of the South. Not only were they ruled by oppressive and exploitive alien forces, but they were specifically targeted for extinction by the Congress. By federal law, families with more than $20,000 in property or other assets were denied the amnesty extended to less wealthy Southerners. Disenfranchised from citizenship and voting, they formed their klans and they rode.

They justified themselves by saying they were filling the need for local justice, trying and punishing horse thieves, murderers, highwaymen, rapists, and the like. Their true aim, however, was to restore local government to former Confederate officials.

Bingham's father, Robert Bingham, felt the North had turned loose the blacks on Southern society. By his view, the Southern whites didn't deserve such treatment.

Early in the Century there was a deep and strong movement among the slave owners against holding slaves; and but for the agitation inaugurated by the abolitionists, some scheme for the gradual emancipation of the Negro would in all probability have been worked out, and this might have settled the Negro question peaceably. My father thought of going to Ohio in the '20s to be relieved of the burden and responsibility of slaves; but he found the condition of the African in the North West worse that in slavery. Everybody in the South knew that the condition of the ante-bellum free Negro among us was worse than that of the slave, though the free Negro had the right of suffrage in North Carolina till 1835. My father offered his nurse her freedom and support for a term of years in Liberia and she declined the offer. Many of the slaveholders in the South felt as my father did, and a bill for the gradual emancipation of the slaves failed to pass the Legislature of Virginia in the early '30s by only *one vote*. It is safe to say that we of the South dealt more successfully with the Negro up to '65, when he was taken from our hands, than our race has ever dealt with any other race on the same soil since the dawn of history. He came into our hands from overseas, by the action of the people of New England chiefly, not by our own, as we did not own a single ship. . . . [The vote] which was given by law to every adult Negro male in the South, is still denied to illiterates of our own race in New England.[4]

From the moment it was born in the congressional legislation of 1867, Reconstruction was under attack. But it held fast against even the strongest opposition. Indeed, in fighting against the excesses of Reconstruction, President Andrew Johnson was impeached by the U.S. House of Representatives, but the Senate fell one vote short of convicting him. The Republicans replaced Johnson with President Ulysses Grant, 1869–77, who supported Reconstruction with the full force of federal troops and marshals.

The Thirteenth, Fourteenth, and Fifteenth amendments to the Constitution, passed in the years 1865–70, guaranteed blacks to be the legal and political equals of whites in all matters including voting. Indeed, they were more than equal, being the most enfranchised class of people in the nation. In its zeal to gain a political constituency in the South, the victorious Republican administration had created a situation where the only classes *guaranteed* the right to vote were Northern white males who could pass certain literacy and property-holding tests and Southern black males, who were allowed to vote regardless of literacy or property.

Not allowed to vote, and otherwise denied equal rights, were (1) women, Indians, and Orientals of all classes, education, and property; (2) illiterate white males; (3) in certain states, literate but propertyless white males; and (4) men like the Binghams, Worths, and Kenans—that is to say, Southern gentry who had owned more than $20,000 in assets and had fought for the Confederacy.

This unequal citizenship arrangement was completely offensive to the Colonel:

We of the South believe that some plan of gradual enfranchisement on the educational basis which is demanded of white men in Massachusetts, or on the combined educational and property basis which is demanded of white men in Rhode Island, would have been adopted if President Lincoln had been spared. And nothing could have stimulated the illiterate Negro and the illiterate white man as much as making the right of suffrage a prize to be won by an educational qualification. . . . [These amendments were] done, not for the benefit of the Negro, but as a move on the chess board of party politics.[5]

Accordingly, Southerners of Bingham's class rode at night to protect the neighborhood, as it were, from any unacceptable voting. Even their costumes were designed to terrify the newly enfranchised blacks. Riding in armed patrols, they posed as spirits of the battlefield dead returned to restore Confederate justice and law. Dressed in capes, masks, and hoods, they rode in silence, their horses' hooves muffled by wrappings of leather and cloth.[6]

The klans were often able to achieve their goals by fear alone, making simple nighttime appearances and burning crosses in the farmyards and encampments of blacks. When that failed, however, they were not slow to use whippings and lynchings without discrimination against blacks, carpetbaggers, and scalawags alike.[7]

□

While it is easy to scorn those masked vigilantes, were they any worse than their oppressors? The North had imposed on the South a reign of barbarism the likes of which have not been seen in this country before or since. The boy who was Bob Bingham viewed his father and the riders as heroes. The KKK was operating beyond the law, but the law was unjust and that, he felt, was the sort of thing that had made the American Revolution.

In riding with the klan, the Colonel in effect was continuing the Civil War. He rode against Yankees and he did not, he recorded, take action against Southern blacks. Indeed, he claimed, Southern whites and Southern blacks were members of the same large family.

I believe that in the history of the whole world there never were as kindly relations existing between two races on the same soil as between the slave owner and the slave in the South before the Civil War, and nothing vindicates these kindly, and in many cases these tender relations so clearly, or falsifies the pre-conceived opinions of many Northern people on the subject so clearly as the confidence with which the white men of the South left their women and children to the protection of the Negroes during the Civil War and the unexampled faithfulness with which the Negroes discharged this trust. . . . I have always loved the Negro and I shall never cease to love him. My father and mother reared seven children in a slave woman's lap. She loved us better than her life. We loved her next to our parents, and I look with a sort of yearning pity on my grandchildren, because they can never know the love of a "black mammy." And I am sure that this kindly feeling between the outgoing generation of slave owners and slaves is mutual. When the Negro wants work, he comes to us for employment. When he is hungry, he comes to us still for food. When he is naked, he comes to us for clothing. When he is in trouble, he comes to us for counsel. When he wishes to buy a little piece of land so that he may own a home of his own, he comes to us to "stand for him." When his child is sick, he comes to us for medicine, and when it dies, he comes to us to help him buy its coffin.[8]

The Colonel felt his class was the race of "Teutons, God's kings of men."[9] His views, condescending and trenchantly racist, may appall the modern reader. But they were common attitudes of the time, the racism constituting a powerful force in the American environment. The Southerners felt they had treated their black slaves justly, and now, with Reconstruction, they felt betrayed. It was this perception of political betrayal that enraged the Colonel:

When the election comes on, he [the black] does not come to us, but goes to our political opponent and his political master and gets his orders how to vote and a dollar or two perhaps in addition and often nothing but promises, accompanied by assurances that we want to put him back into slavery, and with this all connection between him and his political master ends till the next election. . . . We delivered the African man over to the nation in 1865 orderly, fairly industrious, without vices, without disease, without crime. In the hands of the nation he has become disorderly, idle, vicious, diseased; three times more criminal than the native white and one and a half times more criminal than the foreign white, consisting largely of the scum of Europe. . . .[10]

Having thus seen the Colonel trash most of America's ethnic minorities, it is surprising to learn that he was also a liberal-thinking educator of national influence.

He was a man of ironic contradictions, being almost alone among private educators, North or South, who was convinced of the value of a public school system. Furthermore, he lent it considerable support. As early as 1870 he was advocating free public schools for blacks, although he wanted the schools segregated.

He also was a strong lobbyist for greater opportunities for women.

Originally opposed to women's education as a waste of funds, he was converted by a tour of the Massachusetts school system, which in the elementary grades was staffed overwhelmingly by female teachers. Accordingly, he publicly advocated the recruitment of women as an answer to the nation's teacher shortage. In North Carolina, he successfully lobbied for the establishment, in 1891, of the state's first college for women.

□

Eventually, the yoke of Reconstruction was lifted—not by klan riders such as the Colonel, but by the American electorate. The remedy, however, involved perhaps the biggest election scandal in the nation's history: the presidential election of 1876 was won, both the popular and electoral votes, by Democrat Samuel Tilden, who was backed by the South. However, the Republican Congress denied him the presidency.[11]

The effect of the stolen election was so traumatic that although he was but five years old at the time, Bob Bingham remembered it well:

I had a little tin bucket with Tilden's picture on it. I can yet recall my father's face, his hope at first, the cruel blow when the Republicans stole the Presidency, but always the unflinching courage, his and my mother's unconquerable souls. Nor were they unique. Our breed, nearly all the men, all the women, so far as I can recall, stood fast to the death. I know every phase of it all; the poverty and the pride, the gentility, the gracious manners, the romance, the preservation of dignity and high and generous humanity in rags and semi-starvation. I know the whole story of the Negro. Most of ours would not leave us. I know the problem of feeding them when the family was barely able to subsist.

My grandfather Bingham's barns were burned under the direct supervision of the carpetbag Judge Albion W. Tourgee, and three thousand bushels of wheat destroyed, the first crop made after the surrender. The same grandfather put one hundred thousand dollars in gold into Confederate bonds immediately after the defeat at Gettysburg. My maternal great-uncle was Jonathan Worth, justly famous as Governor of North Carolina, and my maternal grandfather was John Milton Worth, who, with his brother, fought the carpetbaggers and scalawags to the death. Two of my mother's three brothers were killed. The one surviving was a small child. . . .[12]

Against this background, that of the defeated South, were raised Bob Bingham, his future wife Mary Lily, his friend and future law partner Dave Davies, and his friend and future physician Hugh Young.

In those hard times for the South, the rest of the country was booming. The commercial production of petroleum had begun and in Ohio, Henry Flagler and John D. Rockefeller had formed the world's first great industrial monopoly—the Standard Oil Company.

In the South, family pressure to repair financial conditions would determine the course of the lives of both Bingham and Mary Lily and to a lesser extent those of Davies and Young.

Of the lot, the injustice of the times seems to have most heavily affected Bob Bingham. And he was so impressed with the power of politics that he served the Democratic party with a dependence rarely seen in American careers, viewing the party as his protector and *padrone.*

Dependency was not new to him.

Bob grew up in the shelter of the Bingham School, walking no further than the building next door for a quality education in the sciences, languages, and liberal arts.

Graduating in 1888 at the age of sixteen, he enrolled in the fall at the University of North Carolina in Chapel Hill, 20 miles from the Bingham School, where he was remembered as "being extraordinarily handsome, a charmer of the fair sex, a gifted debater and a star football player." [13]

"I would say that he was the handsomest man I ever saw," said Bingham's former classmate, Charles Mangum. "All of the women loved him and all the men admired him. What a fine physical specimen he was, charming and gracious to the superlative degree. He was the social lion of our day." [14]

Social indeed. "He was at home anywhere," said classmate William Andrews of Raleigh. "I have seen him many times entertain a party of 20 or 30 after a dance and had the full attention of all. He was one of the finest chaps I ever knew. A social success always." [15]

At Chapel Hill, Bob was a member of Alpha Tau Omega fraternity and participated in many campus activities, including debating. "But his most important student achievement," recalled Mangum, "was his captaincy of the first University of North Carolina football team to engage in an intercollegiate contest. The players were limited to members of the sophomore class. The game as then played was more like English Rugby than present-day football," and Bingham's team "cleaned up other campus outfits to win the university championship" and the right to play Wake Forest College. In a game played at Raleigh on October 18, 1888, Bingham's team defeated the Wake Forest eleven, although the score seems to have been lost to history.[16]

He was the fourth generation of Binghams to attend the school. His great-grandfather had been a professor of English there from 1801 to 1805, his grandfather had graduated there in 1827 and his father in 1857. He was proud of his family's ties to the school.[17]

□

Bob Bingham's closest friend at the school was Dave Davies, born William Watkins Davies, a fellow North Carolinian whose family likewise dated back to the American Revolution. Small, handsome, fair-haired Davies still carried a bit of the family's Welsh brogue. He was some two years older than Bingham but in the same class, his entry into school being delayed by financial considerations.

Bingham, primarily carrying pre-law courses, was a desultory student, carrying a lighter than average class load but compiling a respectable 89.0 grade point average during his four semesters of enrollment, from September 1888 through May 1890.[18]

In the last semester, he, Davies, and classmate Shepard Bryan founded the Order of the Gimghouls, a secret fraternity lodged off-campus in Chapel Hill at Rosemary Street and Boundary Lane.[19]

In the summer of 1890, Bingham left the university without graduating. There is no documentation in the school records as to why, but there must have been a strong reason. He was an established hero and leader on the Chapel Hill campus, enjoying a status which was of utmost importance to his ego and which he would not regain for nearly twenty years.

The move was costly, and neither he nor his family were well off. Furthermore, there are strong indications that Bingham resented leaving school. In future years, Bingham always listed the "University of North Carolina, class of 1891," as his school, suggesting that he had graduated, although not precisely stating it.

If pressed, he would list the University of Virginia in a manner suggesting he had taken post-graduate law courses there, but he did no such thing. As for studying law, there was an excellent law school at the University of North Carolina, the very same law school from which Dave Davies graduated in 1892. But records show that Bingham took law courses at the university only after a six-year absence in the summer of 1896.[20]

Although there is no direct evidence, the likely cause of Bingham's departure from Chapel Hill and the state of North Carolina seems to have been a conflict with the Kenan family.[21] The very same Kenan family which had ousted his grandfather in 1805. This time, however, the irritant wasn't politics. It was romance.

□

It began at a commencement dance in the spring of 1890, when Bob Bingham took up with Mary Lily Kenan.

She and Bingham had known each other for several years. Bob's sisters, Sadie and Mary, had been classmates of Mary Lily's at the Peace Institute in Raleigh. Through the sisters, Bob was introduced to Mary Lily and the pair met occasionally thereafter at various social functions, dances, and parties. Though both were attractive, they seemed indifferent to each other.[22]

Mary Lily was four years older than Bob, but it was not a factor in their dating. Indeed, Bingham seemed to have a preference for older women—many women he courted, including Mary Lily, were older than he. In addition, older women and younger men were acceptable to the time and place. The slaughter of the Civil War had reduced the white male Southern population to such an extent that relationships between slightly older women and younger men were not unusual. For example, Mary Lily's mother was three years older than her father. Bob Bingham's mother was about a year older than the Colonel.

Mary Lily had come to the commencement at the insistence of friends: There would be dances and all sorts of delightful times. She knew such affairs, while chaperoned, weren't sedate. She accepted with that in mind, expecting who knows?—sort of a civilized bacchanal, rowdy and high-spirited—a *release* from the stress of the college year and the gray winter months.

For her, it began slowly. We can imagine that she sat demurely in the chapel listening to the baccalaureate sermon. They strolled about the grounds and explored the white-columned buildings. Romance seemed to brood among the treetops, reflected in the faces of the fine, strong young boys and men who came in and out at the great doors, and who looked with open admiration into the glowing face of the girl from Wilmington. It was here that young Bingham reintroduced himself. She would have been pretty, very desirable in her low-cut white gown. According to Kenan family sources, they met each day and night during the week, dancing and swirling to "The Blue Danube" and "Tales from the Vienna Woods" and other waltzes of Johann Strauss.

Such waltzes were still considered risqué. In her parents time, they had been banned. Only Scotch reels and quadrilles were danced. From the moment of its introduction, the waltz was looked upon as most indelicate, indeed, an outrage on female delicacy. Preachers denounced it as a heinous sin and an abomination. They wrung their hands over the circumstance of a man who was neither lover nor husband encircling a lady's waist and whirling her about in his arms.[23]

But this was a new era, a "Gilded Age," and a time of music and art. Sousa had just composed "The Washington Post March," Tchaikovsky had published his ballet *Sleeping Beauty,* and Richard Strauss had released his *Don Juan.* Rimsky-Korsakov's *Scheherazade* had crossed the ocean, and a novelty called "cinema" was being exhibited at the university.

□

Mary Lily and Bob Bingham became lovers, in the soft contest where she resists, but not too quickly, and he persists, but not too strongly.

Almost immediately she saw the dark side of him, a self-centered youth who was obsessed with the acquisition of power. She was appalled at his conceits. She was equally shocked by what she saw in herself: that she was attracted both by the fiery aura of power which surrounded him, and by her own need for adventure and danger. And she knew better than most lovers that her yearning for him was not only an indulgence of the flesh, but a step into self-destruction.

Perhaps it didn't matter. Perhaps there was no danger to his ambition. The world was theirs. The South had changed and the times were optimistic. Speaking like an Old Testament prophet in Louisville, Kentucky, the legendary editor Henry Watterson had proclaimed the New South·

The whole story of the South may be summed up in a sentence: She was rich, and she lost her riches; she was poor and in bondage; she was set free, and she had to go to work; she went to work, and she is richer than ever before.[24]

□

In the fall of 1890, Bob enrolled at the University of Virginia. Located in Charlottesville, among the foothills of the Blue Ridge Mountains, the university was within four hours' train ride of Washington, D.C. During this same period, Mary Lily is known to have visited relatives in Washington and, judging from statements made by both of them in later years, the couple met in both Washington and Charlottesville for liaisons. "We had an affair," said Mary Lily.[25]

The affair may have been the reason Bob chose the Charlottesville school. He certainly did not resume the career course he had laid out at Chapel Hill. Despite Bingham's later claims that he attended the law school at Virginia, his college records show him enrolled in pre-medical courses—an unexplained shift in plans.

Bingham's presence in medical classes is confirmed in the autobiography of his friend, the brilliant medical student Hugh Young.

Young was born in San Antonio, Texas, on September 18, 1870, to William Hugh and Frances Michie (Kemper) Young, a descendant of Hugh Young, who came to America from Bally-gown, County Antrim, Ulster, Ireland, in 1741. He would say later that part of the bond between him and Bob Bingham was the Civil War background of their families. Young's grandfather, Hugh Franklin Young, was an officer during the Texas revolution and a brigadier general in the Confederate army in the Civil War. His father also won distinction in the Civil War, as the youngest brigadier general in the Confederate army.[26]

□

At Virginia, the older, more studious Hugh basked in Bingham's society. They played together on the football team in the fall of 1890 and Young said he was in awe of Bingham.

I was trying for the team, and we soon became fast friends. His father was the celebrated Colonel Bingham who commanded North Carolina troops in the Civil War, and as my father had commanded Texans, we quickly formed an offensive and defensive alliance against the Virginians, who were prone to belittle soldiers from other Southern states.[27]

Young comments that it is ironic that he had entered college intending to become a journalist and instead became a great doctor. Bingham, on the other hand, entered as a medical student and later became a great journalist.

□

Living conditions at the University of Virginia were primitive. There were no bathrooms. Under their beds, they "had a washtub which a Negro boy filled with hot water on Sunday morning. It took a long scrub to make up for the absence of bathing during the week."[28]

Despite the rigors of the lodging, the meals were good and cheap. They lived at mess halls that were remarkably inexpensive, varying in cost from $14 to $16 a month, and with very good Southern cooking.[29]

□

In December 1890, the liaisons of Mary Lily and Bingham were discovered by the Kenan family. Apart from the shock of scandal, the Kenans were appalled by the persistence of the lovers. The Kenans were looking for a far better match than poor Bob Bingham. Unimpressed by his family background, good looks, or athletic fame, they focused on his apparent character and found him wanting. He was a rascal, a rake, an indifferent student, and a man with few prospects for improvement.

In their eyes, Mary Lily was the sparkling diamond of the Kenan jewel box, and she was a prize too good for a Bingham.[30] Bob Bingham would not do at all. They thought they had been rid of Bingham in Chapel Hill. Now the family took further steps. Mary Lily was ordered home to Kenansville. There, within the month, she met Henry Flagler and he seemed to take Bingham out of her mind. She even seemed relieved that the romance had ended. Perhaps the flame had burned too fast and too intensely for her to handle. Bingham entreated her for meetings, but she refused. It was over.[31] Shortly afterward she turned completely to Flagler. Bob Bingham was handsome and charming but, upon reflection, only a boy who knew little beyond the social boundaries of the South. Henry Flagler was a man who could deliver the world.

□

Bingham, who was given to sulks, dropped out of his classes but continued to live at the university, perhaps hoping that Mary Lily would again slip off to Washington.

To pass the time, he spent much of the remaining school year on romps with winsome young women, including a local married belle.

"Bob's good looks," said Young, "soon won the favor of the great college vamp, a Mrs. Du Bose, a grass widow who had a fine stable of riding horses. Bob was soon elected to ride with her over the mountainous bridle paths of Albemarle, much to our envy."[32]

□

That summer of 1891, the Colonel moved his school from Mebane some 200 miles west to Asheville. There he had bought 250 acres on a site overlooking the French Broad River. Its facilities included the first gymnasium and swimming pool ever built in the South specifically for secondary instruction.[33]

The mountain town chosen by Colonel Bingham was more than 200 years old. It sat comfortably on a plateau ringed by the Blue Ridge and Smoky ranges, so named because above and around the peaks there arise smoky hazes which give a ghostlike mystery to the locale, the former hunting grounds of the Cherokee Indians.[34]

In July, which was the end of the school year at the University of Virginia, Bob left to join his father's school as professor of Greek and Latin. He was broke, in need of income, and Asheville was far enough away from Kenan territory to ensure peace.

But why did he go at all? Here was a young man with the world at his feet who suddenly abandons his education and career and virtually exiles himself in an isolated mountain resort. Why?

And why did his father, in that eventful summer of 1891, decide to move his school to Asheville? Why did he move so far away from any college or university or large population center from which he might hope to draw students? Did the Colonel foresee that within a few years Asheville would enter a boom period? Perhaps. But it is unlikely, given the Colonel's lifetime track record for bad business judgment. The Colonel had inherited the school in 1873 upon the death of his brother, William, and he had operated it profitably in the shadow of Chapel Hill. Why did he move? Was it pressure from the Kenans? Not entirely. Two commentators on the move say it was done in part because the Colonel was "seeking a better climate" and chose Asheville because of its "health-giving" environment.[35]

And why did the son choose to follow him? Or was it the other way around? Did the father choose the healthy climate of Asheville so that his son would have a place of recuperation? From what?

Whatever the causes, with no degree, having no more than five semesters of college to his credit, and no profession of his own, Bingham spent the next four years in Asheville. He taught at the Bingham School, being listed on the faculty roster as a full professor of Greek and Latin. This handsome and restless bachelor, this ambitious star athlete had dropped out of sight. For the first three of those four years, there are no surviving letters, no diaries, no financial information, no references by friends, lovers, or foes. There is only a blank as to what he was doing and why he was doing it in the seclusion of Asheville.

□

To summarize the mystery so far: We know from Dave Davies that Mary Lily and Bob Bingham began their affair while Bingham was at the University of North Carolina.[36] We know from Mary Lily and Bob Bingham that the affair continued while he was at the University of Virginia, where it broke off. That spring of 1891 saw Mary Lily's introduction to Henry Flagler and Bingham's fling with Mrs. Du Bose. Then, for no apparent reason, the Bingham School is moved from Mebane, an ideal and profitable location, 200 miles westward to a small mountain town that has few facilities other than a train depot and some inns that serve as health spas.

There Bob Bingham's career and education stop dead in the water and he enters sort of a self-imposed quarantine. Was he ill? Was he a fugitive from some crime or scandal?

With those few facts, we will leave the mystery for now.

□

In the meantime, Henry Flagler's life was changing dramatically.

His wife, flying into terrible rages, had become noticeably insane. She confided to friends, mind you with some cause, that Flagler was unfaithful to her. She became convinced, through Ouija board messages, that she herself was being romantically pursued by the Czar of Russia. On one occasion, she tried to kill her doctor. On another, she attacked Henry with shears, attempting to kill *him*. Psychiatrists were called in and she was literally taken away in a straitjacket, beginning a series of confinements in mental institutions.

During Alice's absences, Mary Lily spent more and more time with Flagler, and it was generally agreed among the more polite friends that her gaiety and charm were responsible for lifting him out of the heavy mood of depression caused by his wife's illness.

Less tactful gossips said that Mary Lily was providing more than gaiety to lift Henry out of his moods.

Flagler did his best to observe the dictates of respectability. Although his private car was frequently at Mary Lily's disposal, she was usually accompanied by Elizabeth Ashley, and there were long times when she was alone. To console herself, she developed a dependence on bourbon whiskey.

In the meantime, the ties between Mary Lily and Flagler grew tighter and more complicated. In the summer of 1894, shortly after his graduation from the University of North Carolina, William Rand Kenan, Jr., Mary Lily's brother, met Flagler. Almost immediately, Kenan, a brilliant chemical engineer, began work on the various Flagler projects in Florida. His first job with Flagler was the design of the power plant, laundry, steam heating, and refrigeration of the Breakers Hotel in Palm Beach.[37]

About this time, too, in the mid-1890s, at the height of the Gilded Age, the gossip columnists finally caught on that Flagler and Mary Lily were lovers. It was then, when the affair became public, that Mary Lily's brother began to brood—first on the family's disgrace, then on Flagler's millions.

Of Will Kenan, Flagler said, "[He] got more for his dollar than any man I ever knew. . . . Will Kenan was 21 years old when he was born."[38]

Also that summer, Bob Bingham's self-exile in Asheville suddenly ended when he, too, was brooding—on money and on a way to break free from the confines of the Bingham School.

Eleanor

BOB FOUND the solution to his problems sunning herself on the balustrade of his own Bingham School. Her name was Eleanor Miller, nicknamed "Babe," and she was a gorgeous brunette who had come to Asheville for vacation.

By 1894, Asheville had graduated from a frontier trading post into a fashionable spa. It was a town—one might even call it a *city*—of hotels, mountain lodges, and millionaires' mansions, the latter market being spurred by construction of the Biltmore, the 8,000-acre estate of George Vanderbilt, grandson of the railroad magnate.[1]

Among the sights to see in Asheville was the Bingham School. Continuing to grow in reputation, situated on a bluff with a magnificent view, it was now the oldest preparatory school in the South and one of the most prestigious in the nation.

Thus, on a warm summer day, the school was visited by some bored young women from Louisville, Kentucky, who had nothing much better to do. Among them was Miss Miller, a winsome twenty-five years old with a stunning figure, dark blue eyes, and a dazzling smile.

□

The Miller family was historically important to Louisville and had a lot of money, a fact which had no more chance of escaping

43

Bob's keen interest than would the scent of a fox from a tracking bloodhound.

The fortune came from the maternal side of the family, primarily from Eleanor's grandfather, Denis Long, who was a builder of Ohio River steamboats and bridges from the 1830s through the 1880s.

The details of Bob and Eleanor's courtship are not known, but is likely that after the initial chance meeting at the school, they encountered each other at summer dinners and dances. A handsome, eligible bachelor of good background, Bingham would have been among the first choices on any hostess' guest list.

Their courtship was swift.

As professor of Greek and Latin at the Bingham School, Bob was obligated to remain in Asheville for the coming year.[2] But in late August of 1884, just before Eleanor returned to Louisville, Bingham wrote to her parents expressing his desire to marry her and asked their consent for an engagement. His duties at the school prevented him from pleading his suit in person, so he asked only to become engaged until he could see them.

Bingham was anxious to impress his would-be in-laws that he was a decently brought up young man who had only the best concerns of Eleanor in mind.[3]

□

Throughout the letter, there is a tone of walking on eggshells to avoid riling the Millers. Such delicacy is significant because he and Eleanor were adults and had the right, in custom and in law, to marry. Indeed, the choice was almost certainly Eleanor's, not her parents. It was a long-standing tradition in the American South that parents seldom oppose their daughters in the choice of a husband.

This custom was commented upon as early as 1832 when the visiting Prince Murat, son of the King of Naples, wrote:

The interference of parents is looked upon as an indiscretion in these matters. Nothing can be more happy than the lot of a young American lady from the age of fifteen to twenty-five, particularly if she possesses the attraction of beauty, which they generally do. She becomes the idol and admiration of all; her life is passed amid festivities and pleasure. She knows no contradiction to mar her inclinations, much less refusals. She has only to select from a hundred worshippers the one whom she considers will contribute to her future happiness in life.[4]

Nevertheless, Bingham pledged not to even *engage* Eleanor without her parents' consent. Perhaps to ensure domestic tranquillity, he was only observing the proprieties. More likely, however, being the person he was, Bob was taking every step possible to ensure that there was no break between Eleanor and her family inheritance.

□

Astounded, the Millers responded that Bingham needn't bother to come to Louisville. They were coming to him.

They arrived in mid-November.[5]

Their meetings with Bob Bingham were more in the nature of brawls. Eleanor's mother, Henrietta, did not like him on sight. To further cloud the skies, almost immediately after the initial skirmishes, Eleanor's father, Samuel Miller, suffered a nervous breakdown and was placed under a doctor's care.[6] At the time, Miller, a prominent capitalist, was fifty-six years old with a history of tuberculosis and mental disturbance.

He was ordered to rest.

Anxious to be good hosts, Bob and his father persuaded the Millers to be the Bingham family's guests for the Christmas holidays. Miller's physician, Dr. T. E. Lynne, agreed, saying that Asheville's dry climate and mountain air would lead to a speedier recovery than could be had in Louisville.

To complete the holiday arrangement, all three of Miller's children, his son-in-law, and his two grandchildren converged on Asheville.

They had come to give peace to his spirits. Gathered round him on that Christmas and New Year, in addition to the Binghams and Eleanor, were his wife, Henrietta; their daughter, Mrs. Katherine Miller Callahan, and her husband, Americus Franklin Callahan; the Millers' son, Dennis; and the Millers' two grandchildren, Franklin Callahan and Samuel Miller Callahan, aged six and three, respectively.

Upon the conclusion of the holidays, the Callahans and their son Franklin returned to their home in Chicago. Their youngest son, Samuel, remained in Asheville to bring some cheer to his grandfather. Also remaining in Asheville were Eleanor and her nineteen-year-old brother, Dennis.

Six weeks passed with Samuel Miller showing increasing signs of improvement.

On the first of February, Dr. Lynne notified the anxious Mrs. Miller that her husband seemed to have recovered. Celebratory telegrams were sent to family members and, from Chicago, Katherine Callahan replied with an immediate wire saying to hold the train until she could come down, via Knoxville. She wanted to ride home to Louisville with her father, son, and family.

The following afternoon, February 2, feeling much improved and in a cheerful frame of mind, Samuel Miller was permitted to take a carriage to the depot.

He was accompanied only by his son and grandchild.

As the train carrying his daughter pulled in, he leaped from the carriage as if possessed by demons. Eluding his pursuing son, he ran between two of the train cars. Caught by the wheels, he was pulled under and instantly killed.

He died under the wheels of his daughter's train.

Dennis, in attempting to save his father's life, was knocked down by the car and narrowly escaped being grabbed by the same deadly wheels.

Two days later, the family returned with the body to Louisville.

Eleanor's mother never recovered from the trauma, being a demanding and suspicious figure throughout her long life.[7]

Following her father's death, suffering from melancholy and insomnia, Eleanor grew distant from Bob. When she left Asheville with her father's casket, she said she would not return.

For Bob, the ensuing spring and summer were seasons of bleak anxiety in which nine out of his every ten letters to Eleanor went unacknowledged. Seizing the bit in his teeth, he borrowed

$300 from some Asheville friends and resigned from the school early in December.

Christmas morning, 1895, found him in Louisville on Eleanor's doorstep.[8]

Five months later, in May 1896, they were married. It was done in the usual swift Bob Bingham style, he having obtained the license on the morning of the event.[9] His old school chum, Dave Davies, now a lawyer in Atlanta, quickly came up to be best man.

Robert had not only married Eleanor Miller, he had married Louisville. The city would be his home for the rest of his life and the birthplace of the Binghams of Louisville.

Kentucky Home

LOUISVILLE lies on a level plain that curves for 8 miles along the Ohio, a river first mapped by the French and called "La Belle Rivière." Slightly more than 100 miles downstream from Cincinnati, the town's original name was Falls of the Ohio, until, as a gesture of gratitude for the aid given by Louis XVI and the French nation to the American Revolution, the name was changed to Louisville, usually pronounced and often spelled "Lewisville" by early Kentuckians.

The falls are the only interruption of the mighty river in its 1,000-mile sweep from western Pennsylvania to its meeting with the Mississippi at Cairo, Illinois, some 120 miles below St. Louis, Missouri. The falls are rough, but navigable, being actually a long, rock ledge with boulder-strewn rapids and not much of a waterfall at all.

The first settlement was attempted by the English in 1773, but failed. The first permanent settlement was in May 1778, two years after the United Colonies proclaimed themselves to be the independent United States of America.

Under orders from Virginia governor-elect Thomas Jefferson to establish a base in the British rear, George Rogers Clark led a small force of militia—about 150 men—and a group of perhaps eighty settlers, which included families and a few adventurous young bachelors. They camped on a little island a short distance off the Kentucky shore near the foot of present-day Twelfth Street.[1]

Whether Clark had built his fort or not, a city would certainly have risen at this site because of the falls.[2] Boaters would lighten their vessels at the head of the falls and portage the cargo and passengers to calmer waters downstream, where the vessels could be reloaded. Few travelers, however, went beyond the falls, there being litle to the west but Indian country and the hostilities of the British and Spanish. Usually the boats were aimed right at Louisville and newcomers either stayed in the settlement or pushed further inland to the Bluegrass Country, a limestone region whose calcium and phosphorous-rich soil yielded a grass high in protein. It is prime stock-raising country and when the grass blooms in early May it is blue, hence the name.

Settlers from the Tidewater area of Virginia, from the mid-Atlantic, and the upper South swelled Louisville. In 1830, a canal enabled river traffic to bypass the falls and Louisville began a profitable trade, including the production of bourbon whiskey and cigars.

After the immigrants disembarked, their boats helped build the town, providing inexpensive sawn timbers and boards for houses and buildings.

In 1818, not long after the town began, Eleanor's great-grandparents came to America from Ireland and settled in Erie, Pennsylvania, where they raised three sons: Denis, Matthew, and John.[3]

Trained as a boat builder's apprentice in Erie, Denis left home in 1838 and journeyed to the frontier wilds of Louisville, where he tried his hand as a master builder. Within two years, at the age of twenty-four, he had established himself as an expert steamboat builder.[4] That same year his father died and he was joined by his mother and brothers.

Denis became a major mover and doer in Louisville, often acting in concert with such local entrepreneurs as Benjamin F. Avery, William B. Belknap, Thomas Coleman, and Theodore Ahrens. The group, known as "the Iron Men" both because of their trade in iron and their resolute business honesty, symbolized the best of the age of individual enterprise. Their ties to

Louisville were intensely personal and their local prestige enormous.

□

In those ante-bellum days, Louisville was a center of steamboat building and it was a very common thing for Long and his friends to meet upon some newly launched boat every Sunday morning between the hours of nine and twelve o'clock.

They were men of muscle, energy, pluck, and success—men who built steamboats and the machinery for them, who furnished boats, and took great interest in steamboats and steamboating.[5] They were the primary steamboat men on the Ohio.[6]

Long was soon a millionaire in a time when there was no income tax and the average American skilled working man made less that $700 a year. The average woman's wage as a teacher or factory worker was even less, about $400 a year. Unskilled labor of both sexes earned proportionally less.[7]

In 1842, Denis Long's wife, Catherine Elizabeth Young, had given birth to Mary Henrietta who grew up to marry Samuel Adams Miller and on July 11, 1870, their second child, Eleanor, was born.[8]

□

Samuel Miller, Eleanor's father, was a classic capitalist and had as much talent for making money as did Eleanor's grandfather. A native of Louisville, he built the first railroad bridge to cross from Louisville to Indiana. By the time of Eleanor's birth in 1870, he was president of an iron foundry in Louisville and owned the Danville (Illinois) Water Company.

In 1883, Henrietta and Samuel Miller erected one of Louisville's finest downtown mansions. Built of red granite and done in the French Second Empire style, it had four storys of turrets and bay windows capped by a magnificently coppered mansard roof.[9]

□

By 1896, the year of Eleanor's marriage to Bob, Louisville had a population of 200,000 and had surpassed Cincinnati as the queen city of the Ohio River.

Perhaps the preeminent figure in Louisville at the time was Henry "Marse" Watterson, who would be at various times Bob Bingham's patron, protector, and fierce enemy.

Editor and part-owner of the *Courier-Journal* for many years, Watterson was born in 1840, the son of a prominent Washington journalist. Much of his childhood was spent in the nation's capital, but at age sixteen he started his own paper, *The New Era*, in his father's Tennessee summer home and printed a political editorial that was copied all over the country. During the Civil War he served with the Confederate cavalry and also managed to get out a newspaper called *The Rebel*, which delighted Lee's soldiers because of its "modern" style.[10]

His capacity at liquor was considered startling even for Kentucky. During poker games at various Louisville saloons, he would send relays of messengers to his office for supplies of bourbon and cash to tide him through the game. Once, when he had cleaned the office out and there was nothing left but some Mexican money, he commandeered that.[11]

Watterson hated the Grant administration, and in his opinion the Republican party was no better than a band of highwaymen and horse thieves. Accordingly, he and his paper did much to give Louisville its Southern flavor. He used the *Courier-Journal* to support a more liberal national Democratic party by championing the newly attained rights of the blacks and vigorously condemning the Ku Klux Klan.

His main partner at the *Courier-Journal* was publisher Walter Haldeman. While Watterson supervised the gathering of news and wrote his editorials, Haldeman gave the *Courier-Journal* financial balance. He turned its plant into the most modern outside New York. In 1876, he erected a state-of-the-art publishing plant at Fourth and Green streets. Ten years later, he dazzled Louisville by installing electric lights throughout the building. The next year this newspaper plant became the third in the nation to adopt Ottmar Mergenthaler's revolutionary Linotype machine, which had ended setting body type by hand.

Louisville by 1896 was a city of broad avenues, well paved and well shaded, with ample spaces of abundant foliage and flowery lawns. "A beautiful city: a beautiful, healthful city in a temperate climate, surrounded by a fertile country," said *Harper's* maga-zine.[12] One-third of all the tobacco grown in North America was handled in its warehouses.

Following his marriage, Bob, who still had no university de-gree, enrolled in the University of Louisville law school for the 1896–97 academic year, graduating in May 1897 after compress-ing a two-year course into a single year, a privilege granted to "students whose knowledge and training are such that they will not be an impediment to the class." [13]

It is likely that he was granted such privilege because of the influence of his wife's family. As detailed earlier, Bob had no legal experience and had shown no sustaining interest in law. What he did have was an erratic college career with an acceptable grade point average and a flirtation with the idea of becoming a physi-cian.

So one wonders about the new arrangement, but not for long. There are some likely answers. First, law school was easier to enter than medical school and required less time to obtain a de-gree. Second, law practice was a direct path to politics. And that is where thirty-year-old Bob Bingham was now aiming his career.

Following graduation, Bingham bought himself a partnership in the Louisville law firm of Pryor, O'Neal and Pryor. It lasted less than a year, however, and in 1898 he was given $2,500 to set himself up in a real estate agency. The donor was his maternal grandfather, John Milton Worth, who gave Bob the money in lieu of an inheritance.[14]

Around this time, Bingham began to dignify himself, chang-ing his signature from "Bob" to "Robert Worth Bingham," for example and otherwise straightening up his rakish image. He began representing himself as a man not given to drink and ca-rousing, although letters surviving from the late 1890s and early 1900s provide ample, if not enthusiastic, testimony to the oppo-site.[15]

For example, in October 1900, a visiting businessman wrote a letter congratulating Bingham on "two fine days . . . of debauch-ing influences" and said he got home to York, Pennsylvania, "still a little dazed by the bourbon influence. . . ." Indeed, Bingham's trade in bourbon was so great that over the years the head of the

Green River Distillery wrote him several notes of grateful thanks, a testimonial indeed.[16]

Nor did Bob give up his habits entirely. He simply moved them to Atlanta, Georgia, where, on "business trips," he would cut loose with his old Chapel Hill friends, Dave Davies and Shepard Bryan.

The three lawyers were running with a fast crowd in Atlanta and one woman, feeling she had been discarded by Bingham, sent word up from Atlanta that while Bob was "doing his great club and society act in Louisville . . . [he] was nothing more than an ordinary drunkard . . . a club house man" with a long list of now-neglected "lady friends." [17]

Bingham could not afford to have such gossip circulate in Louisville, and quickly enlisted the help of Davies to squash the rumor. Davies traced the source to "one *particular* lady" who felt Robert had been ignoring her. Davies somehow convinced her to cease and desist.[18]

Shortly afterward, Davies went off to the Spanish-American War, serving as captain in a company of Georgia volunteers which he had recruited. After four months of combat in Cuba, he returned home.[19]

In the meantime, Louisville was preparing for the twentieth century. In April 1899, the last ten gas streetlights were turned off, replaced by electricity. A few months later, the Louisville Country Club, complete with swimming pool, opened near River Road on the rocky bluff above the river. And John E. Roche, president of the Louisville Carriage Company, became the first resident to own an automobile. It was steam propelled. He exchanged it for an electrically operated machine the following year. By 1902, some thirty-six automobiles contested with horses for Louisville street space and there was an auto race at Churchill Downs in 1903. Electric trolleys replaced mule cars in 1901, a seemingly innocent event which would have tragic consequences for the Bingham and Kenan families.

□

Things still weren't working well for Bingham. His real estate business very quickly ran into trouble of an unknown nature, and he was informed by stockholders that unless he agreed to surrender control, court action would be taken. He so agreed.[20]

Having extricated himself from that debacle, Bingham started a new business by persuading Davies to move to Louisville and set up a law partnership. Davies, newly returned from Cuba, arrived in late August 1899. They opened their law firm, Bingham and Davies, on September 1, with offices in the Louisville Trust Company building.

Davies' input of cash allowed Bingham to cover some bounced checks and to finally pay off the original $300 loan which had financed his original trip to Louisville.[21]

Despite Davies' support, it was not a good time for Bingham. He was in debt to his grandfather and others. His initial two business ventures—the Pryor law firm and the real estate company—were failures. And the once strong athlete was beginning to have severe health problems.

The nature of his illness is unknown. It may have been a recurrence of the mysterious quarantine in Asheville, or it may have been a souvenir of his Atlanta adventures. Whatever it was, he would not or could not have it treated in Louisville. Instead, in February of 1900, he went to see Hugh Young at John Hopkins Hospital in Baltimore, Maryland. Young was not only a urologist, but also an expert in venereal disease. Apparently on Young's advice, Bingham also took treatments in Asheville and Philadelphia, imploring confidentiality in every case.[22]

In this same year, Davies fell in love, a whirlwind romance culminating in marriage with one Sadie Coonley of Chicago. In a series of letters, she refers to Bingham's mysterious illness being so severe that Davies was forced to remain in Louisville and tend to the law practice while she went home alone to New York to inform her parents of her wedding plans.[23]

Despite the illness, the Binghams were having children. Their son Robert, named after the Colonel, was born in 1897; a daughter Henrietta, named after Eleanor's mother, in 1901; and another son Barry in 1906.

During the first five years of their marriage, Eleanor and Bob lived in the upstairs apartment of the Miller mansion.[24]

After the birth of Henrietta, however, grandmother Henrietta Miller gave her daughter and son-in-law $48,000 in securities and a $50,000 house in the wooded suburbs. The house, significantly, was deeded to Eleanor and not to Bob.

About the same time, Bingham saw a further chance to enhance his finances by challenging the last will and testament of his maternal grandfather, Dr. John Milton Worth.

When the eighty-nine-year-old Worth died, he was the president of three manufacturing companies, owner of banks, former state treasurer of North Carolina, and a man so respected that when he passed away in April 1900 the state flags of North Carolina were displayed at half mast.[25]

When Worth died, Bingham went after the legacy like a lawyer after an inheritance. And here we have a fine example of Bingham's ethics in action. In the pursuit of his grandfather's estate, he (1) ignored the fact he had already spent his share of the inheritance; (2) bribed a witness; (3) tried to cheat his clients, namely his two sisters and a cousin, out of their full shares; and (4) slandered whole platoons of opposing members of the Worth family.

The performance was rather numbing and caused one Louisville attorney to remark, "When it comes to money, Robert Bingham is the most ruthless attorney I've ever seen."[26]

The circumstances were these. Following Dr. Worth's death, two wills were filed in court. The first will was written in 1888 at the home of his son Thomas Worth and divided the estate into four equal parts for the four branches of the family. The second and superseding will was written on December 2, 1899, at the home of daughter Addie Worth McAllister, with whom old man Worth had lived since the death of his son Thomas following a "whiskey spree" in 1891.

Most of the bequests were of stock in the Worth manufacturing companies, and because various Worths and McAllisters were officers of the firm, it was a corporate fight for control as well as a money fight.

The case is somewhat complicated but worth following because of the light it sheds on Robert Worth Bingham.

The competing family branches were:

1. The Addie Worth McAllister branch. She was a daughter of Worth, with seven children.
2. The heirs of daughter Delphine Worth Bingham branch. She was Worth's daughter and Bingham's mother who died in 1886. Her heirs were Robert and his sisters Mary Kerr Bingham (McKee) and Sadie Bingham (Grinnan).
3. The Allie Worth branch. She was the widow of John Milton Worth's deceased son, Thomas, and on the board of directors of Worth Manufacturing.
4. The Roberta Collins and Hal M. Worth branch. Mrs. Collins was Dr. Worth's granddaughter and represented by Bingham. Her brother, Hal M. Worth, was opposed by Bingham and was president of the manufacturing companies.

While the 1888 will divided the state equally among the branches, the 1899 version and its codicils greatly favored the McAllister and Worth branches, who got virtually everything, at the expense of the Binghams, who got nothing. This was probably to reward the former for keeping the old man in style after his son died.

About two weeks after Dr. Worth's death, Robert Worth Bingham entered the case by filing as attorney in "the matter of Dr. Worth's will," saying that he was representing himself, his sisters, and his cousin, Mrs. Collins. That same day, Bingham wrote attorney Oscar Sapp of Asheboro, North Carolina, enlisting his aid to shelter and pay a male nurse who would provide testimony to break the 1899 will. Bingham said it would be a good idea to keep the witness in North Carolina rather than to bring him to Louisville, "which would lay us liable to the charge of bribery." [27]

Attorney Sapp went for the arrangement, thus proving he was well named. Bringing the witness to Louisville would have made Bingham liabel for the bribery charge. Leaving him in North Carolina made only Sapp liabel.

In March of 1902, Bingham received an informal offer from the opposition to pay $25,000 in cash if the Bingham clients would drop legal action and hand over their stock. At the time, the stock Bingham and his clients owned was worth $18,500, broken down thusly: Bob had $1,700, or approximately 9 percent; his sister Sadie Grinnan $4,500, or 24 percent; his sister Mary McKee $2,500, which was 13 percent; and his cousin, Mrs. Collins, $10,000, or 54 percent. In a move that would have defrauded his cousin, Bob made a counteroffer to settle for $40,000. The four of them would split it evenly—$10,000 each— he said. His idea of proportionate math was unusual. He had raised his and his sisters share to 25 percent each while lowering the share of his cousin accordingly.

Unable to negotiate the settlement, Bingham saw the case through two trials, the final result was a ruling by the North Carolina Superior Court in July 1902 saying that the 1899 will was *the* will and that the executors were authorized to buy back the 195 shares owned by Bob, his sisters, and his cousin for $21,750. This amounted to $100 per share, plus $2,250 in legal costs. Bob's percentage gave him about $1,960. It was a three-way legal defeat: he had gained less than the settlement offered; he was unable to break the will; and he was unable to gain control of any of the companies.

Win or lose, however, Bob was no miser. He used his share to take his family on a summer trip to England and Continental Europe. It was a custom that would continue each year for the next ten years.

Politics as Usual

ROBERT BINGHAM's true profession in Louisville was not the practice of law but the pursuit of politics. He was never a good lawyer and he was not one of your pie-in-the-sky politicians. To him, politics was a game of excitement and money and he loved it wherever it led him—from the seamiest precinct levels to the carpeted halls of the White House.

There is a tendency among American intellectuals to ennoble themselves by taking on the causes of the downtrodden. If the causes don't exist, they invent them. So it is today. So it was yesterday.

In the first half of his life, Bingham was not guided by such fashion. He did not saturate his politics with thought. Although generally faithful to the Democratic party, he gave no loyalty to person or creed. Throughout his career his politics were as changeable and as varied as the colors woven into Joseph's coat. The one constant seems to have been his own advancement and welfare.

Such clear focus on his goals fit right in with the time and place. In Louisville, such intellectual life that existed was funneled into politics and the law. To Kentuckians, politics was not a noble class struggle. It was more in the line of Voltaire's idea of transferring as much money as possible from one class of citizens to another.

Louisville at the turn of the century was one of a long list of American cities politically corrupt and under boss rule. When Bob Bingham arrived in the 1890s, the city was run by Boss John Whallen, who with his brother had come downriver from Cincinnati and established a political machine built around the Buckingham Burlesque Theatre and Saloon. If that seems to have been an odd site for a political headquarters, bear in mind that only males could vote. Using beer, women, and political favors, Whallen captured the labor and immigrant loyalties in a male-only political environment where wages were low and labor unions were firmly repressed.[1] Miners died daily half a mile beneath the ground. Farmers labored until they were old before their time. Clerks worked for a lifetime in old business houses for little pay and felt themselves honored to have the job. Let well enough alone. That was it.[2] The men compensated for their helplessness by drinking and arguing and boasting at the Whallen saloons. There they were recruited for their votes, assigned petty jobs at the polls, and occasionally picked up a dollar or so from the overflowing coffers of the bosses.

The machine was fed by three main sources of income: graft, usually in the form of kickbacks from public contracts; tithes, another form of kickbacks in which city and county officeholders kicked back 10 percent of their salary to the machine; and donations, the largest coming from the Louisville and Nashville Railroad, known as the L&N.

Not just Louisville, but all of Kentucky state politics of the post–Civil War era was dominated by the L&N. Its lines, most of which were laid down after the Civil War, reached to nearly all the major river and seaports of the South, connecting Louisville to the iron smelting areas of Alabama, and the agricultural and lumber markets of Mobile, New Orleans, Pensacola, and Jacksonville. The L&N tapped the freight from the green pine forests of Georgia and the black coal mines of Kentucky and Tennessee. To build and expand such a railroad called not only for large amounts of capital, but for a protective and predatory network of lawyers and politicians who could seize land with one hand and protect the railroad from restrictive public regulation with the other.

The L&N had been spending money since 1880 to control Kentucky politics. It didn't matter if the candidates were Democrats, Republicans, Populists, or whatever as long as they agreed to further interests of the L&N.

Like many an aspiring lawyer with an eye on politics, Bob Bingham applied to the L&N right away, seeking cases to handle. The railroad obliged by tossing a few small assignments his way.

In later years, after he had become a powerful and respectable newspaper publisher, Bingham was described in articles and book references as a reform politician. In fact, his political rhetoric never attacked capitalism and throughout his legal career his main clients were railroads, banks, and manufacturing companies.[3]

His early career began with the L&N and spanned some of the shabbiest elections in Kentucky history.

In 1899, the year Bob Bingham began handling L&N cases, the railroad tried to prevent the election of antimonopoly Democrat William A. Goebel as governor. The L&N succeeded in giving Republican William S. Taylor a slim victory of 2,000 votes, but the railroad's tactics were too corrupt even for Kentucky and an abused populace forced the election into the Democratic-controlled state legislature for final decision. To help the representatives make up their minds, the L&N transported a thousand armed men to Frankfort, the state capital. Despite those subtle lobbying efforts, the legislature feared Democratic voters even more than the L&N gunmen and announced Goebel to be the victor. The next day, he was shot by a hidden rifleman as he stood on the statehouse steps. He lived long enough to be inaugurated and when he died the legislature passed the gubernatorial baton to his running mate, J. C. W. Beckham. Some suspicious people thought the L&N had a lot to do with this rearrangement, Beckham being quite acceptable to the L&N bosses.[4]

□

Throughout Bingham's career, his involvement with the railroad increased steadily until he eventually became a board member and one of the bosses of the company.[5] He also stood solidly with Beckham, who would become one of Bingham's political patrons.

Bingham's overt political debut came in the 1899 election, working as a polls inspector. He was courted by several factions but chose the Whallen machine, which was bitterly opposed to Goebel and ardently in favor of the L&N candidates.[6]

At the time, Louisville held municipal elections of one sort or another almost every year, a frequency which kept donations rolling in and the political machinery well-oiled with money. Every year, the entire election apparatus of Democrats, Republicans, Prohibitionists, and things in between could count on activity and payment, from the greediest party boss down to the poor black and white men selling their votes. In Louisville, Kentucky, as in most of the South, politics was both an entertainment and an industry.

And so it was for Bingham, who increased his political activity in the mayoral election of 1901 by making speeches on behalf of the winning candidate, Charles Grainger, a Democrat backed by the Whallen machine and the L&N.[7]

His success at public oration gave Bob an inflated view of his popularity and, to the astonishment of all, in early 1902 he tested the waters of Congress, coyly informing supporters he appreciated fully their support and was glad to have friends that felt he could run without embarrassing them or himself.[8]

It was a bit premature. The *Louisville Times* sneered that "Mr. Bingham, although not long a resident of Louisville, [has] interviewed numerous Democratic leaders with a view of becoming a candidate for the Democratic nomination for Congress."[9]

Failing to get the approval of Whallen and the machine, Bingham backed down from entering the primaries.

His first real chance to feed at the public trough came a year later, just prior to the November 1903 elections, when the county attorney, Sam Kirby, stepped aside to accept the Democratic nomination for circuit judge.

The vacant county attorney job would be filled by appointment until a special election could be held. It was a prize plum, providing $5,000 in salary, an office, and a staff paid for by public funds. For politicians, it was a publicity dream, the county attorney being also the district prosecutor. But the real harvest came from inside information on government contracts, which could be exploited financially.

No less than eleven lean and hungry lawyers went after the spoils, and at the head of the pack was Robert Worth Bingham.

He began his approach in a traditional manner, by recruiting friends to lobby on his behalf to the man who would make the interim appointment—Circuit Judge James Gregory.

One of the more influential lobbyists promoting Bingham was William Richards, a patronage chief for Whallen and Governor Beckham, who agreed to have party hacks write endorsing letters to Judge Gregory.

Inasmuch as Richards, Whallen, and Gregory were all part of the same political machine, simple ordinary people might not think such letters were necessary. The three men could simply meet, go over the candidates, and select Bingham. But politics is a system of deceits, and with so many candidates the party needed a written record of Bingham's political popularity to show to backers of his rivals. Accordingly, Richards caused letters to be written to Judge Gregory, as follows:

Dear Judge Gregory,

Realizing the fact that you may soon be called upon to appoint a county attorney, I beg you to permit me to ask your consideration of Mr. Robert Worth Bingham for that office. You doubtless know Mr. Bingham, but I feel constrained to express my appreciation of him as a man, and as a lawyer, and also express my conviction of his eminent fitness for the position. No man can more faithfully and successfully perform the duties of the office, and no man be more satisfactory to the citizens of the county. Trusting you will give Mr. Bingham's name earnest consideration, I am, sincerely . . . [followed by signature].[10]

The above letter was written by Charles Ray, a machine "enforcer" who was described by the *Louisville Evening Post* as a party gunman, a "sure thing" thug "of a class [which] should be chased out of Louisville, but which instead of being under the ban of the police is held in the highest esteem. . . ."[11]

At the bottom of the letter was scribbled a note to Richards saying, "Dear Will—as promised," followed by Ray's initials.

On November 18, announcement was made of Bingham's appointment, a newspaper article noting that he was prominent in the Sons of Confederate Veterans and that there were a number of aspirants.[12]

Had he been an honest, idealistic, and unreasonable man, he would have bitten the hand that fed him by opening a grand jury investigation of a crooked city election which accompanied his appointment. As a machine election it was a classic with wholesale frauds committed throughout the city. In some places "the ballot boxes were stolen and the effect was no election at all. In others, Republican voters were driven away" by club-wielding Democrats such as Charles Ray "while the police stood passively" nearby.[13]

The police were not the only law enforcement officials to watch passively. In the two weeks following the election, Bingham, now among the anointed, was writing friends not about the frauds but about a job which paid $5,000 a year. He noted that in addition to his appointment, he was still conducting his business.

His business, of course, was making money, which he began to do from the day of his appointment, although there is no evidence that his rise to modest fortune was accomplished illegally. There were a number of reasons why his income began to grow in this period, including the aforementioned access to county information, his increased prominence, normal political patronage, an investment partnership with his brother-in-law, Dennis Long, and maybe just plain luck.[15]

Along with the sudden increase in business came the furtherance of his political career, Bingham presenting himself to voters for the first time in 1904, in the special election for county attorney. Victory would only give him the job for one more year, but it was important because the regular election scheduled in November 1905 would keep him in power until 1909. That would give him six consecutive years as an elected official in Kentucky's most populous city—an official, furthermore who occupied a power position, both as a prosecutor and as the city and county's lawyer for business contracts.

The stepping-stone was the 1904 special election, and to Bob it meant a great deal. He curried favor with the Whallen machine in many ways, including looking away from election frauds. Nor did he close the saloons of the Whallen machine and others which operated on Sundays illegally, to the affront of the growing local and national Prohibition movements.

Instead, he kept his alliance with Whallen and as early as July 1904 he felt that he would obtain the nomination for county attorney, which was tantamount to election.[16]

Supported by the machine, Bingham easily won his 1904 election. Harvesting some political spoils, the one-time desultory student was appointed "professor of forensic medicine" and "professor of medical jurisprudence" at the University of Louisville, moderately prestigious sinecures which he would hold for several years of good pay and little work.[17]

At the medical school, he became influential in the medical community and made many friends, most especially Michael Leo Ravitch, a Russian-born dermatologist, and Walter Fisk Boggess, a pediatrician.

In addition to the social friendship, Ravitch was a physician to Bingham. At the time, dermatologists were specialists in skin disease and in syphilis, again suggesting that Bingham may have been having difficulty of a venereal sort.[18]

□

In the summer of 1905, following the Ravitch treatments, Bingham took his wife and two children to Paris. Davies, who was running the law practice in Bingham's absence, as he often did, informed his partner by mail that they were defending the L&N railroad in two damage suits, both involving men killed instantly on the tracks, "one of them a very good case, but the other seems to be a case of contributory negligence [by the railroad]."[19]

Davies also wrote that he had won a case for the Citizens of Oakdale Committee, which was seeking to block a $30,000 graft-laden street improvements contract in their neighborhoods. But in a move which would chill the heart of any lawyer, the clients made an under-the-table deal which looked as if it might cost Davies and Bingham part of their fee.

I carried the case into court, and obtained a ruling of the court which gave them every practical result that they could. . . . The contractors came on bended knees and offered us all kinds of graft and bribe if we would let up, and get our clients to sign papers not to resist the [improvements]. . . . Of course, I turned a deaf ear to their entreaties, but finally our bunch of clients got together and made some kind of satisfactory outside agreement. . . . The only thing that remains now to be done, is to collect our fee. If Schuster says anything to you about this fee, tell him to wait till I get back, because I do not intend to let them [off], because I attained every objective that they sent me after, and if they compounded and agreed with the contractors on the outside, then that is their own affair.[20]

Davies, who was leaving for a month-long fishing trip to Canada, lived in downtown Louisville. In the above letter, he offered Bingham the use of his house during the upcoming election campaign, saying it would be more convenient for Bingham than commuting from the suburbs. And in that general mood of distrust which seems to surround many lawyers, he added that it would provide a check on the servants.

My room is exceedingly comfortable and cool, and my electric fan is installed, and you need never suffer with the heat in the room. You will have the whole floor to yourself, and there are unlimited bathing facilities. . . . That will not entail any additional expense, because I have to maintain three servants there anyway, and I believe that your being there will be a check upon the propensities toward epicurean practices.[21]

Bingham by now had begun to view himself as an important man, too important for the tithe system and upon taking up residence at Davies' house he sent Whallen's machine a contribution of only $300, a mere 6 percent of his salary.

He got a sharp and quick reprimand from F. R. Bishop, secretary of the Democratic Campaign Fund.

"I return the enclosed check," said Bishop, "as it is not correct.

The amount should be $500—being ten percent of your one year's salary."[22]

In the meantime, the campaign for the citywide elections of November 1905 were gearing up and by October, the Whallen machine had completed its ticket. It announced that the Democratic candidates would include Paul Barth for mayor and Bingham for county attorney.

Bingham stumped the district for the ticket headed by Barth and denounced in the bitterest words his rival candidates for mayor, and any number of other Republican leaders—all of whom he would later lie down with, cheek by jowl.

The election that followed was characterized by almost total voting fraud, violence, and near anarchy. It was like a modern Mexican election where the political machine, fearful it is doomed by anything approaching an honest election, outdoes itself in villainy.

The main opposition was a group which called itself "The Fusionists" and was composed of a coalition, or fusion, of Republicans and alienated Democrats, the latter including some genuine reformers such as attorney Helm Bruce and businessman William R. Belknap.

To protect their interests and themselves on election day, the Fusionists purchased a large stock of ax and pick handles and distributed them to workers with the strong advice that they should be used on the heads of those Democrats who might interfere with the electoral process.[23]

They never got much chance, however. It was the Democrats who did the assaulting, quick and early, beginning in the early morning when a policeman clubbed down Fusionist polls inspector Arthur D. Allen, auditor of the Belknap Hardware & Manufacturing Company. Knocked unconscious, the bleeding Allen was arrested and dumped without medical attention in a jail cell. Belknap's efforts to have Allen released or transferred to a hospital were rebuffed. Bingham was called upon by several citizen delegations to prosecute either the policeman or Allen. Not wanting to alienate either the Democrats or the Fusionists, Bingham passed the hot potato onto the city attorney. Ultimately, the policeman who assaulted Allen was acquitted in the city court, while the man whom he had beaten up was fined.[24]

In other displays of political preference, Whallen toughs stamped about one hundred Republican ballots with the name of the Democratic candidate for mayor, thus giving Paul Barth one hundred votes that really belonged to his Republican opponent. Election repeaters were openly taken from one polling place to the next, and voted first in one and then in the other. Early in the day the Democratic election officers excluded blacks from voting, knocking and shoving them out of line. At the same time, Democratic voters were advanced to the front of lines and Republican voters were made to stand back. When a Republican judge protested, he was assaulted, dragged into the street and beaten in the presence of policemen who refused to interfere, although called upon to do so. Republican workers who were taking pictures of those felonies were driven from the streets by police.[25]

Elsewhere, in precincts with high Fusionist votes, the Democrats burned the ballot boxes before the votes could be counted. A gang of policemen went from precinct to precinct breaking up voting lines or the counting of ballots. In another clubbing, Fusionist poll watcher Harry Browning was hit over the head by a detective when he insisted on remaining at the polls to see that a fair count of ballots was made.

The reader will not be surprised to learn that when the votes were counted, the Democrats had won by a substantial majority.

Screamed the *Louisville Herald* on November 8, 1905:

What happened! With a boldness unparalleled even in the history of Louisville, hired robbers, the commonest type of manhood, went into your polling places, stole from the law's receptacle the ballots you had cast, and carried them away as so much junk.

Where was Bingham, the county's chief prosecutor, in all this?

Right in the thick of the conspiracy. As county attorney, he had not only the power but the duty to suspend the election results and take the evidence before a grand jury. Instead, he did nothing except to ratify his own illegal election and swear to uphold the duties of his office as the county attorney. But he did more than just passively accept the results. Grinding salt into the voter's wounds, he swore in a courtroom affidavit that the election was fair, peaceful, and orderly.[26] That was akin to saying the Mongol ravaging of Europe was a tourist trip.

Bingham also wrote a toadying testimonial to the newly elected mayor, Paul Barth, praising Barth for giving Louisville an honest election.[27]

The Fusionists, with financial backing from a wide segment of an abused community, took their charges of election fraud to court. Attorney Helm Bruce led the legal offensive, which cited as defendants all the Democratic officeholders, including Bingham.

Bingham, as county attorney, led the defense of the office-holders. In addition, his law firm, Bingham and Davies, acted as consultants and received a substantial fee for their services, although Bingham was a defendant in the suit.[28]

In other words, as county attorney and consultant, Bingham managed to be paid twice from public funds for defending himself in a crooked election.

As the case wound its way through the courts, the Democrats went about their business, and Bingham, who was becoming almost impossibly confident, stretched out and enjoyed himself. He had no doubt that he would win the case. But as we have seen, when it came to lawyering, he would have made a good window washer.

□

In the meantime, flushed with his new prominence and power, he ordered, not requested, top seats for a visiting performance of Sarah Bernhardt. He was explicit in his instructions for two aisle seats on the main floor in the last five rows.

He was having the time of his life.

In May, he was the governor's guest at the Kentucky Derby.

"Preparations for this Derby are unprecedented," wrote the *Courier-Journal* the day before.

The management is prepared to take care of anywhere from 25,000 to 50,000 people. The infield for the first time in years will be thrown open and a big balcony has been built on top of the betting shed. The town is filled with visitors from all over the country. . . . Every box in the grandstand was disposed of more than a week ago. Most of these desirable places were secured by society people not only of Kentucky but of the entire South. The new Seelbach Hotel has had to turn down 200 applications for rooms.[30]

Bingham found the clubhouse and lawn ablaze with colorful costumes. Dainty parasols in light pink, blue, white, and coral lent a festive touch to handsome ladies gowned in "organdies and dainty muslins."

The crowd favorite in the race, although not the betting favorite, was Sir Huon, a Louisville colt born and bred at Bashford Manor Farm, owned by Bob's uncle-in-law, George James Long.

As the horses burst from the starting line:

Sir Huon came on fast, on down the stretch, past the battling bettors, past the huge throng pushing and heaving against the fences, past judges and jury, past society glittering in its glory, with Sir Huon galloping along with the greatest of ease while behind him, foam-flecked and punished to the limit of animal endurance, Lady Navarre and James Reddick are fighting it out for second place. And behind these two come all the heart-burnings and disappointments and hopes that have been wrapped up in Hyperion II, Velous and Debar.

It was a fine race won by Sir Huon, "the best horse that has finished front in the Kentucky Derby field in many years."[31]

□

That summer Bingham wrote the University of North Carolina suggesting some ceremonial note be made of the fiftieth anniversary of his father's class at the school.

With characteristic humility he added that four generations of Binghams had connections with the university, which wasn't the case with any other family in relationship to any university in America with perhaps the exception of the Adams family of Massachusetts at Harvard.[32]

The grand tone of the letter was particularly absurd for a student who had barely survived four semesters. Nevertheless, the school agreed, saying that they had planned on a fiftieth anniversary anyway and would be pleased to include Colonel Bingham.

Bob responded with an instruction to a school official that "it is my intention to attend the commencement and to take my oldest son with me so that there will be three Robert Binghams representing three generations there together. . . .

With the tone of a Russian prince addressing his servant, Bingham instructed Chapel Hill to attend to his accommodations. He intended to arrive with his oldest son, and requested notice to be made that three generations of Robert Binghams—the Colonel, the Judge, and the son—would be in attendance. He also requested adjoining rooms for all three of them.[33]

□

Life was cozy. Then, in May 1907, the bomb hit. The Kentucky Court of Appeals ruled the election of November 1905 to be corrupt and invalid, and ordered all elected Democratic officeholders in Louisville and Jefferson County removed from office.

It appeared that the Fusionists had won. Reform and justice had triumphed after all. But had it? To protect Democratic party interests, Governor Beckham reached down and appointed as head of the new reform city government not one of the Fusionists but none other than his supporter and the Whallen machine man, Robert Worth Bingham.

Reactions to this monstrosity were remarkably low-keyed. *Courier-Journal* editor Henry Watterson noted that the court decision "came like a peal of thunder from a cloudless sky," but proclaimed Bingham to be marginally acceptable. Fusionist reformer Helm Bruce expressed similar sentiments. The *Evening Post* hoped that the new mayor would be "animated by a zeal for the righteous conduct of public office." And ousted Mayor Barth asked that Bingham, his friend and supporter, give Louisville "a businesslike administration."[34]

On June 29, 1907, Bob, who had remained on county attorney salary until the day he was ousted by the Court of Appeals, walked from the courthouse into the City Hall where he took the oath of office as mayor. During the next few months as chief executive of the city, his closest adviser, his boon companion, "his ideal and the hero of his dreams was Colonel John H. Whallen, who was at all times at his elbow or at the other end of the telephone lines that led out of the mayor's office. . . . Bingham regarding Colonel Whallen as one of Louisville's best and most influential citizens and a person eminently fitted and qualified to give advice and counsel." [35]

Louisville had no civil service, and the mayor presided over a city payroll which included more than 1,000 patronage jobs. In Bingham's first days in office, hundreds of patronage chiefs and workers were lined up outside the mayor's door. His job was to calm them, and he did, reassuring the multitude that only a few job changes would be made, and those only at the top.

These changes included the appointment of police judge Randolph Blain to enforce the Sunday closing laws against saloons. This, in fact, was Bingham's most publicized reform and it was a cosmetic, the Sunday closings being a symbolic gesture toward the Prohibitionists and their Fusionist allies.

Bingham also fired police captain Thomas Riley, the commanding officer who stood by idly during the election riots. However, when the publicity subsided, he secretly appointed Riley inspector of gasoline lamps, a sinecure which actually allowed Riley to stay off the streets and enjoy, at full captain's pay, an unofficial retirement. Riley knew too much about Whallen machine secrets to be treated badly.

Bingham kept the police thoroughly in control by appointing his law partner, Davies, as head of the Public Safety and Police Department. To assist Davies, he named as board members his banker, John Stites of the Fidelity Trusty Company, and his political patron, Judge James Gregory.

Thus, Bingham had masterfully stacked his reform administration entirely with Whallen machine men, including himself. The foxes were still in charge of the chicken coop.

To provide some illusion of action, Bingham ordered the police to conduct vice sweeps, a traditional cosmetic employed by corrupt regimes.[36] Throughout July, August, and September more than 200 men and women were arrested for such major crimes as prostitution, drunkenness, and gambling.

Bingham, however, could not escape Fusionist pressure to investigate city contracts awarded by the Barth administration. It must have been an uncomfortable chore for Bob, who had ardently supported Barth and had enjoyed good relations with the mayor during nearly ten years of association.

Nevertheless, better Barth than Bingham. He appointed Fusionist committees, which investigated the Barth administration with zeal and found deplorable conditions in the hospitals and jails. Ironically, one of the major wrongs reported was the politicalization of the Louisville University medical school, where Bingham had enjoyed his own patronage job.[37]

Despite the findings, little happened. Bingham's reform administration was much show and little substance. Although his investigations uncovered boatloads of felonies in the Barth administration, Bingham withheld any move toward prosecution. He wanted to keep his fences mended with the Whallen machine. One prosecution, and no convictions resulted from the Fusionist evidence.

□

All this while, Bob was keeping closely focused on his own political ambitions. He wanted to run for mayor in the election scheduled for November 1907. The Fusionists and the Republicans had split, and as both parties were dissatisfied with Bingham, each chose other candidates, leaving Bingham with the Democrats.

And here occurred a moral instruction for all who are on the fast track and moving. Even as Bob reached for the Democratic nomination, his arrogance caused him to alienate the one man who might have given him the prize.

The man was Will Richards, the Beckham patronage chief who had lobbied for Bingham to obtain the county attorney job in 1903. Now, on instructions from Governor Beckham, Richards met with former mayor Charles Grainger and machine officials on Friday, July 19, 1907, to work out a "deal" whereby the machine could get the posts it wanted and Bingham would be the party nominee for mayor.

Following the meeting, Richards wrote Governor Beckham that the results were a complete success. The Democrats "decided not to bring out an opposition ticket, and the individuals would do what they could to secure Mr. Bingham's election in November." It was agreed that Grainger and his people would meet with Bingham in a week to close the deal.

The Monday after the meeting with Grainger, Richards went to Bingham, where he was left cooling his heels in Bingham's outer office for more than three days.

The enraged Richards detailed the snub to Governor Beckham:

Following the [Grainger] meeting, I immediately determined to advise Mr. Bingham of the facts, and to tell him that all he had to do [for the nomination] was to attend the meeting called for the 26th, and to work with his friends in the Democratic party for the success of the ticket. . . .

I waited until half past four o'clock, when his private secretary came into my office, which opens into his, with a message from Mayor Bingham that he had been too busy to see me during the day, but would see me sometime during the next day. I waited through Tuesday and Wednesday and hearing nothing from him, I stopped in his reception room the first thing Thursday morning and asked his private secretary to arrange an interview for me during the morning as I expected to leave the city that afternoon. I heard nothing from him during the day. . . . I still have no response to my request for an interview. . . .[38]

The immediate result of this incident was that Bingham had alienated the governor, patronage chief Richards, and ex-mayor Grainger.

Grainger did not respond by getting mad, he got even. In late July, he and his backers took over the Democratic caucus apparatus, a move which ensured that Grainger, not Bingham, would emerge as the party nominee.

Rejected, Bingham turned on the machine like a rabid animal. Accusing the local party and Grainger of corrupt elections—a fact of which Bingham seemed just recently to have discovered—he asked the state Democratic party to take control and run a primary election and thus honestly determine the nominee for mayor. The state party, headed by Beckham, succinctly and distinctly said no.

Now Bingham turned completely vicious, attacking the Democratic party and its nominees at all opportunities. His denunciations of Grainger were energetic, but tragically, his most devastating attack was against ex-mayor Barth, his friend and former running mate.

Barth was the man for whom Bingham had made speeches. The man to who he had written fawning letters a bare ten months earlier. The man he had praised, publicly and privately, as "honorable, wise, and patriotic."

But those were different times and an enraged Bingham found Barth standing in his way.

The ammunition which destroyed Barth was this:

In the course of his investigations, Bingham had uncovered a secret about Barth. Mayor Barth had approved the purchase of numerous city horses and mules which had died or disappeared under mysterious circumstances—probably never having existed in the first place or having been secretly passed on to private users.

One of these horses, however, had "died" and passed on to Barth's private stables. He was a fine saddle stallion named Marc Hanna and at the time of Bingham's split with the machine, Barth still had the horse.

Originally, Bingham had sat on the information, part of his plan to keep things friendly with the machine. But now, denied the nomination, it was time to release the news.

Enormous publicity ensued, much of it in the form of editorial cartoons ridiculing Barth. In his own defense, Barth lamely claimed that the horse was indeed the city's but had been boarded at his stables to save the city money. Bingham sneeringly pointed out the absurdity of Barth's explanation. In interview after interview he hounded the ousted mayor to return the horse or reimburse the city. After continued pressure from Bingham, editorial cartoonists, and the Fusionists, Barth sent Bingham a personal check for $750 to buy the horse.[39]

For Barth, described by the sympathetic *Courier-Journal* as a "sensitive man," the strain had proved too much. On August 21, 1907, two days after he sent Bingham the check, he fatally shot himself in his Main Street office.

The *Courier-Journal* blamed Barth's death on Bingham. Watterson was especially hot, noting in an editorial that he "hoped that the young gentleman who poses as a Reformer in the City Hall, and his newspaper and other satellites, who are making such efforts to be spectacular in front of the grand stand, whilst keeping such equivocal company under the cover of darkness, are now entirely happy." When the police could not handle the huge crowds at Barth's funeral, the *Courier-Journal* claimed it was done deliberately by the administration to further humiliate a "Victim of Relentless Persecution."[40]

Bingham vigorously denied being the cause for Barth's "unbalanced" condition, but he seemed neither shocked nor saddened by Barth's death. Certainly there is no indication of remorse by Bingham, either in contemporary interviews or surviving letters, diaries or other materials.

Barth, however, may have had some sort of revenge. The furor over the ex-mayor's death quickly eroded Bingham's political stock. He did not run for mayor and having resigned his county attorney job, he was out of political jobs, including his appointment to the medical school.

Further humiliations began to pile up on Bingham, who did not seem to know that his time was finished, that he had used up his coupons with the common man, that his fleet window of popularity had come and gone.

Blissfully ignorant, Bingham continued to offer himself to an indifferent public.

In 1909, he again sought the Democratic nomination for mayor, but was rejected. The following year, the orphaned Democrat became the Republican nominee for judge of the Court of Appeals. By now, he had thoroughly clothed himself in the robes of reformer and, like an actor hiding behind the illusion of theater, cast himself as David going against the Goliath of the Democratic machine. He was roundly defeated.

Ultimately, his political activity cost him his law partnership. Davies got tired of holding Bob's coat and carrying the bulk of the case loads. In October 1909, Bingham agreed to Davies' request to dissolve the law firm. Under a new arrangement, Davies remained in Louisville pursuing his own practice while Bingham joined the law firm of Kohn, Baird, Sloss, Kohn and Spindle.

□

Despite his defeats and his inability to woo the common man, Bingham remained politically influential, partly because of his increasing wealth gained through stock investments, partly because of his connection to the Long family, but mostly because he had somehow charmed the liberal establishment into believing he was a courageous reformer. He was written up in the national press, invited to important conferences, and visited Washington in 1909 at the invitation of Theodore Roosevelt.[41]

Furthermore, he was growing wiser in politics. In January 1911, he was appointed chancellor of the Jefferson County Circuit Court. An election for the post was scheduled in November of that year, but after sampling his chances, Bingham decided not to run.

He resigned the judgeship on November 30, 1911, returned to his law practice, and concentrated on his family life.

In the spring of 1913, his wife went to Asheville to pick up the children from boarding school. In Asheville, just prior to leaving, she told her sister-in-law, Mrs. Sadie Grinnan, "[I]f anything happens to me, take care of the children."[42]

It happened a few weeks later.

On April 27, 1913, Eleanor, her brother Dennis Long Miller, and two of Eleanor's children, Barry, seven, and Henrietta, twelve, were returning from downtown Louisville in Miller's big touring car. At an intersection near the Bingham home, their vehicle stalled on a trolley track crossing.

Barry remembered looking at his mother. "A charming, delicate, high-spirited person. She was quiet small, with curly dark hair and blue eyes. We used to sing duets."[43]

As his uncle got out to look at the engine, there was no alarm. It was raining, but the scene was pastoral. Looking up the tracks, Eleanor could see pleasant little farms, with the corn waving in the breeze, cows standing knee-deep in clover, the fresh, cool air from the river blowing in the faces of the family. The view in the opposite direction, however, was obstructed by a barn and power-house station.

Barry may have been the only one to see the trolley car.

"It was raining very hard. My uncle, who was driving, became temporarily blinded and we stalled on the track. I remember a terrible white light coming toward us. It was the interurban car crossing the track!"

The boy was knocked unconscious. "The next thing I remember was coming to in a strange house."[44] Dennis Miller and the Bingham children were only slightly bruised.

Eleanor's skull was fractured and she never regained consciousness. She died the following day. If the city had retained its old mule cars, there would have been no accident. What followed wouldn't have happened.

The Flaglers

O N T H E D A Y Eleanor Bingham died, Mary Lily Kenan was at an oceanfront cottage in Palm Beach, Florida, nursing her husband.

Henry Morrison Flagler, age eighty-three, had fallen down a flight of stairs and broken his hip. Tied up in a sand-weighted body cast, he had been bedridden since March 15.

For security reasons, Mary Lily was among the few to see him. The town was alive with private detectives and spies who had descended on Palm Beach after word got out that Flagler was stricken. Financial speculators were doing everything possible to find out his condition, including interviews with druggists and bribes to telephone and telegraph officials to intercept information. To counter this, Mary Lily had sealed him off from visitors and Flagler's lieutenants used a code to communicate with the Standard Oil headquarters in New York. Flagler himself, loaded with narcotics to relieve the pain, was nearly comatose and wildly out of his mind, babbling as if he were still a boy in Ohio.

□

Although married just short of twelve years, Mary Lily and Henry had been almost constant companions for twenty-two years. They had met when she was twenty-four and he was sixty-one, but what a sixty-one.

A native of upstate New York, he had come into Ohio at the age of fourteen and with hard work, good sense, and mostly making his own luck, he and John D. Rockefeller had built the world's first and greatest oil monopoly.[1]

The only undeserved piece of luck he had in his life was the timing of his arrival in Ohio. He was a young man when a forty-year-old jack-of-all-trades named Edwin Drake drilled a well in the creek beds of western Pennsylvania. From somewhere below ground, Drake auguered up oil, and as far as anyone knows, it was the first time ever that man had tapped a subterranean supply of petroleum. Previously, oil could only be soaked in small amounts from the ground by blankets and other such "sponges." At the time Drake struck oil, Henry Morrison Flagler was living in central Ohio, about 100 miles west of Drake's well. In 1867, Flagler and Cleveland refinery owner Rockefeller joined to create a company which would set a standard of quality and practices in a chaotic industry. Appropriately, they called their company Standard Oil.

Almost overnight, the name Standard Oil became a household word throughout the world—from Europe to the Middle East, India, Siam, Sudan, Liberia, Morocco, the Congo, and China. It did business with, and obtained franchises from, kings, presidents, emperors, mandarins, and warlords. The Standard oil can was a familiar object in every village of Europe, Asia, and Africa. The Standard emblem was as familiar along the Nile and the Ganges as it was in America. Camel caravans carrying Standard cans crossed the desert of the Sahara. Even elephants in India wore caparisons showing the ubiquitous Standard Oil white-and-red symbol.

Standard Oil was not only a great producer and seller of oil, but it was the first of the modern corporations. And it was highly predatory, swallowing up competitors right and left. Ida Tarbell, biographer, historian, and investigative reporter, said that oilmen regarded a business offer from the Standard as the moral equivalent of a highwayman's command to "stand and deliver."

The front man for Standard, the partner who took most of the heat, was Rockefeller. Behind the scenes, however, was Flagler. It was Flagler who created the company, drew up the contracts, set the prices, and connived with Rockefeller in shaping takeover plans.[2]

There came a time when the money-making machine of Standard Oil was not only perfect, it was permanent. The only concern of its engineers became personal: What to do with the profits? The yearly incomes of Flagler and Rockefeller were in themselves princely fortunes—and growing princelier. Rockefeller was content to pile dollar upon dollar, but not Flagler.

He began to withdraw, to look for other challenges. And it was then, at the time of withdrawal in 1881, that his wife Mary Harkness died of consumption, a victim in large part of Henry's neglect. To escape his guilt, he retreated to other women and the party life of New York. But inevitably, being a thoughtful man, he turned away from the shallow and frivolous. He began to think about Florida. He and Mary Harkness had made their first visit there in the 1870s when it was a wilderness sparsely populated by a few families in the north and a scattering of settlements of fishermen and ship scavengers in the south. Florida was a frontier, its interior of sawgrass, swamp, Spanish bayonet, and desertlike plains was largely unexplored. Lake Okeechobee, the nation's sixth largest freshwater lake, was unknown to geographers. It was the last American wilderness, and it appealed to him.

□

Henry Flagler began investing in Florida in the early 1880s. He had come to St. Augustine on vacation and rented a room in an old hotel. At the time, he had about $50 million in his pocket and was ready to spend it.[3]

The Florida that Flagler came to had a population of 269,000. It was the most backward of all the American states. Its few railway lines were located for the most part in the northern tier of counties bordering on Georgia. Its largest city was Key West, with a population of 10,000. Jacksonville, the chief city on the mainland, had a population of 7,000, Tampa less than 1,000. On the 550 miles of Atlantic coastline, the only towns between Jacksonville and Key West were St. Augustine, with 2,300 inhabitants, and Daytona, with 321.

He did not stumble into his fortunes in Florida. His move was purposeful. Two important motives fired him. First, he felt he owed it to Mary Harkness, who had wanted to settle in Florida. Second, he wanted a chance to put some of his social theories to work, to see if private capital, and not government funds, could be used to open a wilderness and create railroads, cities, banks, farms, orchards, bridges, harbors, buildings, newspapers, telegraph lines, and the other features of a modern civilization.

And he did it, converting a subtropical jungle into a 400-mile-long garden of groves, agricultural colonies, and tourist resorts.

Ultimately, his personal holdings, which he said he owned like he owned his cigar, included 3,125 square miles of land. Representing nearly 6 percent of Florida's total of 54,090 square miles, Flagler's holdings were about the size of the states of Delaware and Rhode Island combined. Furthermore, much of it was waterfront property on the Atlantic Ocean.

He gave work to thousands of people, from black and white common laborers who were paid equally at the rate of $1.10 per day, to architects John M. Carrère and Thomas Hastings, who established their reputation by designing his hotels, and jeweler Louis Tiffany, who did the same when he created Flagler's stained glass windows.[4]

During much or most of Flagler's Florida adventure, Mary Lily Kenan was at his side, although at the time Flagler was married to a second wife, Ida Alice Shourds, his first wife's former nurse.[5]

He called the buxom Mary Lily, "Pudgy."

□

Flagler started his work in St. Augustine at a time when it was a primitive pesthole peopled with a shiftless population.

Fresh nutritious meat there was not. It was the land of early vegetables, but no friendly hand ever strove to put them on our table. In place of wholesome, well-cooked food, we were served with canned meats, canned vegetables; and, as if in compensation, all sorts of fancy tarts and meringues. Orange trees were not very plentiful in the city, although the perfume of the blossom often enough greets one as we walk through the streets.[6]

Nevertheless, he saw the town's climate and charms. It was an architectural spectacle, more than 300 years old. He saw the old slave market; he saw the old Spanish town. He saw the old city gates and ancient houses. He felt ocean breezes and saw palm trees—palms!—this man who grew up in Ohio amidst the wheat. St. Augustine was a magic Fountain of Youth, rejuvenating him, and he began to spend his millions building hotels, houses, churches, roads, sewerage, and railroads. Yet he was careful not to overwhelm the region with his millions. Unlike his rapacious Ohio career, in his new Florida life he was not an exploiter. He never went into anything that local capital would or could do. Nobody else would build the railroad, because it would not pay, nor the hotels, nor the waterworks or electric light; and so he did. He wouldn't even run the stage line in St. Augustine, nor permit his hotels to do a livery business, because other people could make a living at it.

His first hotels were the Ponce de León and the Alcazar. Architectural marvels done in Moorish style with castellated towers and roofs of red tile, the two hotels immediately became the show places of the Atlantic coast.

By the end of the 1880s, a traveler could leave New York and within fifty-five hours be in St. Augustine, leaving New York, for example, at ten o'clock Monday morning and arriving in front of the Ponce de León hotel at five o'clock Wednesday evening after a pleasant journey and no fatigue deserving the name. The Moorish palaces awaited and from the moment the train stopped, the service was worthy of royalty.

From St. Augustine, Flagler ran his railroads south, along the pinelands, through marshes and cypress hammocks. Cabbage palms grew thickly along rivers and creeks, and the undergrowth was often dense, impenetrable, and teeming with wolves, panthers, bears, and alligators. The iron rails ran through sandy ridges, forested with blackjack oaks, and skirted cypress ponds, the dark waters studded with tiny yellow flowers.

To encourage railroad building, the state of Florida made land grants along the right-of-way and Flagler obtained more than 2 million acres as his subsidy.

To develop those land holdings, Flagler established the Model

Land Company, which created agricultural colonies from Jacksonville to Key West, contributing in large measure to the agricultural and industrial growth of the state.

Many of the settlements survive today. Linton and Boynton were established by pioneers who purchased land from the railroad. Modelo was built in the same vicinity by colonists from Denmark and from Illinois, Michigan, Wisconsin, and Iowa. Other settlements of the 1890s which were directly founded by the Flagler land policies included Delray, Deerfield, Dania, Holland, Ojus, Perrine, Homestead, Kenansville, and Okeechobee, in addition to principal cities such as Fort Lauderdale, Miami, and West Palm Beach.

Flagler made many concessions to people who came to colonize. In order to encourage and stimulate the planting of lemon, grapefruit, and orange groves, he made a temporary reduction of 50 percent in freight rates on nursery stock shipped over his lines and frequently gave a variety of seeds to people in the area.

Time after time, Flagler refused to stamp his name on Florida. The people asked him to put his name on towns, on lakes, on rivers, on cities, even on his own railroad. And in each instance, with 100 percent consistency, he refused.

He kept building, and he would keep building until the end of his life. With hard work and rare genius, he was able to transform his visions into reality. He was driven to do it; to create life in the form of towns and farms and colonies and cities and railroads and churches and schools.

His greatest accomplishments in Florida came after he met Mary Lily. The blue sky began to take on meaning for him. So he had his engineers survey lines for railroads and build into undeveloped wilderness. Then people came and planted orange trees.

The first was Palm Beach, a lush, semitropical island which he had reconnoitered in the early 1890s. It was a long, slender island with coconut beaches on the Atlantic Ocean and about a dozen inhabitants, most of whom lived in huts made of grass, palm leaves, and thatches. It was bordered on one side by the ocean and on the other by brackish Lake Worth, and in its center was a freshwater lake with shores lined with palm and mango trees, making it a bountiful breeding ground for millions of mosquitoes.

Flagler filled in the lake and set to building his houses and a hotel, the Royal Poinciana.

The largest resort hotel in the world, it opened in February 1894 and introduced more than a hundred of the most beautiful acres on Palm Beach, land covered with perhaps the greatest variety of tropical growth found in Florida. Fronting on the lake, the building was a huge sprawling structure with six floors, 540 rooms when it opened, and soon after expanded to 1,150. It accommodated 2,000 guests and was usually filled to capacity. Suites cost $100 per day, and a couple occupying a double with bath would pay $38 per day—a month's wages at the turn of the century. Like most of Flagler's enterprises, it was painted a vivid lemon yellow.

Immediately, the Royal Poinciana became the gathering place for wealth and fashion, known throughout the United States for its service and food, and with a staff of 1,500.

The mirrored, chandeliered dining room was like a crystal palace and could seat up to 1,600 people. It was so big that humorist Ring Lardner claimed that communicating from one end of the main dining room to the other was a long distance "toll call."

During the season, from December through April 1, the hotel employed a chambermaid for every four rooms; a bellman in every hall; and 400 waiters, one for every four diners at capacity, not counting an exalted headwaiter who had a secretary and twenty-six assistants. There were separate dining rooms for the help, for the first officers among the help, for the second officers, for the servants of guests, and for children. The help had its own orchestra for their dances and other social functions. The head housekeeper had a three-room suite.

The Poinciana was the *in* hotel for the Northern social set. At the onset of each season, more that a hundred private railroad cars, each luxurious in its own right, would arrive at the hotel with their masters obtaining suites while the servants slept in the cars.

The trains which pulled the private cars were technological marvels of the day. The baggage car contained an engine and dynamo for lighting the coaches electrically. Dining cars were usually attached and included refrigerator, storerooms, and complete kitchens. Menus were first class and four cooks and five waiters worked each dining car. Orders were placed from the waiters to the kitchen through speaking tubes. Electricity made possible the arrangement of berth lighting, which not only furnished the occupant with light before retiring, but after the berths were made up one could lie at ease and read if so disposed. The rear coach was an observation car, one end of which was used for a smoking compartment. A library contained the works of popular authors and a writing table was at the service of the traveler. The entire train was connected by vestibules, and so came to be called "vestibule trains." A child could walk from one end to the other with perfect safety. A porter was provided for each coach.[7]

□

Flagler himself was seen regularly in this period with young Mary Lily. Although it is unknown exactly when their affair began, it seems to have been somewhere about 1894.

Often Mary Lily and Elizabeth Ashley accompanied him on trips between New York and Palm Beach. They traveled in his private railroad car and had every imaginable luxury. It seemed obvious to many that Flagler was using Elizabeth as a "beard," a disguise to protect his involvement with Mary Lily,[8] who was with Henry during these profound changes in his life.

In building the Ponce de León and the Alcazar, with his wife Alice as his companion, Flagler seemed to be freeing his mind from his memories of his first wife and his fascination with the Oil Trust. For Henry, the 1880s were characterized by the awakening of a dormant sense of aesthetics.

But as his estrangement from Alice increased, and his involvement with Mary Lily grew, his preoccupation with the aesthetic mutated, shifting from the creation of buildings to the development of a state.

He did not care so much for the tourists as for the fruit growers now. Therefore, in Palm Beach he did not take the interest in the Royal Poinciana Hotel, architecturally, that he had in the Ponce de León. He gratified his love of beauty with the marvelous grounds.

In the winter of 1895–96, however, subtropical Palm Beach was hit by a freeze and orange trees were killed, perversely, in what up to that time had been a section safe from freezes. At the height of the cold, a lieutenant showed him a spray of lemon blossoms from mainland groves located 90 miles to the south. Henry was astonished because the lemon tree is even more delicate than the orange. The lemons came from a very small settlement on a ridge of limestone which was bisected by a clear, cool river which the Calusa Indians called "Mayama," meaning Big Water. So he carried his railroad to Miami. He built the town. He felt safe there. He had a city below the frost belt, a city which he designed and laid out.

In Miami, he built roads which were absolutely white—literally streaks of blinding glare in the sunlight. Where nothing was, he built streets, brick buildings, hotels, banks, churches, schools, and cottages. And these were built for residents, not "resorters."

The Royal Palm at Miami was completed and opened for the 1896 season. But he did not stop there. With Mary Lily at his side, Henry opened steamship service to Nassau and built for guests the Colonial Hotel, a 400-room house. Also in 1896, he inaugurated steamship service to isolated Key West, and in the winter of that year the operation was extended to Havana.

In the meantime, he and Mary Lily had been seen so much together that society writers began to speculate. Despite the growing scandal, Mary Lily and Elizabeth Ashley continued to travel and visit with him. Mary Lily's family became increasingly uneasy about her association with one of the wealthiest men in the country, most especially since he was married. Her grandmother strongly advised her to end the relationship, not on grounds of morality, it seems, but because the publicity was annoying.

As a result, Henry turned his attentions to divorce. His only grounds, however, was insanity, Ida Alice by this time having been permanently institutionalized. But neither of the states in which he was a legal resident, New York and Florida, allowed insanity as a cause for divorce. Accordingly, Henry changed the law.

Step one came on April 23. Less than three weeks after his proposal of marriage to Mary Lily, he announced he was changing his legal residence from New York to Florida. He said he was doing it for business reasons, and Florida newspapers, such as the *Florida Times-Union,* commented favorably on the "state's newest number one citizen." The *Times-Union* was secretly owned by Flagler.

Step two came on June 28, less than three months after his proposal to Mary Lily. He successfully petitioned for a ruling by the New York Supreme Court that Ida Alice Flagler was insane and incompetent. The court so certified.

Step three was one of preparation. Although Flagler was now a citizen of Florida, divorce was not allowed except in cases of proven adultery. It seemed that he was in no better fix than he had been in New York. But, where he felt blocked by the New York laws, he felt he could do something about the Florida laws.

Step four came on April 9, 1901, at the convening of the Florida legislature. A bill was introduced "making incurable insanity a ground for divorce. . . ."

At the time, Flagler's name was a household word throughout Florida. To most citizens he was a benevolent developer of the state, although some politicians, including Governor William Jennings, had been critical of the vast influence wealthy Northern developers were exercising in the state.

After the divorce bill slipped through the legislature as if it were a greased pit, there were widespread charges of payoffs to legislators, but no official evidence of bribery was uncovered.

For whatever reason, few bills ever sailed through both houses and were signed by the governor with greater speed. Rushed through, Standard Oil style, it was law a mere two and a half weeks from the day it was introduced: The divorce bill was introduced in the Senate on April 9 and passed on April 17 with little opposition. On April 19 it won approval of the House by a vote of 42 to 19 and on April 25 was signed into law by Governor Jennings.

The *Tampa Herald* objected to the bill, saying, "It is a queer thing to see a state wake up so suddenly to the enormity of being a slave to Flagler. Scarcely a day has passed since he came into Florida that Flagler has not done worse and more atrocious things than cause a Legislature to pass a divorce law. . . . He has had many newspapers at his feet, so to speak, and he has been a little tin god on wheels to an army of politicians. . . ."

Rumors that he had bought the legislation, and the legislature, spread quickly. The *Tampa Tribune,* on April 30, noted: "The opposition to the measure doesn't seem to be directed at the bill itself, but to the unconcealed fact that it was passed for the special benefit of Mr. Flagler. And whenever the Legislature passes a bill that is supposed to benefit that distinguished gentleman, the average country editor always jumps at the conclusion that somebody, in some way, has gotten some money out of it. It's this idea that provokes the howl."

When Frank Harris, the editor of the *Ocala Banner,* said in an editorial that the divorce law was sensible, he was roundly condemned by his fellow newspaper editors.

"Harris needs the prayers of the brethren of the press," editorialized the *Palmetto News,* "Has he shared some of the favors bestowed upon the Legislature?"

The *Pensacola Journal* accused Harris of selling out to Flagler because of a $20,000 gift from Flagler to Florida Agricultural College (later to become the University of Florida). Harris was a trustee of the college.

Numerous legislators were defeated because of their support of the bill. It was a major issue in the 1904 governor's race, almost resulting in the defeat of Jacksonville's Napoleon Broward, who as a House member, had voted for the bill.

Broward, who would succeed his friend, Governor Jennings, was shocked by the criticism of his vote.

"I received nothing," he said. "No one solicited my support. I felt under conditions outlined in the bill it was a reasonable ground for divorce."

Flagler indeed had made payoffs, more than $125,000 worth. But it would be more than seventy years before researchers obtained access to the Florida East Coast files, which showed the disbursements. Flagler had paid former Governor Francis P. Fleming $15,000 for allegedly defending his insane wife. He had paid George Raney, an important member of the House, $14,500 to act as Flagler's attorney. He also had paid Raney $106,942, which was listed as "expenses incurred."

If Flagler was bothered by this sharp criticism in Florida and other states, he didn't show it. He was accustomed to getting what he wanted.

Nevertheless, even Flagler must have been shaken when, in the very midst of his divorce scandal, a New York husband, C. W. Foote, filed a divorce suit in Syracuse naming seventy-one-year-old Henry as co-respondent. Foote filed papers and affidavits showing that Flagler had maintained Mrs. Foote in a New York apartment from December 1896 through June 1897. Henry didn't formally reply to the accusation, but his name was later dropped from the suit as co-respondent and it is probable that he made a financial settlement with the aggrieved Mr. Foote. The scandal is known to have caused Flagler's younger partner, John Rockefeller, nursing a bad stomach at Pocantico, to shake his head mournfully.[9] As Ida Alice was already confined in her mental institution when the news got out about the adultery, there was no known complaint from her quarter. We may assume there was some coolness from Mary Lily, but not enough to put off the marriage.

As for Flagler, public furor mounted even more sharply against him when, on June 3, 1901, he filed for *his* divorce in a Dade County court. Represented by a prestigious New York law firm and a bevy of witnesses brought down from that state, Flagler was granted a divorce on August 13, 1901, two months after filing under the new law.

As a settlement, Ida Alice received Standard Oil stock worth about $2.3 million. Financially, the arrangement was quite comfortable. Her annual living expenses at the New York asylum where she lived luxuriously were about $20,000. Her yearly income from the Standard stock netted about $120,000. Furthermore, Alice Flagler never realized she had been divorced, living in her world of delusions and hallucinations, she thought herself to be the mistress of the Czar of Russia.[10]

□

Henry and Mary Lily were married on a Saturday, August 24, 1901, a bare ten days following his divorce. An elaborate ceremony was held in Liberty Hall in Kenansville, seat of the Kenan family estates. For the event, the old ante-bellum mansion had been completely renovated and painted during the summer. Always a showplace, the house glowed from the work of hordes of plasterers, painters, decorators, and gardeners. Shutters were painted dark green. The house was given a new coat of white paint. Inside, rose-colored Chinese silk wallpaper covered dining and drawing room walls. Rare Aubusson and Savoronne rugs were placed on the floors. Large vases of roses were set in corners. The only items left untouched by the workmen were the family heirlooms.

The night before the wedding, Flagler brought the wedding party down on private railroad cars from New York. Henry's guests were put up in hotels. The Kenans invited only immediate relatives. There was no admission to the home during the ceremony, and press representatives were given only the simple announcement of the marriage after it had occurred. As wedding gifts, Henry gave Mary Lily's brother, Will, and her two sisters each a substantial block of Standard Oil stock.

Mary Lily was dressed in a white chiffon gown, trimmed in rare lace, delicate as a flower, which had taken her seamstress months to create. From a window she could see the guests arriving by carriages on a new road that Flagler had had constructed from the train depot to the front of the house. His private railroad car not only had carried in dozens of friends but also a fifteen-piece orchestra.

Mary Lily looked again into the mirror and placed the veil of ancient lace trimmed with orange blossoms on her hair. Someone tapped on the door. She picked up her bouquet of white orchids and lilies of the valley. After several minutes, the orchestra played the wedding march as she descended the stairs, escorted by her father. Louise Wise, a niece, was the flower girl and the only attendant. Flagler looked impressive in his black Prince Albert coat and light-colored trousers.

After the ceremony, a wedding breakfast consisting of turkey, ham, roast pork, caviar, cakes, ices, and champagne was served.

That afternoon, the couple boarded Flagler's private train car and sped away to New York, to his summer home at Mamaroneck. En route Henry presented her with a necklace of Oriental pearls worth $500,000, a certified check for $1 million, and another $2 million in registered government bonds.

From courtship through engagement to divorce and marriage, Henry Flagler spared no expense to give Mary Lily anything she wanted that money could buy.

□

Eight months after the wedding the couple moved into a marble mansion Henry had built for her in Palm Beach. For their home, Flagler had chosen a 6-acre site bordering Lake Worth, just south of the Royal Poinciana Hotel. To create a place with the view of the lake that he wanted, he built a lot for the house by filling in part of the lake. The result was that the house stuck right out into the lake with a magnificent view in three directions.

Inside a wrought iron fence, Flagler's engineers dumped thousands of carloads of earth and created gardens of palms, hibiscus, orange trees, and native Florida vegetation mixed with plants from around the American tropics. Lawns had been seen before, but not these spectacular trees and strange shrubs with polychromatic leaves; uncanny screw pines with clumps of exposed roots like sculptured snakes upholding the trunk; the gaudy red blossoms of the hibiscus that suggest the crimson lights on a Christmas tree; palms of divers kinds and borders of century plants grown to huge size. And over it all the blue splendor of the Florida sky covering a scene of such exotic beauty that it seemed one was on another world.

Designed by Carrère and Hastings, with interior decorations by William Stymus, the mansion was a tremendous structure that cost $2.5 million to build and $1.5 million to furnish.

Mary Lily named it "Whitehall."

A romantic press called it the "Taj Mahal of America," because both were palace-tributes to brides. The *New York Herald* called it "more wonderful than any palace in Europe, grander and more magnificent than any other private dwelling in the world." [11]

The main floor was dominated by a marble entrance hall, behind which was a tiled courtyard and a huge Louis XV ballroom. Also on the main floor were an Italian renaissance library, a Louis XIV music room, a Swiss billiard room, and the south porch. On the second floor, built on two sides of the courtyard, were fourteen bedrooms and suites, including the Nellie Melba room, a master suite and bath, and a "morning room."

The mansion featured a dozen blending tones of marble, Persian rugs, fifty sets of dinner service, and a hostess who seldom wore a dress twice under any circumstances.

In the billiard room, double walls concealed closets, a lavatory, and a hidden staircase to the second floor which Flagler used when he wanted to escape early from parties.

Upstairs, the fourteen guest chambers, master suite, and Mrs. Flagler's sitting room were decorated in an array of styles reflecting the influences of Italy, France, Spain, England, the Orient, and Colonial America. All the rooms had double doors for privacy and ventilation, most had individual baths and dressing closets. The west side of the second floor had thirteen servants' rooms, each equipped with a marble basin. Two of the rooms had private baths; the others were served by facilities accessible from the central hallway. A staircase at the north end of the second floor led to the third floor, which contained bedrooms used by the guests' maids and valets, and storage rooms.[12]

Mary Lily's private sitting room was used to store her collection of bric-a-brac and materials for correspondence, music practice, and bridge playing, making her an early player of the game.

The master suite consisted of a bedroom in the Louis XV style, a large bath, and two elaborately fitted dressing rooms. The furniture was two-tone pearl gray.

Mary Lily kept her clothing in glass-fronted cabinets, and another bedroom was turned into a wardrobe for her when her clothing overflowed the original dressing room. Her bathroom measured 17 by 11 feet, and the upper walls and windows were hung with gold silk to match the bedroom walls. Besides a double "toilet stand," or sink, of green onyx, the master bath contained a sunken bathtub and a "needle bath," or shower, which had a shallow marble basin below and a casing of pipes with nozzles on the sides as well as above. The tanks and seats of all the house toilets were maple.

The Flaglers were constantly entertaining, starting even before they officially moved into the house. Guests were received at monolithic bronze doors which were balanced to turn on their massive hinges at the touch of a child's hand. A pair of liveried doorboys was on duty at all times.

The doors opened onto a marble foyer or great hall 40 feet in length and 110 feet wide. It was, and is, finished in seven shades of delicately veined marble ranging from cream-yellow to dove-gray and from sea-green to off-pink, rich brown, and pure white. On January 26, 1902, just after a state-of-the-art Odell pipe organ had been installed, their first entertainment was a musicale. Guests included Admiral and Mrs. George Dewey, Mr. and Mrs. Frederick W. Vanderbilt, and the famed American actor, Joseph Jefferson.

The Admiral and Mrs. Dewey, he of Spanish-American War fame, returned on February 6 for another musicale. By that time, the Flaglers had moved into Whitehall, although it wasn't finished until March 5. Other guests included Mr. and Mrs. William Rockefeller.

Two nights later there was yet another party, the first formal dinner at Whitehall. The guest of honor was Sir William Grey-Wilson, governor of the Bahama Islands. They sat at the head of a wide table. On Flagler's left was the Duke of Manchester, and on the governor's right was Dr. Woodrow Wilson, president of Princeton University.

All indications are that Henry and Mary Lily enjoyed their home and entertained with a warmth calculated to make their friends comfortable, rather than to make Mary Lily a super-society hostess. It might be noted, however, that Flagler's wealth and holdings in Florida automatically put Mary Lily at the top of the social list, whatever her activities.

Despite the grandeur of it all, Flagler quickly made himself comfortable. Near the ballroom, he built a second stairwell protected by a secret panel so that he could slip out of parties and go upstairs to sleep or read. He had his office set up in a wing of the house, allowing him to come and go without notice. The parties continued, but often without Henry. Mary Lily adored entertaining and was a great hostess. She loved theme parties and she went overboard on them. He began to avoid them, slipping up the hidden stairway earlier and earlier.

Published accounts of the early days of marriage, at the time and afterward, state that Henry and Mary Lily were enthusiastic newlyweds and well-matched despite the age difference of thirty-seven years. But it appears that it was only the first year that was romantic. After that, Henry began to tire and wanted to go to bed at eight o'clock. He wanted her to go, too.

On several occasions, Mary Lily accompanied her husband on business trips to the Bahamas and Havana. However, they never ventured to Europe.

After the first couple of years, despite all the guest rooms, they had very few house guests. When Flagler was away, or unwilling to socialize, Mary Lily would go out with her first cousin, Owen Kenan, a sort of ladies' man.

Visitors found Mary Lily to be utterly charming, and without pretensions. A house guest in 1907 was Arthur Spalding, who had been hired as a live-in organist. He was immediately impressed with Mary Lily:

[A]n unaffected, cordial, homelike and charming woman. She invited me to sit down, and we had a very pleasant chat, becoming acquainted at once. Then "the old man" as many people call him down here, came over and we chatted pleasantly until it was time to prepare for dinner. Thus did I become a member of the household!

The people in the hall whom I did not recognize upon entering proved to be a party that had come down from St. Augustine with the Flaglers. They were Mrs. Flagler's mother, Mrs. Kenan, a sister, a sister-in-law, and several friends. . . . [That] evening we had an informal sing in the music room, there being no one there but the family. . . . Mrs. Flagler used to sing considerable before she was married but has given it up since. Her voice now shows lack of practice, but I should judge it was pretty good in its day. After we had sung a while, Mr. Flagler suggested that I play one or two "Great Big Things" as he expressed it (he is so deaf that he can't hear the soft things that other people are always calling for), so I played the March from Tannhauser, and the March of the Priests from Athalia, and he began to clap before I got through either piece. He likes a lot of noise and one of his favorites is the Anvil Chorus from II Trovatore, which unfortunately I haven't arranged for the organ yet.[13]

Mary Lily, secure in her social background, was the opposite of Flagler's second wife. Not a snob at all, said Spalding.

The more I see of Mrs. Flagler the better I like her and she is not at all the kind of woman I was prepared to see. Of course she is not perfect any more than the rest of us are, but there is nothing snobbish about her. If you treat her well and don't appear to be using her for what you can get, you can't ask for better treatment than she will give you in return. Last evening I went hunting for the first time—insect hunting. It began when Mrs. Flagler spotted a mosquito reposing on my shirt stud and destroyed it with her fan, thereby committing my shirt to the laundry. She, Mrs. Mitchell, and I were chatting in the music room, Mr. and Mrs. Percy Rockefeller having left and Mr. Flagler having gone up to bed. Suddenly I saw Mrs. Flagler's eyes become fixed on a dark spot on the drapery across the room, then grow wider and wider until finally unable to stand it any longer she crept over to the spot and gave a blood-curdling shriek which would have made the car-mule wild with envy and which brought Mrs. Mitchell and me to the spot and Edward the foot-man into the room on the dead run. There in the folds of the drapery reposed the nearest approach to a tarantula that I have seen yet. I was perfectly contented that Edward was there so that my gallantry would not be put to a test. Mrs. Mitchell was going to bravely gather it into her handkerchief, but you might as well try to squeeze a soft-shelled crab between your fingers, so Edward was despatched for a broom while Mrs. Flagler withdrew to the farthest corner of the room.

Mrs. Flagler remarked this morning that she was afraid if last evening's experience should be repeated, I would think there is more insect life down here than social life.[14]

Flagler himself was equally easy to get along with, despite his awesome accomplishments and reputation:

As I went into the church today, a woman asked me if Mr. Flagler ever went to that church and if so, where he sat. She said she wanted to see the man as she thought he had done so much for the state of Florida. So I pointed out his seat, she fixed it in her mind and sat down to wait for the king to enter. What she said is absolutely true and I know of hardly a man who has brought more pleasure to thousands of people than he has. As I keep hearing of the condition in which this east coast was only a dozen years ago, the things that Mr. Flagler has accomplished are mirac-ulous and he is still at it in his 77th year. As Mrs. Flagler says, he wouldn't be happy if he wasn't working and accomplishing unusual things. To be sure most of the improvements are carried out in the name of the East Coast R.R. but he is the whole thing and almost sole owner of it—the one man who instigates every improvement. Yet, he's the most modest appearing man about the place.[15]

Spalding also found that the household loosened up consider-ably when Flagler was on the road. Flagler was an early-to-bed, early-to-rise type and insisted on punctuality at meals, teas, and other gatherings. However, when Flagler was gone and Mary Lily was in charge, the wine flowed at night, people slept late and took their breakfasts in bed. They would have boat outings, stopping on islands where they would have picnics of clam chowder, fried crawfish, crawfish salad, boiled groupers, baked porkfish, fried red snappers, fried chicken, mashed potatoes, Saratoga potatoes, tomato and lettuce salad, asparagus on toast, ice cream, crackers and cheese, coffee, punch, and Poland Spring water.

"During and after lunch," said Spalding, "we had singing and mandolin and guitar playing by a colored quartet that was brought along with us.

"It was a very congenial crowd, with no formality, and after lunch we had songs by Mrs. Flagler, ragtime on the piano and popular songs by the whole crowd." [16]

Mary Lily enjoyed such picnics more than she did the more formal gatherings, said Spalding:

Many people, especially the [George] Wards, seem to think that Mrs. Flagler has the society bee in her bonnet and rejoices in all the entertainment that takes place at Whitehall, but I must confess she doesn't appear that way to me. To me she never seems happier that when she is off with a few friends whom she knows well and can act as she pleases without the restraint of all the formality and conventionality that is necessary in Whitehall functions. At any rate we all cut up merrily . . . Mr. Flagler acting as kittenish as the rest. [17]

Whitehall was only one of four homes used regularly by Mary Lily and Flagler.

Normally, to avoid the heat and mosquito season of Palm Beach, he and Mary Lily would stay until a week or so after Washington's Birthday, February 22, then move up by train to the cooler climate of St. Augustine, where they'd stay until mid-May. They'd then go further north, by train or yacht, to the estate at Mamaroneck, New York.

Situated on a narrow extension of land, almost surrounded by water, the 32-acre estate, called "Satan's Toe," was accessible by both water and rail from New York, being about 20 miles northeast of downtown Manhattan. There they lived in a forty-room mansion, plus guest houses, with a dock for yachts and a smooth bathing beach made of sand imported from New Jersey.

They also had a mansion in New York City at 685 Fifth Avenue, a large brownstone very near the similarly designed mansion of John D. Rockefeller.

For many summers, when Henry and Mary Lily weren't at Mamaroneck, they would be at the Hotel Mount Washington in Bretton Woods, New Hampshire.

□

Eventually, Henry and Mary Lily's social differences began to grow, and in the last few years of their marriage, she was restless and unhappy but stayed with him.

In the last years of his life, Flagler was to attempt his riskiest stroke. He put everything he had gained, his entire fortune, on the line, to build an "overseas railroad" to Key West and add Florida's largest city to the mainland. At the time, it was considered an engineering feat second only to the Panama Canal.

In 1909, for the first time, they had no house guests at all because of Flagler's involvement with the Key West project, and in 1910 they gave no social functions at all.

Spalding relates that the railroad had also become an obsession with Mary Lily. After a series of hurricanes crippled the construction, the Flaglers left for an immediate inspection:

Yesterday morning Mr. Flagler got a telegram and last night he and Mrs. Flagler started for the extension. . . . They [boarded] a boat at Miami and proceeded slowly along the line clear down to Key West stopping here and there to inspect the work, which Mrs. Flagler has never seen.

The family arrived home late yesterday. . . . Mrs. Flagler, as I could see when talking with her, was prouder than ever of her husband. She says she has actually lived with the blue prints of the extension since it was first conceived, but she had no idea of the size of the undertaking and of the many obstacles they had had to overcome until this trip. It is costing far more than they ever anticipated and her only hope is that it won't swamp Mr. Flagler before it is entirely completed, but in the end it will certainly stand up well alongside the Panama Canal as an engineering feat.[18]

During the building of the railroad, Flagler's subordinates were accused of using "slave labor," of forcing men to remain in the mosquito-plagued swamps as virtual prisoners. Charges were brought against several Flagler engineers in court, but a federal jury found the charges to be without foundation. Nevertheless it hit the people at Whitehall hard, particularly Mary Lily. The pressure on her infuriated Spalding.

It is a cruel blow to deal at such sensitive and kind-hearted people as the Flaglers. The truth is that Mr. Flagler has spent thousands of dollars in merely improving the living conditions of the laborers along the extension, and they live in far better houses than they ever knew before or will know after they leave the employ of the East Coast Railway.

The article is simply a sample of the hysterical raving that is now going all over the country against men of capital, and alas, probably will either be believed as gospel truth or else passed over unread. The injustice and cruelty of such articles becomes apparent when we know the persons at whom they are aimed and find them to be as sensitive as the rest of us even though they are in the limelight much of the time. . . . Mrs. Flagler cried her eyes out the afternoon she read the article.[19]

Flagler had begun the Key West job in 1904, determined to finish it before his death. He just barely made it, but make it he did. On January 22, 1912, as the last piece of rail and tie were hammered down, he and Mary Lily rode a supertrain into Key West.

When the train rolled into the city 1,000 children and 10,000 other citizens greeted Flagler's "Extension Special." For many Key Westers it was the first train they had ever seen. He was greeted with the roar of bursting bombs, shriek of whistles, and bands playing. Flagler, now old and feeble, but cheerful, made a brief speech including the remark, "Now I can die happy. My dream is fulfilled."

After the speech, he was escorted to a platform to be serenaded by a group of schoolchildren. They scattered roses before him and sang. In this moment of triumph, tears welled from the old man's eyes. "I can hear the children," he said sadly, "but I cannot see them." He was nearly blind.

He was frail, but he carried on as ever, showing attentions to his wife with a final anniversary gift in August 1912 and a note saying, "To my darling wife in loving remembrance of the day you became my wife and the many happy days you have given to me since our marriage. May the dear Lord reward you for what you have done for me."

He died at the height of the morning, 10:00, May 20, 1913.

The Agreement

ND NOW came the time of reunion. With hindsight it seems inevitable, what with Mary Lily and Bob both losing their spouses in the spring of 1913. Each was certainly aware of the other's loss. Both deaths were well publicized—Henry Flagler's because of his worldwide prominence; Eleanor, partly because of her family name but mostly because of the untimely freakishness of the accident. Surprisingly, however, it took more than two years for them to come back together in even the slightest and most formal way.

□

Mary Lily had inherited more than $100 million from Henry. In addition to substantial holdings in cash and Standard Oil stock, she received all of the Flagler System, including the Florida East Coast Railroad; the Model Land Company, which controlled about 4 million acres of model farms; the Florida East Coast Hotel Company, with eleven hotels; the Florida East Coast Car Ferry Company, which ran railroad freight cars to Havana, Nassau, Miami, and Key West; the East Coast Steamship Company, which ran cruise and freight ships to the same ports; the Miami Electric Company, which became the mammoth modern utility Florida Power and Light; the Miami Water Company, the West Palm Beach Water Company; and newspaper publishing companies, including the *Miami Herald,* the *Palm Beach Daily News,* and the *Jacksonville Times-Union.*[1]

Flagler's will left virtually everything to her, with the condition that for the first five years the businesses should be run by three key executives.[2] This thoughtful clause would allow her some breathing room while she learned the management of the businesses.

Following funeral services, Mary Lily accepted an offer from the Pembroke Joneses to stay with them in New York, and for the next several months she alternated her residences between their homes in New York and Newport, Rhode Island. She did not return to Whitehall at all during that time. While in mourning, her vast business interests were taken care of by William Blount, the Flagler System's main lawyer, who was also the executor and trustee of the Henry Flagler will.

□

There ensued a period of "terrible loneliness" for Mary Lily, according to Kenan family members. She was seemingly without friends and ignored by relatives. Shunned, as often happens with widows, rich and poor, for no reason other than she was *awkward,* difficult to place at a dinner table or a party, difficult to talk with.

In a pathetic attempt to arouse some attention from her family, she published her will, listing as heirs her brother, two sisters, and a niece. The will stretched over sixteen pages and in detail parceled out the pearls and jewelry, the hotels and railroads, the Standard Oil stock (New Jersey, California, Kansas, Kentucky, Nebraska, as well as New York and Ohio). Money was left to relatives and servants, including a telling bequest to "Mary —— my cook." Last name unknown. She wanted to share with even the least known of her companions.

She expected her chief heirs to spend more time with her out of gratitude. When they didn't, she sulked. She closed Whitehall and moved to a permanent apartment at the Plaza Hotel in New York. The richest woman in America wanted to be closer to her family and former friends, but to no avail.

Her summers, divided between the estate in Mamaroneck and a mansion in Asheville, were equally lonely.

Mary Lily singled out her seventeen-year-old niece Louise Wise, daughter of her sister Jessie, as her principal heir. Louise, who would become a gorgeous adventuress and darling of the rotogravure magazines, was grateful and became Mary Lily's major companion. But she was, after all, only seventeen.

The press followed Mary Lily closely and any association with a male provided speculation. In March of 1915, she felt compelled to issue a public denial that she was engaged to a Dr. S. Westray Battle of Asheville, with whom she'd been seen, and protested that there was no foundation for the press reports. "If I were not still in deep mourning and not going around at all, a statement like this perhaps wouldn't upset me so."[3]

Nevertheless, she should not escape the press. The least connection of her name made a story news. It even rivaled the sinking of the *Lusitania* in May 1915, at the beginning of World War I when a German submarine, without warning, sank the unarmed British passenger liner, killing 1,195 people. Among the few survivors was Mary Lily's first cousin, Dr. Owen Hill Kenan.

The story was enormous news, a terrorist attack against unwarned civilians. But the Associated Press picture that ran in papers around the country showed not Dr. Kenan debarking from a rescue vessel, but the doctor and Mary Lily posing in an archival photo on a Palm Beach dock.[4]

In the summer of the same year, the *New York Times* had a field day with a story of a handsomely gowned woman with "blonde hair, sparkling blue eyes and a sweet manner" who obtained the savings of more than a dozen young men by impersonating Mary Lily Flagler. For example, she bilked one Frank Mahoney, a hotel telephone boy, of $4,000 by contending she was coming into a $15 million inheritance within a few weeks and she promised to make him her secretary at $20,000 a year. His friends would share in that wealth by helping him raise the $4,000, which they did. The imposter turned out to be a Mrs. Henry Johnson, a cook and laundress who was duly convicted and sentenced to the New York State Prison for Women for not less than three years. Investigations had brought out she also had lived magnificently in Washington, D.C., under Mary Lily's name, and had rented and elaborately furnished a house formerly occupied by the Russian embassy—all possible because of the magic of Mary Lily's name.

□

In Louisville, things were not going well for Robert Worth Bingham. If he hadn't had bad luck, he'd have had no luck at all.

He was forty-four years old and he had no career or prospects. His wife was dead. His children absent, the two oldest being away at school and young Barry boarding with his Aunt Sadie Grinnan in Asheville.[5] His political career was dead in the water. And to save money on upkeep and servants, he had closed his suburban home and was boarding near downtown Louisville in an upstairs apartment of a rundown, wooden frame house that was owned by his insurance agent.[6]

His sole regular income, it seems, came from his late wife's estate, being a monthly fee he received for administering the trust funds of their children.[7]

In the year following Eleanor's death, Bingham had taken his father and one of his sisters on a long-promised tour of Europe and the Holy Land.[8]

Upon his return, he found a letter from the lawyer of Eleanor's mother, Henrietta Miller, accusing Bob of improperly disposing of collateral which served as bond for business dealings he was handling for Mrs. Miller.[9]

Bingham deposited new collateral, but it failed to mollify Mrs. Miller, who fired Bingham as rent collector for the Miller family.[10]

The following month, Bingham made a power move against his mother-in-law, trying to obtain from the Fidelity & Columbia Trust the deed to the lavish $50,000 house and lands he and his family had occupied since Henrietta's birth in 1901. He wrote to Fidelity asking them to send him the deed. In a tactful response, made without comment and designed so as not to embarrass Bingham, bank president John Barr sent him a copy of Eleanor's will, which stated the house was part of a trust set up by Eleanor for the children.

Infuriated, Bingham objected that the will was not what he sought. He insisted upon having the deed. An exchange of letters ensued, and finally Mrs. Miller stepped in to block Bingham once and for all. She maintained that the house had been given to Eleanor, not to Eleanor and Bingham, and as such was part of the trust. Bingham could not have it. Accordingly, banker Barr informed Bingham: "I regret that we can not make a delivery to you of the original deed. Mrs. Miller and her advisers are opposed to the delivery of this paper to you. I regret that the situation is such that an amicable agreement in regard to such matters does not exist between Mrs. Miller and yourself." [11]

During this period, even more financial pressure was being applied to Bingham by his creditors. To finance his political outings and his stock investments, Bingham had run up huge debts, and with his political career apparently finished, the banks were pressing for payment. [12]

He said he had no money, but he had a potential sponsor: Her name was Mary Lily Flagler. To the bankers' utter astonishment, Bingham explained that they had once had a relationship. He would arrange to meet her in Asheville, where Mary Lily often visited with his sister, and her former classmate, Sadie Grinnan. [13]

There is no documentary evidence that Bingham and the bankers conspired to pay off his debts by seeking help from Mary Lily. However, the tradition, along with details, is strong in both the Bingham and Kenan families.

Thomas Kenan, the Kenan family historian, and a distant cousin of Mary Lily, contends that Bingham's trip to Asheville had been conceived by his creditors in Kentucky, where the presidents of two banks suggested that a renewal of his acquaintanceship with the well-publicized widow might be a way out of his debts. "Rob Bingham had lots of land but little cash. He had meager financial resources. And this was the way out for him and the banks." [14]

Bingham's granddaughter Sallie Bingham maintains that it was also part of her family's lore: "There is a strong tradition among older Louisville families that bankers sent him to Mary Lily to recoup his debt . . . *our* family story has it that the Judge was one million dollars in debt, mostly because of politics, and bankers suggested he go to Asheville and see if Mary Lily could help him out." [15]

Whatever the extent of the creditors' conspiracy, go he did.

At the time, Bingham's son Barry was boarding with his Aunt Sadie Grinnan in Asheville because of his health: "I had been diagnosed as being 'threatened' with tuberculosis, and medical wisdom at the time held that a climate such as that in North Carolina, along with much sunshine and fresh air, would strengthen my defenses to the disease."

Barry Sr. doesn't remember much about the courtship of Mary Lily, but he recalls that his father spent much of the summer of 1915 in Asheville, presumably visiting Barry's Aunt Sadie. Grove Park Inn records in Asheville show, too, that Mary Lily spent much of the summer there. It is Barry Sr.'s recollection that it was while both were attending a house party that his father and Mary Lily got to know each other again. The following summer, he says, Mary Lily and the Judge were both guests at The Greenbrier in White Sulphur Springs, West Virginia.[16]

The sequence of events is supported by Tom Kenan, and by contemporary newspaper interviews with Mary Lily.

She was paying a visit to friends in the South. Among the guests was Bingham. With him was his son Robert. Mary Lily would later recall that "he looked just as his father did at the same age."[17]

"The Grove Park Inn in Asheville," says Tom Kenan, "is where she re-struck her acquaintance with Rob Bingham. She was utterly lonely and she probably forced the play. She was a powerhouse."[18]

□

Mary Lily left Washington, D.C., at 7:00 P.M. with her private car attached to a regular train of the Southern Railway. She arrived in Asheville at 11:30 the next morning.

The great stone inn, only opened since 1913, had become a fashionable summer spa with guests including Thomas Edison, Henry Ford, John D. Rockefeller, William Jennings Bryan, Woodrow Wilson, and a young couple from New York State, the Franklin Delano Roosevelts.[19]

After refreshing herself in her suite, Mary Lily went downstairs for a late lunch. Rob Bingham was in Asheville and there they met.

"She invited him to come to New York, well-chaperoned, but the brother and sisters and her niece were suspicious," says Tom Kenan. "Mary Lily sent Rob Bingham many telegrams and seemed very happy. 'I wouldn't trade places with anyone in the world right now,' she told them." [20]

She saw Bingham at her apartment in the Plaza Hotel in New York and at the mansion in Mamaroneck. They also were together at White Sulphur Springs and in Louisville.

Her spirits were so buoyed that in February 1916, for the first time since Henry Flagler's death, she reopened Whitehall. The magazine *Palm Beach Life* hailed it as an event:

. . . Although the past week's social calendar was replete with many notable events and hundreds of arrivals were chronicled at both hotels, quite the most important of the week's happenings was the opening of Whitehall and the arrival of Mrs. Flagler. The great showplace of Palm Beach has been closed for nearly three years since the death of Mr. Flagler, and it is a genuine pleasure for her many friends to have Mrs. Flagler back in her accustomed place among them, not that it matters whether Mrs. Flagler be in her palatial mansion or in the most modest abode, for she is always the same and the many persons who are privileged to really know her well appreciate the sterling worth of this modest, unassuming little woman, so small of stature but so big of heart. However, it is a pleasure for everyone to see the big iron gates of Whitehall swung open once more, for we now feel that Mrs. Flagler is really here to stay. [21]

Ignoring her joy, her family and business associates warned her that Bingham was a fortune hunter. Her affair was opposed not only by her family but by the senior Flagler System executives, led by company president William H. Beardsley and his chief aide, J. C. Salter. Both had a "falling out" with her over the matter. Because of the terms of Flagler's will, she couldn't do much about Beardsley but, vengefully, she forced Salter to take early retirement. [22]

□

In the Indian summer of 1916, while both were staying at White Sulphur Springs, Mary Lily and Bob agreed to be married.

To appease her family and the Flagler System trustees,

Bingham signed a prenuptial agreement waiving his dower rights and all other claims to her fortune.

Barry Sr. stated that the initiative for the pre-marital and post-marital agreements came from his father, not from Mary Lily. Barry Sr. also had the will of September 1916, and the will-change of December 1916, examined by his lawyers.

However, the language of the will indicates little input from Robert Worth Bingham. Indeed, his name is unmentioned. There is no reference to him, nor to his waiver of dower rights, roughly 50 percent of the estate.

The will leaves the bulk of Mary Lily's estate to her niece Louise Wise and smaller bequests to her brother, sisters, and sister-in-law; to cousin Owen Kenan; to various servants; to the University of North Carolina to establish a salary fund for accomplished and talented professors; to the Reverend George Ward; and to two friends, Ida Remly and Hannah P. Bolles. A final item concluded, "that if anyone mentioned as a beneficiary . . . tries to contest the will, the will should be carried out as if the person were not in it."[23]

An ominous warning to relatives and friends that she, Mary Lily, would no longer brook interference with her private life.

She had decided to marry Robert Worth Bingham, but she wasn't quite ready to make the announcement.

Honeymooning

LOUISVILLE, Kentucky's calling you on the telephone, Ma'am." Thus began a breathless story on page one of the *New York Evening World*.[1]

This was the message which was brought this morning [November 3, 1916] to Mrs. Henry M. Flagler by a Hotel Plaza bellboy just as she was about to get into the limousine which was to take her to her train for Washington. It came simultaneously also with an *Evening World* reporter's inquiry whether it was true that she was engaged to Judge Robert Worth Bingham of Louisville, Kentucky, and whether, as stated, the wedding would occur on November 15.

Mrs. Flagler, undoubtedly pleased at the long-distance call, paused just long enough to say:

"I do not confirm the report, nor will I deny it. I am on my way to Washington now; ask me when I come back on Sunday. Then I may have a statement to make to you. I know Judge Bingham; he's a most estimable gentleman."

Then she went off to the telephone booth. And when she came back, she was all smiles as she entered her car. . . .

Judge Bingham is a widower. He was at one time Mayor of Louisville.

The *Affaire Bingham* was a welcome relief to American newspaper editors and readers who were long weary of the increasingly unfavorable war news.[2] Mary Lily and Bob became instant celebrities as newspapers around the country tracked their love story.

The *Columbus* (Ohio) *Dispatch* noted that Bingham was in that city, where "he has many friends," and was en route to a meeting in Washington with Mary Lily.[3]

The headlines ran from coast to coast and border to border. Special attention was given by the papers of Louisville and Palm Beach, but the most intense scrutiny came from the highly competitive New York City press, which in that era had a glorious galaxy of seventeen dailies, including the *Herald*, the *Times*, the *Sun*, the *Journal*, the *World*, the *Evening World*, the *Evening Journal*, and the *American*.

The *New York Times* weighed in with its report of the romance, informing readers:

Mrs. Flagler left this date for Washington and left word that she would return on Sunday, when she has arranged to meet Judge Bingham, who is coming from Louisville. Since her husband's death she has spent much of her time at Whitehall—the famous estate at Palm Beach. She has an estate at Mamaroneck where she resides during a part of the winter season, or at the Plaza. She has a permanent box at the Metropolitan.[4]

The *Times* added that they met while he was a student. "But something happened, whether a lovers' quarrel or a mere drifting apart may never be known. Their paths diverged and later both wed elsewhere. . . ."

Since 1908, Bingham's tawdry political career had been essentially dormant. Now, with memories dimmed and hostilities cooled, in the overwhelming flood of ink concerning his romance, he emerged in the press as a full-fledged progressive politician, the mayor who had cleaned up Louisville.

The *Times* report was typical: "A leading reformer . . . in 1907, he was appointed by Governor Beckham of Kentucky the Mayor of Louisville, the former administration having been ousted by the decision of the Court of Appeals on the grounds of an unfair election."

Having thus overlooked the rather central fact that far from being a "leading reformer," Bingham was a *leading member* of the ousted administration, the newspaper painted the image of a golden hero: "Mayor Bingham at once instituted a crusade against the saloons, took the Fire and Police Departments outside of politics, and in general carried out reform work."[5]

☐

On Sunday, November 5, Mary Lily called a press conference in her suite at the Plaza to officially announce the engagement and wedding plans.

The *New York Herald* of the following day confirmed that the wedding would be held November 15, adding that "one of the guests at the wedding will be Miss Louise Wise, a niece of Mrs. Flagler, who is destined to receive a great part of Mrs. Flagler's vast fortune."

Delicately, the *Herald* reporters touched on what seemed to be a mismatch: an obscure Kentucky politician marrying the richest woman in America. Mary Lily responded that it was love, not money, that mattered.

"One of my friends said to me, 'Why, this is not a very brilliant match, is it?'

" 'Yes it is,' I replied to her. 'It is of the heart, and what can be more brilliant than that?' "

Mrs. Flagler then pointed to a portrait of a beautiful young woman over the mantelpiece. "I am so very glad that she can be present at my wedding," she said. The reporter looked at the portrait and ventured:— "And she is?"

"I have no children of my own," Mrs. Flagler said. "That is a picture of Miss Louise Wise, my dear niece, daughter of Mr. and Mrs. J. K. Wise, of Wilmington, N.C. She is the youngest member of the family circle and will eventually inherit the responsibilities that now rest upon me. Great wealth," she said, "brings responsibilities to those who possess it—responsibilities to others who have capabilities, but whose horizon is narrowed through a want of proper means. It was Mr. Flagler's idea that wealth should bring as much happiness as possible to the greater number, and it has been and will continue to be my duty to follow his principles."

Miss Wise, who is destined to become one of the greatest of American heiresses, is now twenty years old and has not as yet been formally introduced to society. She makes her home in Wilmington with her parents, but frequently is a guest of her aunt in this city and at White-hall. . . . Mrs. Flagler's coming marriage will be marked by a gift of more than $125,000 to the St. Augustine Hospital, at St. Augustine, Fla., which was destroyed by fire. Mrs. Flagler's arrangement for the future are indefinite. Following their marriage, Mr. Bingham and she will pass a year at least in Louisville, where he has a large law practice. They will maintain an apartment at the Plaza Hotel and will pass part of the winter at Palm Beach.[6]

In the photos of the time, Mary Lily doesn't appear to be a happy, robust woman. Her hair is grayed and her face is etched with lines of worry. She was obviously disturbed about her age. Initially, the *Herald* and other papers listed the ages of both Mary Lily and Bingham as forty-five, a figure which was probably given out by the bride-to-be. Mary Lily, of course, was four years older. The wedding license, signed by both a few days later, showed her and Bob to have split the difference, each listing themselves as 47 years of age. It was perhaps the last gallant gesture he would make to her.

The biggest surprise, a burst of real estate news, came when she announced that she and Bingham would make their perma-nent home in New York. She would build a new mansion opposite Central Park. She had purchased a block—not a lot but *a full square block*—fronting on Fifth Avenue from Ninety-sixth to Ninety-seventh streets. The fashionable architect John Russell Pope, son-in-law of the Pembroke Joneses, was engaged to design the mansion for the newlyweds.[7]

Prior to the wedding, Mary Lily gave Bingham an engagement gift of $50,000 in cash. There is no indication that he gave her anything.[8]

For the ceremony, each chose a single attendant. Mary Lily had Louise Wise as her maid of honor. Bingham chose as best man Hugh Young, who despite his world fame in medicine, was repeatedly misidentified as "Dr. Luke Young" in the newspapers, which were copying each others' material.

Young checked in at the Plaza Hotel the day before, on No-vember 14. In Young's eyes, Bingham was still a hero, a classic gentleman, responsible to family, devoted to duty. Left with three small children, said Young, Bingham had become:

The most devoted parent I have ever known. His life with Robert, Henrietta, and Barry was beautiful to behold. But his home sadly needed a mistress, and in 1916 I was delighted when Bob told me he was going to marry again.[9]

That night, Bingham joined him at the hotel and after celebrating briefly at the bar they went to the barbershop to get polished up for the "very distingué dinner that was being given Bob and his fiancée by the Pembroke Joneses."[10]

The wedding was held on Wednesday afternoon, November 15, in the music room of the Pembroke Jones home.

An hour before the four o'clock ceremony, the guests arrived. They found simple but artistic decorations in the entrance hall and drawing room, while in the music room on the second floor were palms, Easter lilies, and white chrysanthemums to suggest a chapel. Across the front of the lower hall was a tall screen of palms. The music room had been reduced one-third in size by the erection of a screen of vines, back of which was stationed an orchestra that played classical music while the guests assembled.

Among the few guests were Mary Lily's brother and sisters; Bob's sisters; the Joneses; the Wises; cousin Graham Kenan; Mr. and Mrs. Pope; and about six other friends. Significantly absent were the three Bingham children.[11]

The most elaborately dressed at the wedding was bridesmaid Louise Wise, who had become the darling of the society pages. The *Times* reported she wore a full, ankle-length dress of white broadcloth, with "bodice and bottom of . . . white fox fur. Her white hat was of satin and fur," and she carried pink roses.

Mary Lily was dressed much more simply, as people can afford to do when they own million-dollar pearl necklaces. The necklace and a ring, in fact, were her only jewelry. She wore an afternoon gown of pale gray velvet and tulle embroidered in pearls and carried a cluster of pale pink roses and white orchids.

Henry Flagler's former pastor, the Reverend George Morgan Ward, came up from Palm Beach to conduct the service. There was no reception. Soon after the ceremony, the newlyweds boarded Mary Lily's private car. Bingham, incredible as it seems, had scheduled business in Louisville the next day.

□

From this point onward, the man behaved monstrously. He had sold himself. He had been bought and delivered. And now it seems he set his mind to a deliberate revenge.

As mentioned, there is no indication that he gave Mary Lily even a modest wedding gift. To the press, he remained a background figure, never commenting. There is no indication of the least affection. He doesn't even allow time for a honeymoon, leaving unaltered business appointments in Louisville, which a review of his correspondence shows could have been easily put off until December.[12] The facts speak quite bleakly. He collected a bride and dowry in New York, returned home immediately, resumed business as usual, and was quite a bit richer.

The newspapers were unaware of this, reporting that the couple had left on a grand "honeymoon tour of the South. . . ."

Mr. and Mrs. Bingham plan spending most of the coming year at the bridgroom's Louisville home, and later will divide their time between Whitehall, the Flagler estate at Palm Beach, New York, and Louisville. The bride's apartment at the Plaza will be kept in order for her whenever she comes to this city. Mrs. Bingham also has an estate at Mamaroneck.[13]

What was there in him for her to love?

On the train, did she ponder that question, even now, nearly thirty years after they first met? Was there anything there? Perhaps we can't see Bob's value, but she did. Or thought she did.

Even on their honeymoon, they were not alone. Bingham had invited his sisters to ride back to Louisville with them. Mary Lily had been married that afternoon and now, in the late evening, riding in her private car with relative strangers, probably tired by the excitement of the day, she listened. The Bingham sisters remarked how pretty she was, how nicely her gray traveling dress fitted, and how well the pearls looked at her throat. At the other end of the richly carpeted private car sat her husband, drinking a brandy and reading a book.

No one met them at the station in Louisville and there was no house prepared for the bride. Instead, Mary Lily was taken to the Seelbach Hotel, a magnificent hostelry, mind you, but nevertheless a hotel. Opened in 1905, it was the business and political center of western Kentucky. It was shiny, somewhat famous, and had sparkling service, but it was a hotel primarily for men. The Seelbach had two entrances, with a ladies' parlor, or sitting room, between. The lobby looked like a men's club, full of spittoons.

Only married women were allowed as guests, no bachelorettes, and for the wives there was little to do. For example, women couldn't enter the dining room during the day. Meals, including breakfast, were either taken in their rooms or outside the hotel.

For men, the Seelbach was a playhouse of considerable resources, what with its saloons, bars, restaurants, oyster houses, and billiard rooms. For women, there was only the ladies' lobby sitting room, and at night they could visit the main dining room, provided they were accompanied by their husbands or relatives. They also were allowed, but only at night, to attend a magnificent roof garden above the tenth floor, which served as a nightclub and concert hall. Other than that, they stayed in their room or suite.[14]

Do not imagine that the restrictions on females was placed there thoughtlessly by the men. It was a calculated business decision. Downtown hotels of that era had mostly men for customers and the restrictions on visiting women was designed to reassure the men's wives. A virtually womanless hotel provided scant opportunity for temptations or adventures.

The Seelbach wasn't as grand as the Flagler hotels, but it also wasn't nearly as expensive. Rooms with baths cost about $2 a night and the best suite, the one occupied by Mary Lily and Bob, was but $5 a night.[15]

The food was excellent. The Thanksgiving Day menu for that year shows Canapes à la Seelbach, oyster cocktail; clear green turtle soup or *consommé à la reine;* fresh shrimp or broiled Spanish mackerel; rissoles of quail with cauliflower in cream or sweetbread patties with *petit pois,* kirschwasser punch; roast turkey with oyster dressing and cranberry sauce; sliced tomatoes and celery mayonnaise; almond biscuits; mince pie, baba au rhum or assorted cakes; Camembert or Edam cheeses; and coffee.

It was at "the most prominent location in the city, being in the midst of the retail business district surrounded by all of the leading theatres, within a block of the Post Office and Custom House and within five minutes' walk of all the public buildings." [16] All this mattered little to Mary Lily, of course, being a stranger to the city and having little use for Custom House, Post Office, or public buildings.

The hotel was her daily prison, with her husband leaving in the morning and often not returning until late at night. Sometimes he would be gone for days. Unseemly anxious to invest his newly acquired funds, he spent the "honeymoon" making business trips throughout Kentucky, and to Indiana and Ohio.

In his absence, Mary Lily set out to find a house to rent for a year or more, until the New York mansion was completed. She decided on a 22-acre suburban estate known as "Lincliffe," which included a stucco mansion done in Georgian style, and a Currier and Ives view of the Ohio River.

Lincliffe had been built for the former Fusionist political leader William Belknap in 1912, but had been vacant since his death in 1914. Mary Lily rented it for a bargain of $50 per month. Needing many minor repairs, it was to be repainted, refurbished with her own furniture, and ready for occupancy by January 1.[17]

In the meantime, Mary Lily's lawyers informed her that the marriage had invalidated the September will and the prenuptial agreement. Under Kentucky law, her husband was now entitled to one half the estate, regardless of any previous wills. Accordingly, she had her lawyers draw up a new will, one that included a specific waiver by Bob of all claims to the estate. The will was mailed to her in early December and on December 8, on the morning of their departure for a two-week stay in New York, she and Bob summoned lawyers to the hotel to witness their signatures and to accept the documents for safe-keeping.[18]

The purpose of the new will was simply to reaffirm the main provision of the September document, namely that Robert Worth Bingham would not share in the estate.

It remains open to speculation whether the idea came from Mary Lily, who had much pressure from her family and business associates, or from Bingham.

Their wedding invalidated the September will. Thus, on the wedding day, the Judge held his full statutory share, one half, of Mary Lily's fortune. At that time the law stated that a wife could not exclude her husband from her estate without his consent. Nevertheless, with half of the vast Flagler fortune in his hands, the Judge willingly agreed to sign away his rights. This led to the republishing of her will, along with the Judge's waiver of dower rights, in December 1916.[19]

Robert Bingham certainly did not go empty-handed. In addition to the $50,000 wedding gift, Mary Lily also paid off his debts to Kentucky banks and private individuals, New York brokerage houses, and Florida and Georgia real estate brokers. The amount came to nearly $1 million.[20] After the signing of the December will, she provided Bob with an annual income of more than $50,000 by giving him $696,500 in securities, mostly Standard Oil stock.[21]

Bob was not the only Bingham with his hand out. His father, the Colonel, incessantly nagging, pressured Mary Lily into making new bequests to the University of North Carolina, establishing a salary fund for professors.[22]

In the meantime, Mary Lily was apprehensive about the three children, then aged ten to nineteen.

On December 21, Mary Lily and Bob returned from New York. Within the next twelve hours, sixteen-year-old Henrietta arrived from Stuart Hall school at Staunton, Virginia; nineteen-year-old Robert from the University of Virginia; and little Barry from Asheville.[23]

As a surprise, Mary Lily had covered a bed in the hotel suite with presents for the Bingham children and invited them up to see. To her shock, their reaction was sullen gloom—the children, resentful of their mother's replacement, set a tone of hostility which would last thereafter.

Mary Lily did not immediately give up, however.

To mend fences with Henrietta, Mary Lily gave her a Christmas party at the Seelbach, decorating the hotel's Red Room to represent a Louis XV garden and filling it with more than a hundred of Henrietta's friends.[24] But Mary Lily's attempt didn't work. Throughout the holidays, Henrietta made it *the* project to study Mary Lily, keeping her under constant surveillance and recording her movements and activities in notebooks. In a private seventeenth-birthday talk with the Judge on January 3, Henrietta announced that her stepmother was a drug addict. Furious, Bob reprimanded his daughter, but it was without effect. Henrietta continued to spy on Mary Lily at every meeting, then run to her father with reports.[25]

In Mary Lily's behalf, let us say that at this point in her life there is no indication she used narcotics, although opium and morphine were easily obtained with prescriptions. Mary Lily did hoist a few bourbons now and then, but, married to Bob and left alone for days in a hotel suite, who among us would blame her?

□

In late December, Mary Lily wrote her family that she was disheartened by the treatment she received from the children. Shortly thereafter her health began to deteriorate.[26]

The Judge at that point made perhaps the most incriminating move of their married life. She was ill, but, from the perspective of seventy years later, the nature of her illness isn't clear. Bingham would later claim she suffered from chest pains. But to treat her, he didn't call in a chest specialist or a heart specialist. He called in a dermatologist, his old friend Dr. Michael Leo Ravitch.

His selection of a physician is worth thinking about. *The richest woman in the world has chest pains and he calls in a second-rate dermatologist?*

Even Bingham's friend Davies was puzzled by the selection. "I don't know the details . . . I think he [Ravitch] visited her before she went away . . . to Palm Beach, along after Christmas. I think he attended her then because I remember she mentioned having [seen Ravitch] when she had some sickness or indisposition of some sort."[27]

Among Louisville's 626 physicians, Ravitch had little prestige. Some colleagues regarded him as not much better than a hack.[28] Overall, he seems to have been something of a political hanger-on, grubbing out an existence from patronage jobs.

He was certainly not a financial success. A native of Kiev, Russia, Ravitch had come to Louisville in 1896. He had a meager private practice, obtaining most of his income from politically appointed jobs on the teaching faculty at the University of Louisville and on the medical staff of the Eastern Kentucky Asylum in Lexington.[29]

After ten years of medical practice, he was still unable to afford a house and he and his wife and daughter lived in a downtown Louisville apartment in a lower-middle-class neighborhood.

This is the man Bingham called in even though he was able to afford the best medical help in the country.

A monstrosity was building.

Although Flagler System documents show that the ailing Mary Lily continued to function effectively as a businesswoman, Bingham increasingly took over their mutual affairs. For example, in mid-January, he canceled plans for the New York mansion, instructing architect Pope to sell the property.[30]

He was determined to stay in Louisville, where he could pursue his favorite mistress—politics.

An important round of elections was coming up in November and he put out feelers, testing the waters for another run at the mayoralty. Finding them cold, he decided instead to run for county commissioner, making his public announcement for the office on January 27.[31]

In the meantime, the renovations at Lincliffe had fallen behind schedule and Mary Lily and the Judge remained in residence at the Seelbach. To console herself, Mary Lily ordered up her private car and took a trip to Tiffany's in New York where she bought herself a necklace of 111 pearls. Price tag: $228,000.[32] Those are 1917 dollars; today they would be worth sixty times that amount, $13.7 million—for a necklace![33]

Mary Lily had still not given up on putting some love in her marriage and she figured she might do so by temporarily removing both of them from Louisville, away from his business, his politics, and his cronies. On February 13, she ordered servants to reopen Whitehall. She and her husband would be there for the Easter holidays.

Judging by surviving correspondence, she was sincerely welcomed by friends, who found her new marriage much easier to deal with than her old widowhood.

Palm Beach Life observed, "It was a joy to many friends of Mrs. Robert Worth Bingham . . . to see Whitehall open once more and to know that Judge and Mrs. Bingham had arrived at Palm Beach for the season."

The Binghams, said the magazine, were expecting Mr. and Mrs. Pembroke Jones, of New York.

Who will reach here in a day or two and who will be their guests at Whitehall for several weeks. Though no plans have been laid for any large functions, Judge and Mrs. Bingham will have a number of house guests from time to time and will entertain their large circle of friends informally.[34]

Mary Lily and Bob had traveled to Palm Beach in her private railroad car, and shortly after their arrival, Mary Lily called in her lawyers and added yet another codicil, a change, to her will.

In substance, it was minor, simply raising a bequest to the Flagler Hospital in St. Augustine from $10,000 to $125,000. What was significant about the codicil was (1) she used her own lawyers, and (2) once again, she had omitted any bequests to her husband. It was the third successive change in six months, from engagement through marriage, and Robert Worth Bingham was excluded each time.[35]

□

On April 1, two weeks prior to Easter, they had the biggest fight of their brief and unhappy marriage. The children refused to come to Palm Beach for the holidays. They preferred Louisville, wanting to stay in either the unfinished Lincliffe or the Seelbach.

This caused a huge scene at Whitehall. Bingham, dealing a hurtful blow, sided with the demands of his children, telling Mary Lily that he would be leaving her to spend the holidays in Louisville.[36]

In tears, she gave in. She would go with him, which probably wasn't what he wanted at all.

She closed Whitehall, canceled the parties, and returned with her husband. A bleak announcement in the *Louisville Courier-Journal* told much more than the words said.

Judge Robert Worth Bingham and Mrs. Bingham, who spent the winter at their home at Palm Beach, have returned and are at their apartment at the Seelbach.[37]

Bingham did not even stay with her there. He immediately left for Staunton, Virginia, where he picked up Henrietta, and then to Asheville where he met Barry. After several days there, he returned to Mary Lily, on Easter Sunday.[38]

About this time, Mary Lily and her sister announced the engagement of Louise Wise to Lawrence Lewis, son of Mr. and Mrs. Thornton Lewis of Cincinnati, a family that also maintained a residence at White Sulphur Springs.

On May 1, Bingham accompanied Mary Lily to Wilmington for her niece's marriage. Upon their return, they found Lincliffe ready for occupancy. After five months of intermittent internment, Mary Lily could finally quit her hotel prison.

Lincliffe, however, would be far worse. It would be her tomb.

The Codicil

O N T H E M O R N I N G of May 29, Robert Bingham was awake in a guest room adjoining the master bedroom. He had moved his clothes and articles four days earlier. Mary Lily was often delusional now and it unnerved him to be around her.

He had been awake for hours and had propped himself up in the bed, positioning the pillows high so that he could read the letter yet one more time.

It came from Hugh Young's wife, Bessy. Two weeks earlier, Hugh had sailed to France as part of the American Expeditionary Force and Bingham had written Bessy to cheer her up.[1] Now she was responding and some of what she had to say was alarming.

My dear Bob, the photograph came. I am delighted to have it, it is very good indeed, perhaps a trifle stern and judge-like. I am awfully glad you don't look at me with that expression. . . . It is too ridiculous for you to talk about being "old" to even discuss. Though I know you feel so sometimes. When all you have been through piles up on you . . .

I have a favor to ask of you, but don't feel you must grant it. It is that, if it is possible, when you re-invest your money, as you spoke of having to do, this summer, you do a little of it through my brother, George Colston. . . .[2]

He reread the offending paragraph again: ". . . if it is possible, when you re-invest your money, as you spoke of having to do, this summer, you do a little of it through my brother, George Colston."

It unnerved him. In an unguarded moment, he had told Bessy that he might be coming into sums of money. He did not intend the news for public circulation, however. Putting down the letter, he rose from the bed and began his bath.

The house was nearly empty. The children had been sent away almost as soon as they had arrived home from school. Henrietta and Barry had gone with their grandfather to Asheville. His son Robert was in an army training camp.[3]

Other than a few servants, the only people remaining in the house were himself and Mary Lily. He was emptying the house for privacy. Tomorrow, the good doctor Michael Ravitch was arriving as a house guest to keep Mary Lily under twenty-four-hour supervision.[4] She was to be kept sedated, pacified, and *at home* because Bingham needed her signature on a change in her will.

This change was at the core of his plan, the reinvestment scheme to which he had unguardedly referred in his letter to Bessy Young.

What he had in mind was nothing less than a takeover of the *Courier-Journal* and the *Louisville Times*.

Through his confidential relationship as a lawyer for editor Henry Watterson, Bingham had learned that the combination of Haldemans and Watterson which had dominated Kentucky journalism for half a century was coming to an end. It had fallen victim to splits created by the death of co-founder Walter Haldeman, editorial positions, and the spreading movement to prohibit liquor. The dissension was further exacerbated by a long-standing quarrel between Haldeman's sons, Bruce, fifty-five, and William, sixty-one.[5]

The result was a nasty fight for control that ended in the Kentucky Court of Appeals where Bruce Haldeman lost. Watterson, now seventy-seven years of age, was elected president of the corporation, a post he held reluctantly. Neither he nor William Haldeman had suitable heirs to succeed in taking over the two newspapers. They began looking for a buyer.

That's where Bingham figured to make his move.

To take advantage of his inside knowledge, he needed to

make a firm offer and soon, before the newspapers were put up for public sale and the price became subject to auction. After months of dealing with Watterson and the other principals, he was convinced that a majority control of the newspapers could be bought for $1 million, provided the money was in cash and without encumbrances.

It was a considerable sum for a man virtually bankrupt a year before. But Bob had a plan. He could raise maybe 60 percent of the $1 million by selling the securities given to him by Mary Lily, or by borrowing on them.[6]

The remaining $400,000 was the reason Dr. Ravitch was staying in the house.

Bingham needed to persuade, or somehow force, Mary Lily to write a codicil naming him as beneficiary to at least some of her millions.

It doesn't seem that he planned to kill her. Not at this point, anyway. Murder would be too obvious, and it would be unnecessary. His need for funds would be satisfied merely by the existence of the codicil. It would serve as ample collatoral for a loan of $400,000.

The question was how to persuade her. Already, he had been excluded from her estate in three successive will changes. In addition, the agreement that he would not share in her estate was by now well known to all involved. Any deviation would bring down on him not only a howling pack of her relatives and business associates, but also the Flagler and Standard Oil lawyers. So he needed not only a codicil, but a secret codicil, the papers of which he would keep in his possession.

To accomplish his plan, he had two confederates, one a full accomplice and the other an unsuspecting one. The first of these was Ravitch, who would break down her resolve through addiction to morphine. The shots had begun in small doses in January, represented as part of her treatment for chest pains. They had been increased by increments until now she wanted them every day.[7] She was a woman of pluck, but the drug was too powerful, too seductive to resist.

□

The casual use of morphine was much more common at the turn of the century than it is today, and it is possible that neither Bingham nor Ravitch regarded the doping of Mary Lily as criminal.

Narcotics had been sold freely over the counter in the United States until 1909, when the Opium Exclusion Act was passed. Cocaine was an ingredient of the new popular drink Coca-Cola. Opium and morphine were widely sold by prescription in drugstores and were especially popular with discreet ladies who were otherwise respectable except that they were "on dope." In the early twentieth century, the profile of the typical drug addict matched Mary Lily exactly: white, female, and middle class. There was as high a rate of drug addiction in 1900 as in the drug-ridden era of the 1960s through the 1980s.[8]

□

Bingham's second, unsuspecting, accomplice was a lawyer to draw up the will. Bingham could do it himself, but that would certainly be challenged in court. He wanted to be as distant as possible from the codicil's creation. Any lawyer could do it, but *any* lawyer would notice Mary Lily's drugged condition. The best of them would certainly report their suspicions to the authorities. The worst would extort blackmail.

No, the job called for someone who would believe Bingham's tale that Mary Lily's condition was a result of medication. Dave Davies was the obvious choice. He had just returned from a year's service in France as a Red Cross ambulance driver and was therefore unfamiliar with the systematic drugging of Mary Lily and her rapid decline in health. He was loyal to Bingham and an old-time acquaintance of Mary Lily. He would believe what he was told, and even if he did develop suspicions, he would never resort to blackmail. In fact, Bingham figured, if Davies ever did discover he was a dupe in the plot, he most likely would keep his mouth shut and just retire from the scene. He and Bingham had been in too many previous adventures for one to blow the whistle on the other.

□

In the meantime, Mary Lily had been reclusive since she and Bob opened Lincliffe on May 2. Social etiquette required a housewarming and when none was forthcoming, resentments began to build. "People expected parties and when there were none, they got mad," says Sallie Bingham.[9] Whispers began. Was Mary Lily too good for Louisville society? Even Mary Lily herself, although ill and drugged, seemed aware of the necessity for a party.

Accordingly, to ease the talk and pacify his wife, Bingham set up a housewarming for Saturday, June 9.

It was a sumptuous affair with special streetcars shuttling guests between downtown Louisville and Lincliffe.

In the several newspaper accounts of the party, there is curiously no description of Mary Lily other than the mention that she was present and that she was the hostess. This is contrary to normal coverage of such events in that era, which routinely dwelled on the hostess' costume, frame of mind, and attentions to duty. It was an especially curious oversight in the case of Mary Lily, a woman of national prominence hosting her first party as a *grand dame* of the pretentious Louisville social satrapy.

In contrast, elaborate description is given of Robert Worth Bingham, of the guests, even of table arrangements.

Guests were invited from dusk to midnight with supper being served at eight. The entire 30 acres of grounds were lighted with electric lights hidden under red bunting, which extended from Longview, the streetcar station, through the woods to the lawn. Dinner and drinks were served at small tables under a marquee.

"Following dinner," the social columns relentlessly reported, "the tables were removed and dancing took place. . . . Provision was made for those guests who did not care to take part in the dancing to play cards in the house. A string band from Lexington furnished the music for the dancers." Later in the night, a "moving picture," starring Marie Doro in *Diplomacy,* was given on the edge of the garden.[10]

According to Kenan family sources, after the last guest had gone, in the hot, sweaty early morning hours, Mary Lily wandered the grounds. She was drunk. She was in pain. She had no strength to hold her stomach in. Her chest pains came back. She stopped every few feet to rest.

An artery pumping blood from her lungs to her heart had shut down. It was supposed to be a big artery, big enough to stick one's little finger into, but the years of little exercise or bad eating or stress or whatever it was that caused arteriosclerosis had clogged it with fatty materials and closed the artery down to the size of a pencil lead.

She was helpless. She wanted only to get into bed and rest. Before retiring, she had a mixed drink of laudanum.[11]

Following the housewarming, Ravitch quit Lincliffe as a house guest and returned to his own family and apartment. Mary Lily was by now so addicted that she gladly went to his office for injections.

A shopkeeper across the street from Ravitch's office said Mary Lily would come into his shop almost every time she left the doctor's office. She told him that Dr. Ravitch had her come in several times a week and he would give her a shot that would make her feel terrible at first but then much better. Judging by her conversations, the shopkeeper suspected that Dr. Ravitch was trying to get Mary Lily to do things against her will.[12]

A rumor began to circulate that one of Ravitch's nurses had objected to the medication and had been fixed.[13]

□

By mid-June, Davies had drawn up several tentative codicils and left them with her.

On the morning of June 19, a warm breeze stirred through the muslin curtains.

The dawn's hot, orange light had set afire the steeple of Christ Church Cathedral. Along the willow-lined banks of the Ohio, squirrels and birds scampered about their nests. The city of 237,000 souls was awake. In the kitchens, fires were made and pots of coffee set to boil. At Churchill Downs, stable hands were walking the thoroughbreds. In the Haymarket, farmers had already laid out their produce.

Bob Bingham had left for Lexington. Mary Lily would do as he insisted.

One wonders if the morphine by itself was sufficient to force such an action. Did he have some other hold on her? Was there some sort of blackmail? If so, what? Or was it done out of love?

Putting these speculations aside for the moment, let's follow the indisputed facts. She was, at this juncture, a heavy user of narcotics, according to medical records possessed by the Kenan family, according to the lore of the Bingham family. And she would sign, and never repudiate, the codicil.

□

It was about 10:00 A.M., Davies later testified, that she telephoned him to meet her at Ravitch's office. She did not explain why.[14] Upon his arrival there, Davies found only Mary Lily, Ravitch, and a single nurse present. Inexplicably, the nurse was excused to another room.

According to Davies, Mary Lily told him that she wished to leave her husband a handsome bequest because she thought he had behaved nobly when he made the agreements relinquishing all his rights to her estates. She added, said Davies, that "she wished to exercise her rights over her own property and that she did not care for her trustees and her brother, William, and her family to have knowledge of everything she did with her own property."[15]

The secret codicil, which Mary Lily brought to Ravitch's office already prepared, was based on Davies' previous drafts. But it was in a different handwriting and the language was somewhat different. Davies studied it carefully. He wasn't sure who had written it. It wasn't his handwriting, and it wasn't Bob Bingham's. But he approved of the document. It was short and perfect.

I make this codicil of my last will. . . . I give and bequeath to my husband, R. W. Bingham, five million dollars to be absolutely his, and he shall have the option of taking this from my estate in money or in such securities as he and the administering authorities of my estate may agree upon with respect to market value. . . . [signed] Mary Lily Bingham; [witnesses] W. W. Davies and M. L. Ravitch. . . .[16]

The new codicil was handled with significant difference from those changes made in her will by Mary Lily in December 1916 and March 1917. Following the signing, Davies took the codicil not to the courthouse for filing, but to his office. After two or three days, he returned it to Mrs. Bingham, who said she wished to give it to her husband. It would remain in Bingham's possession thereafter. Unfiled and secret, it was thus protected from any challenge by Mary Lily's family or business associates.

The scheme was complete. Bingham was now a legal beneficiary and only four other people knew about it: Mary Lily, Davies, Ravitch, and whoever had actually written the codicil. Of those, only Ravitch was a paid accomplice. His reward was to be a $50,000 fee.[17]

□

And now life grew even harder for Mary Lily.

Ordinarily, in these hottest days of summer, she and Bob would have headed for cooler climes. She was accustomed to spending Julys and Augusts at Mamaroneck or in New Hampshire. He, too, always went to cooler places in the summer, either a trip abroad or a rest at Asheville, or both. This summer, however, was peculiarly different.

Immediately after the party, Mary Lily vanished. Nothing was seen of her as she resumed her seclusion in the sweltering rooms of Lincliffe.

Bingham, on the other hand, was much in evidence. From the signing of the codicil onward, nearly every day carries a newspaper report of his attendance at rallies, meetings, and committee elections. When he was not politicking, he was out of town on other business. He seems to have spent little time, if any, with Mary Lily.

On July 5, he did a peculiar thing. He bought three expensive lots at Cave Hill, the main Louisville cemetery, where Eleanor was buried. Who were they for? Mary Lily? His father? Him? The three children? The arithmetic did not add. His father's ties were to Asheville, and presumably he would have preferred to be buried there, near or at the school. If the lots were for the three children, then where would Bingham be buried? If for him and Mary Lily, who would take the third grave?

Perhaps he had no one specifically in mind and the purchase of the lots was an investment. The Bingham lots occupy a large amount of ground and there is ample room for eighty-eight graves. However, in the seventy years following Mary Lily's death, only six people were buried there. Barry's father and mother, brother and sister, and two of his own children.[18]

But maybe this was Bingham's one attention to Mary Lily. To be sure she had a place to lie, once dead.

□

In the stress of the heat, Mary Lily's health began to falter. On the sweltering hot afternoon of July 12, with a heat wave sending temperatures to 102 degrees in the shade, she had her maid bring a tray of iced mint juleps to a table beside her bathtub. From the medicine cabinet she took the laudanum pills given to her by Ravitch. Disrobing, she lowered herself into the cool bath waters. A rotating electric fan on a white wicker table whirled and moved the heavy air but did not cool it.

An hour later, a worried maid knocked on the bathroom door. When there was no answer, she cautiously entered. Mary Lily was unconscious, her body draped over the side of the tub as if she had been trying to escape.[19]

Immediately Bingham called Ravitch, who diagnosed a heart attack. In the next few days, Bingham summoned Mary Lily's brother, William Kenan, who conferred with Ravitch and was persuaded that everything which could be done was being done.

Ravitch was understandably nervous, however, and moved to avoid full medical responsibility by inviting two colleagues into the case. It was pure window dressing. Incredible as it seems, believe it or not, neither of the two new doctors had training in heart disease.[20]

The senior of the pair was Walter Fisk Boggess, a colleague of Ravitch's at the University of Louisville and who shared Ravitch's office building. Boggess, fifty-four years of age, was a pediatrician of some reputation, but his practice was limited to diagnosis of children's diseases. He was a consultant, not a practicing physician, and he had no credentials in heart disease.[21]

The junior physician of the team was Solomon Steinberg, twenty-nine, a brilliant but inexperienced doctor who had been a student of Boggess at the University of Louisville.[22] Like the others, he was unqualified for anything but the most basic treatment of heart disease.

Bingham's selection of, or approval of, such a medical team seems inexplicable. Maybe he trusted them because of personal associations. He was certainly a longtime friend of Ravitch and probably a friend of Boggess since all three served on the same medical faculty. He may even have known young Steinberg.

But there were only two things all four had in common. One was association with the University of Louisville medical school. The second was that none, including Bingham, were qualified to diagnose, let alone treat, heart disease. Yet that is exactly what they did. They "treated" Mary Lily for heart disease and she, understandably, got worse.

If it seems strange to include Bingham as a member of the medical team, let us recall that he had a long interest in medicine. It was his choice of career at the University of Virginia. He collected several years of paychecks by lecturing on forensic medicine. And there was his ongoing interest in venereal disease. Indeed, in this July of 1917, even as Mary Lily lay in pain, he received a letter from Hugh Young which commented on Bingham's concern with "social hygiene."

Young, by then in France on Pershing's staff, wrote that he was setting up venereal disease stations throughout the front and wished Bingham was with him "because as a matter of fact you know you really are considerably medical in your makeup, particularly when it comes to problems of social hygiene." [23]

During this time, Mary Lily may have recovered sufficiently to have insisted on leaving the house, or to be given more qualified medical care. Something happened because Bingham wrote her pastor, George Ward, that she felt bitter toward him, that she might be leaving him.

Ward replied, "I am writing with the perfect, absolute freedom to which my love for you all entitles me . . . would it do any good for me to write her just a casual letter?" [24]

What she needed, of course, was a good doctor and a caring husband not a letter from Ward.

Her condition worsened and the morphine injections continued. She began having repeated hallucinations, according to Kenan family reports. Her sisters arrived and reported home that there was blood in her urine.

By now, full-time nurses were on duty. Two were fired in succession when they protested the amount of morphine dosage.[25] Their records were seized by the doctors, who later said they were "kept in a secure place and will be produced when a proper occasion arises." [26] Instead, the records were never produced. They have vanished from history, becoming one of the mysteries of the case.

On July 26, with brother William, sister Jessie Wise, and childhood friend Hannah Bolles at Mary Lily's bedside, Bingham released a statement to the press, nailing down in the public mind that Mary Lily was a victim of heart disease.

"She has been a sufferer from myocarditis, an affection of the heart, for some time, but the illness forced her to bed only two weeks ago," he told the *Courier-Journal*.[27]

The *Louisville Post* reported:

Mrs. Robert Worth Bingham is critically ill of heart trouble at her home, "Lincliffe," on the River Road. She has been a sufferer from myocarditis for some time, but has been confined to her bed only about two weeks. She became unconscious about 6:30 Thursday evening, and the physicians in attendance are fearful of the result. . . . The doctors say that her condition was improving, but the regarded her relapse on Thursday as most serious.[28]

In his interview with the *Post,* Bingham further implanted the heart disease theory by claiming that fourteen years ago, in 1903, she had suffered "a severe attack of angina pectoris." [29]

Although none of the surviving historical documents indicate Mary Lily had a heart condition, the statement may be true.[30] Mary Lily's family was present at the time of the interview and none of them challenged Bingham's statement.

On the morning of July 27, she went into fits and only oxygen kept her alive. That afternoon, at 3:10, she died in horrible convulsions.

Both Bingham and Ravitch avoided any involvement with the

official death certificate, which was signed within minutes by Boggess and Steinberg and witnessed by Mary Lily's sister, Jessie Wise.

It listed Mary Lily's age at fifty years, one month, thirteen days and said that the cause of death was oedema, or swelling, of the brain. A contributing disease was myocarditis, which she had had for at least ten months, said the doctors. In fact, Boggess and Steinberg had not begun treating her until July 6. Ravitch hadn't even met her until December 1916 at the earliest. So how did the doctors know of her alleged health history? From Bingham? Other than Mary Lily, he and Ravitch were the only ones in the world familiar with her health history in the last months of her life. Yet both men distanced themselves from the death certificate.

In a later interview, Boggess became more specific on the cause of death, describing it in medical terms as "cardio vascular renal," a condition that affected the heart and kidneys.[31]

Two days later, her coffin was placed in her private railroad car and taken by train via Atlanta to Wilmington for burial. Although Bingham may have earlier bought a cemetery plot for Mary Lily in Louisville, it appears that he deferred to the wishes of the Kenans.

She was laid to rest in the Kenan plot at Oakdale Cemetery. Her death so surprised the Kenans that no headstone had been prepared.[32] Services were conducted by the ubiquitous Reverend George M. Ward.

The burial statistics were particularly impressive, the grave being over 9 feet deep, with the lower 3 feet and the bottom being built of brick and faced with concrete slabs. The casket, weighing 650 pounds, was encased in a metal box, and after being lowered into the brick and concrete grave, it was covered with slabs of concrete. A cemetery keeper said fully three hours of effort would be necessary to take the casket from the grave.

The grave was unusually deep, exceptionally secure. It was as if the Kenans were hiding something. Perhaps a secret? Perhaps a tragedy.

Upon his return to Louisville from the funeral, Bingham made a verbal agreement with the Haldemans to deposit some of his securities as an option to buy. They, in turn, would hold off on seeking another buyer. If the codicil was uncontested, Bingham would take his millions and complete the sale. If the codicil was overturned, he was stuck.

He began to be very nice to the Kenan family.

Probate

MARY LILY died leaving an estate valued at between $130 million and $150 million.[1] Approximately half of the property was protected by the trusts set up by her and Henry Flagler. The Henry Flagler Trust properties were not to be touched, continuing in trust until May 24, 1918, with the trustees given the option to continue the trust for another five years.[2]

Of the remaining half, approximately $60 million went to niece Louise Wise, $6 million each to Mary Lily's brother and two sisters, and $5 million to Robert Worth Bingham. The personal property included more than $30 million in stock of Standard Oil of California, Indiana, Kansas, Kentucky, Nebraska, New York, New Jersey, and Ohio; $9 million in other stocks; $22 million in bonds, $5 million in accounts receivable; the mansion "Whitehall"; the mansion "Satan's Toe" in Mamaroneck; other real estate in Florida, New York, and North Carolina; furs; jewelry held in the vault at Tiffany's; her private railroad car; four automobiles; art objects; pianos; elaborate clocks; cash, including $1.9 million in New York banks, $700 in drawers at Lincliffe, and $375 in the German Bank of Louisville; and household furnishings.[3]

The art objects and furnishings at Whitehall and Satan's Toe dwarfed the possessions Mary Lily had in Louisville, but the Lincliffe furnishings alone amounted to a maharaja's ransom. They included thirty-one items of jewelry worth more than $2 million with such pieces as a large string of pearls consisting of 213 graduated pearls with a round diamond clasp, a medium length string of pearls consisting of 111 pearls with an oblong diamond clasp; a heavy platinum chain set with diamonds and a large emerald pendant attached; and one short string of pearls consisting of fifty-one graduated pearls with a square-cut diamond clasp.

Lincliffe furniture included a leather sofa with two "illuminated pillows" and two armchairs; mahogany tables and sofas; enameled reed chairs and lamp; velour armchairs; a Dresden paneled Louis XVI cabinet; a Chinese hall table in red; two Louis XV chairs, two Louis XVI armchairs and four Louis XV armchairs; a mahogany and gilded Louis XV bedroom suite, carved, including a bed canopy; chairs, sconces, and tables; a gilt dressing table in the bathroom; and twin brass beds.

For other bedrooms there were a Louis XVI gilt bed, a mahogany bed set, an ash bed set, and a brass bed set in the servants' room on the third floor.

Books were matched sets, with Dickens, Dumas, George Eliot, Thackeray, and Hawthorne, among them.

Floors were covered with thirty Persian or Turkish rugs, many the size of large rooms; several chenille and several silk rugs; and a couple of room-sized velvet rugs.

Bric-a-brac included candlesticks, cloisonné items, urns, a Japanese dragon piano lamp, a large gilt and wood mantel clock, three more piano lamps, Victorian English silver inkstand, cologne bottles, sterling silver writing implements, lots of glass bowls and vases, some old silver items and powder boxes.

Silver table items included baskets, salt and pepper items, bowls, trays, compotes, demitasse sets, jewel boxes, candlesticks, celery dishes, cocktail mixers, and a silver toilet set of twenty-eight pieces all monogrammed "MLK."

There were two major patterns of flatware—the "King's pattern" and the "Gilded pattern." Mary Lily had ice cream spoons, orange spoons and knives, berry forks, oyster forks, and service for anywhere from twelve to twenty-four. China was Limoges and Dresden.

□

The initial publicity focused on Mary Lily's primary heir, her niece Louise, who in addition to all the real estate holdings would receive $200,000 a year in income until her fortieth birthday, at which time she would receive a lump sum of $5 million cash.[4]

"Mrs. Lewis is only twenty-one years old," gushed the *New York Herald:*

Her bequest includes Mrs. Bingham's superb collection of jewels, valued at $2 million, including her $1 million pearl necklace. All the real estate also was bequeathed to young Mrs. Lewis. This embraced the magnificent chain of Flagler hotels at Palm Beach, Ormond and St. Augustine, as well as the Flagler residence at Palm Beach, which is said to be the handsomest private home in the United States

Since the death of her aunt this young woman, who had been quite unknown in social circles until her vast inheritance made her prominent, has been spoken of as "the Queen of Palm Beach." Apart from her own legacies, her mother, Mrs. Jessie Kenan Wise, of Wilmington, N.C., a sister of Mrs. Bingham, comes in under the will for a one-third interest in the trust portion of the estate. . . . Mrs. Lewis is an only child.[5]

Nineteen states made inheritance tax claims on the estate.

"So staggering were the figures compiled in the clerk's office," reported the *Courier-Journal,* "that no attempt was made to compute the actual number of dollars and cents that will be claimed from the fortune."[6]

On August 3, word reached Louisville that the Flagler and Kenan family heirs had filed with the Florida courts copies of her wills—the main will written in December 1916 and the Palm Beach codicil done in March 1917.

Bingham responded by taking the secret codicil from his wall safe and filing it with the Louisville court.

The news hit like a bombshell. Bingham's filing set off front-page headlines across the nation. The *Courier-Journal* reported, "This latest codicil was not attached to the original will and codicil, and was not therefore put to record in the Florida court."[7]

There was immediate consternation. What else might lie in unknown vaults? The news triggered a series of meetings at Standard Oil and among members of the Kenan family. One shoe had dropped. Were there others? Would Bingham end up owning the Flagler System? Or on the board of Standard Oil?

The Kenans and Bingham began testing one another, probing for information.

□

As part of his be-nice-to-the-Kenans campaign, Bingham invited Louise Wise and her new husband, Lawrence Lewis, to accompany him back to Louisville. It will be recalled that Bingham had met the couple at their wedding in May. He set them up in a guest apartment at Lincliffe, well attended by servants, and paid them far more attention than he had paid Mary Lily in the same house.

Indeed, things seemed to be going very well between Bingham and the Kenans until the morning of August 17, when Bingham went into the city on some business. Arriving at his office, he found an emergency message from his housekeeper. He returned quickly to Lincliffe to find that the Lewises had cleared out. They had gone, bag and baggage, leaving only the towels, departing the city without a note of thanks or goodbye, without a hint of explanation.

By the time Bingham next heard of the Lewises they were at the home of Lawrence Lewis' parents in White Sulphur Springs where a meeting of the Kenan heirs had convened.

The departure aroused enormous reaction from the Kentucky press including:

Hard News:

Information of great interest to people of Louisville reached this city Monday morning by way of White Sulphur Springs, West Virginia, to the effect that the brothers, sisters and niece of the late Mrs. R. W. Bingham have decided to contest the $5 million bequest. . . . Mrs. Lewis has done a great deal of talking at White Sulphur during the last ten days and some of her remarks have been keenly resented by Louisville friends of Judge Bingham, who are also at White Sulphur. . . .[8]

Speculation:

It is reported that several important family conferences were held at the Greenbrier Hotel and a contest of Judge Bingham's $5 million was decided upon. According to statements made at White Sulphur, attacks will be made upon Judge Bingham and upon Dr. Ravitch [accusing them] of undue influence.[9]

Fellowship:

The sympathy of the public must and does go out to Judge Bingham. Of his own volition he signed an ante-nuptial contract foregoing the usual husband's share in the estate, and now he is the subject of baseless vilifications. His wife chose to make a codicil leaving him five millions out of nearly one hundred. To her niece went sixty millions; to her brother and sisters, six millions each. Was it not enough? Has the sight of the glittering heaps of the Flagler gold begotten an avarice that brings horror and injuries in its train? Such has been the experience of the world, and this entire affair seems one of unspeakable greed.[10]

And hints of conspiracy by dark powers:

The history of every Standard Oil fortune is a history of fraud, perjury, violence, forgery and bribery; the history of ill-gained power used to debauch courts and Legislatures, as well as to destroy every man or woman who stood in the path of the Standard Oil Magnates.[11]

The general tone was one of indignation.

Mrs. Lewis was married only last May to Dr. Lawrence Lewis, a young man whose family resides near White Sulphur. Mrs. Lewis and her husband were in Louisville immediately after the death of Mrs. Bingham and returned to the South with Judge Bingham and were his guests at the home on River Road. The story of their sudden departure has caused much comment in the city. Judge Bingham left his home one morning to go to his office and when he returned in the evening he found that Mr. and Mrs. Lewis had slipped away from the house and out of the city, without saying goodbye or even mentioning their plans to depart.

Since that time, Mrs. Lewis and her husband have been almost continuously at White Sulphur and it is reported that several important family conferences were held at the Greenbrier Hotel and a contest of Judge Bingham's $5 million was decided upon. . . . Judge Bingham has employed Judge A. P. Humphrey, Edward F. Humphrey, Stanley Sloss and W. W. Davies to represent him in the litigation. . . .

It appears that some of the relatives of Mrs. Bingham did not expect her to leave her husband anything. This belief was based upon the fact that last December Judge Bingham signed on his own motion a waiver of any dower right in the estate. The result of this was that Mrs. Bingham was left free to leave her husband as much, or as little, as she thought fit. Some of the relatives of Mrs. Bingham did not believe she would leave him anything. . . . Some people believe that the matter will yet be settled by payment to Bingham of his bequest.[12]

Unknown to Bingham, the reason behind the Lewises' flight was to clear the way for an investigation in Louisville by operatives of the expert private detective, William Burns. To ensure the Lewises were not connected to the Burns investigation, the Kenans phoned Louise and requested she and her husband leave immediately and meet with the families in West Virginia.

The Kenans had hired Burns and his men in early August, after prominent Louisville residents approached the Kenans by letter and phone and asked why Robert Bingham would choose such medical quacks as the Ravitch team to attend Mary Lily.

□

Burly, red-haired, and mustachioed, Burns was the most famous, the most accomplished, and probably the most brilliant detective of his era. In 1911, after he solved a terrorist bombing in Los Angeles, the *New York Times* called him, "the greatest detective certainly, and perhaps the only really great detective, the only detective of genius this country has produced." His exploits were on a par with, if not superior to, such fictional heroes of the time as Sherlock Holmes and Arsene Lupin. As head of the William J. Burns International Detective Agency, he was connected in some manner to most of the important American mystery cases in the first twenty years of this century and his reputation had spread around the world.

Like his fictional counterparts, Burns sometimes used illegal burglaries and forgeries to solve his cases and in fact just before taking on the Kenans as clients he had served fifteen days in jail for burglarizing a New York City law office and copying papers which he turned over to his client, banker and financier J. P. Morgan.[13]

□

Working in Louisville undercover during parts of August and September 1917, Burns and his detectives eventually compiled a 500-page detective report for the Kenan family. The report included interviews with the four nurses hired by Ravitch to attend Mary Lily.

The nurses gave similar stories, each saying she had complained about excessive amounts of morphine used by Ravitch. Following the complaints or questions, each in turn was relieved of duty. Two of the nurses said they were told by Ravitch that he was going to charge a $50,000 fee for his services to Mary Lily and he would get the fee just as easily whether she were alive or dead.

The detectives also discovered Bingham's purchase of a "brand-new Packard" and reported he had given it to Ravitch as a gift.

□

In the meantime, Bingham misplaced, gave away, or stole a million-dollar necklace—it was the famous necklace given to Mary Lily by Henry Flagler.

One of the first strangers to visit the house after Mary Lily's death, within seventy-two hours of her death, was John Stites, president of the Louisville Trust Company, which was one of the administrators of her estate. He was met at the door by Dave Davies, who showed him around the house. At the conclusion of the tour, Davies took Stites to a wall safe.

Dialing the combination, Davies took out a handsome jewel box, which he laid on a table. With a flourish, he flipped open the lid to reveal the dazzling million-dollar pearl necklace Flagler had given to Mary Lily.

"Have you ever held this much money in your hand in your life?" asked Davies, passing the pearls to Stites.

The banker touched them gently, then spoke a single word, "beautiful."

After both men admired them in the light, Davies replaced the pearls in the wall safe.[14] At that point, the necklace vanished into some great black hole of history—disappeared, from tax collectors and from public display. Except on discreet occasions, it hasn't been seen since.

That was the last time the necklace publicly existed. It was not included in the inventory of the estate filed by the official assessors. Stites himself kept the existence of the necklace a secret for nearly a year before revealing that Davies had shown it to him. Davies confirmed the showing, but said he didn't know what had happened to it.

As for Bingham, he said no such necklace ever existed. Even to this day the whereabouts of the necklace or its remnants is mysterious. No trace of it appears in the inventory of Robert Worth Bingham's estate, nor in the estates of Mary Lily's other heirs.

There are two possibilities as to what happened to it.

Consider, first, that it did exist at one time. It appears in several portraits of Mary Lily from the Whitehall days. Davies and Stites both said they handled it at Lincliffe immediately after Mary Lily's death. And it apparently wasn't stolen, because there was no robbery report.

Pending other evidence, reasonable assumptions are (1) that Bingham pocketed it, or (2) that it was taken away by Louise Wise, who would have inherited it anyway, while she was a guest in Lincliffe following Mary Lily's death.

Where is it now? Either intact or broken up into several pieces it could have passed onto Louise Wise's heirs.[15] Or it could still be hidden in the Bingham family. A third possibility is that Robert Bingham may have given it to another woman. His romantic life was far from over. He would, for example, remarry in 1924.

□

Another mystery came to light on August 23 and it connects to the private detective report about a gift of a "brand-new Packard" to Ravitch.

On that date in August, Bingham walked into the Southern Motors company and bought a new, four-passenger, Packard "325" Roadster costing $3,400. According to the invoice, the car was to be "delivered as soon as possible to Judge R. W. Bingham."[16]

The meager motor registration and ownership records of the era no longer exist, so it is difficult to discern whether Bingham wanted the car for his own use, as his son Barry maintains, or whether it was a bribe to Dr. Ravitch, as the private detectives hired by the Kenan family reported.

It is difficult to believe Bingham wanted it for himself, however. At the time, he had the use of at least six automobiles, including four Packards, two of the latter being owned by Mary Lily and two by him.[17] How many cars can a man drive?

Whether it was a gift to himself or a payoff to Ravitch, Bingham's timing shows a chilling indifference to the proprieties of mourning. It is a confirmation, if you will, of De Quincey's definition of how a man comes to bad habits: "If once a man indulges himself in murder, very soon he comes to think little of robbing; and from robbing he comes next to drinking and Sabbath-breaking, and from that to incivility and procrastination."[18]

Even as the Burns' detectives were in the midst of their work, the opening round of the attack on the bequest began. Probate hearings opened August 28 in the Louisville County Court to determine the authenticity of the codicil.[19]

The Kenan lawyers quickly found they were playing against a stacked deck.

It was like a Bingham courthouse reunion with the judge, witnesses, plaintiffs' lawyers, and defense counsels all well known to each other and each having present or former Bingham ties. For example:

1. The presiding judge, Samuel W. Greene, was a longtime toiler in the Whallen machine sweatshops and a Bingham political ally.
2. Bingham's lawyer, Judge Alex Humphrey, was also Bingham's co-counsel representing Henry Watterson in the *Courier-Journal* litigation.
3. Bingham's chief witnesses, Stanley Sloss and Dave Davies, were respectively his present and former law partners.
4. The opposing lawyer—Helm Bruce, representing the Kenan family interests—was a Fusionist reform leader who had supported Bingham's appointment as mayor.

□

On opening day, in the courtroom crowded with nearly 150 participants and spectators, Bingham could have fired scattershot and never hit a stranger.

He opened the hearings by presenting five papers:

- The last will and testament of Mary Lily, dated September 23, 1916.
- A reaffirmation of that will dated December 8, 1916, which precluded Bingham from sharing in the estate.
- The assent of Bingham to those terms.
- The Palm Beach codicil dated March 1917.
- The original of the secret codicil giving him $5 million.

To beat the stacked deck, the Kenans needed a lean, mean lawyer, one who would be Bingham's equal in cynicism and his superior in law. Instead, they had chosen Bruce, whose primary practice was civil suits and who was unaccustomed to the rough and tumble contest of liars, which the Bingham side was getting ready to parade onto the witness stand.

Bruce's plan was simple and naive. When Bingham and Ravitch took the stand to authenticate the codicil, Bruce in cross-examination would trip them up on their own stories and force them to unveil the truth.

He and the Kenans found it peculiar that with powerful evidence against them, the Bingham team was strangely confident, even smug. And Bruce wondered why. He was soon to find out.

The Bingham team began by lulling Bruce into complacency. As the trial began, Bruce noticed that neither Bingham nor Ravitch was present, but he figured they would be coming in at any moment.

Bingham's lawyer, Judge Humphrey, opened with routine preparation to authenticate the various wills, including the codicil.

Witnesses to the September 1916 will, for example, testified that Mary Lily had been of sound mind and they had witnessed her signature. For the December 1916 will, attorney Stanley Sloss swore that both Mary Lily and Bingham had been of sound mind.

Did Mr. Sloss recall the signing? asked Humphrey.

"Quite distinctly," replied Sloss. "Judge Bingham and Mrs. Bingham were going to New York. I think it was the first time they went to New York after their marriage. As I recall it, they were leaving on the one o'clock train. During the course of the morning, early in the morning, quite early in the morning, Judge Bingham asked me and Miss Overman [Bingham's secretary] to go out to his room at the Seelbach Hotel and witness some papers and we went out and witnessed them."

Miss Overman's testimony was brief, corroborating Sloss' tale and going no further.

Humphrey then surprised the courtroom by announcing that his only other witness would be Dave Davies.

Bruce sat straight up. What about Bingham and Ravitch? Surely they would be on hand to witness the verification of the signing of the codicil. As if in a bad dream, he heard Humphrey say otherwise.

Neither Bingham nor Ravitch would be called for questioning in their own defense. They were both out of town on vacation.

Vacation?

Gasps and ahs rippled through the courtroom. Humphrey had neatly and cynically destroyed Bruce's case before it even began. Bruce had been lulled into an absolute mistake.

The legal strategy was this: By having Bingham and Ravitch disappear, Humphrey had removed them from not only the jeopardy of perjury, but from any questioning at all. Both men were out of state, he said—Bingham being in Atlantic City "for a rest" and Ravitch in Maine "on vacation." In fact, Humphrey was lying to protect his clients. Bingham was across the border in Ohio. Ravitch was in Lexington, a mere 80 miles away.[20]

But, when Humphrey declined to call them, only two agencies could force the deposition or court appearance of Bingham and Ravitch.

The first of these agencies was the court itself, Judge Greene having the power but lacking the motivation to reach out for the truth.

The second agency was Helm Bruce. But he was tied by a legal knot. If he had subpoenaed Bingham and Ravitch prior to the trial, he could have forced their return from anywhere in the country. But he hadn't done so because he assumed, as a gentleman, they would be present. Now, after the trial began, it was too late. His case was headed for destruction like a canoe over Niagara Falls and there was little he could do to stop it.

He heard Humphrey call Davies.

The blond, handsome lawyer took the stand with aplomb. He would be the swordsman whose arm and foil would defend the Bingham case.

Gently, Humphrey led him into the contest. Had Davies known the deceased?

Since the days of their youth, said Davies. "I had met her in North Carolina a good many years before her death when I was a student at the university."

"And what is that you hold in your hand?" asked Humphrey, seeming to notice that Davies had brought a document to the witness chair.

Davies looks at the document in his hand. He examines it, giving it a thorough study, and announces that it is a codicil to Mrs. Bingham's will.

"It is dated Louisville, June 19, 1917."

Q. Did you see Mrs. Bingham sign that paper?
A. I did.
Q. In whose presence was it signed?
A. In my presence and in the presence of Dr. M. L. Ravitch.
Q. Was it signed by her as a codicil to her last will and testament?
A. It was.
Q. Did she request you and Dr. Ravitch to witness it as a codicil to her last will and testament?
A. She did.
Q. Was Mrs. Bingham of sound mind and disposing memory at that time?
A. She was.

That was about the extent of Humphrey's direct examination of Davies. It was now Helm Bruce's turn to question the witness and Davies awaited him with the confidence of a master fencer. This was Bruce's only shot. To arrive at the truth, he would have to break Davies.

"Mr. Davies," asked Bruce, "where was this paper signed by Mrs. Bingham?"

A. At Dr. Ravitch's office. That is, in the little retiring room of his office.
Q. Did Dr. Ravitch give Mrs. Bingham a drug on the day the codicil was signed?
A. Not to my knowledge. . . .
Q. Who mentioned it to you, the idea of a codicil?
A. She did herself.
Q. Where?
A. At her own house.
Q. When?
A. Several days, I should say three or four days, before that [the codicil] was written.
Q. Did you discuss the matter with Judge Bingham?
A. Judge Bingham was out of the city for those three or four days in North Carolina.
Q. Had you ever discussed with Judge Bingham the idea of a codicil to his wife's will?
A. I had not.
Q. Who was present when she signed it?
A. I was present and Dr. Ravitch was present when she signed it.
Q. No one else except Mrs. Bingham herself?
A. No, sir; no one else.
Q. What time of day was this?
A. It was about one o'clock, I should say, maybe a little earlier or a little later, but about that time.
Q. How did she happen to be in the doctor's office?
A. I do not know how she happened to be there. She had me called up and I was requested to meet her at Dr. Ravitch's office, and I think her chauffeur came for me in the automobile. He had come for me on several occasions before that and after that to meet her and take lunch or for a drive, and I think he came for me on that day and I went to her and met her at Dr. Ravitch's office.
Q. Who called you up?
A. I am not certain who came to the telephone. I was called to come there. I rather think it was the chauffeur. I am not absolutely certain about that. I paid very little attention to that.

Q. Did he tell you what you were wanted for?

A. He did not.

Q. Did you know when you went to Dr. Ravitch's office what you were wanted there for?

A. No, sir; I did not; although for four days I had been drawing tentative drafts of the codicil very similar to that for her; but the message on the telephone said nothing about the codicil, just to come to Dr. Ravitch's office. So I went.

Q. Where had you been drawing these tentative drafts of the codicil?

A. In my office.

And now Bruce zeroed in on a central question. Why, he asked, the secrecy? And why did Mary Lily not use her own platoon of lawyers?

Davies more or less shrugged off the questions.

"She had been talking to me about it and I had been drawing the tentative draft. She stated to me that she wanted to exercise her rights over her own property and that she did not care for her trustees and for her brother William and for her family to have knowledge of everything she did with her own property. That is the only thing that I know that would be an answer to your question."

Q. Mr. Davies, you spoke of having several conversations with her, I believe. You said, on the subject of the codicil. Was anybody else present on the occasion of any of those conversations?

A. Nobody else but Mrs. Bingham and myself.

Q. How many conversations did you have with her on the subject?

A. I should say three definite conversations and conferences about it, besides other ordinary remarks concerning it.

Q. Where were those several conversations?

At this point, Davies' composure broke a bit and he shows signs of exasperation.

"The first one, as I said a moment ago, was out at her house and then in the automobile drives that she would ask me to take with her, we discussed this matter."

Q. You mean then that all the conversations except the first one were in the automobile drives?

A. Yes, I am quite certain of that. I am certain of the first conference which was a very full one concerning the matter and the other two I am quite certain were on the automobile drives which she would take very often in the middle of the day along about one or half-past one or two o'clock.

Q. Did she suggest the $5 million?

A. She did.

Bruce turned from Davies; putting his back to him and facing the courtroom, he asked a crucial question.

"Did she tell you at that time or did you know that Judge Bingham and she had executed an ante-nuptial contract, that is a contract before her marriage, by which Judge Bingham had waived all interest in her estate?"

Davies was unsurprised. He was ready for the question

"She did. She told me that plainly. She said in that connection—I suppose it would be competent to say what she did say—that that was one reason she wanted to make that codicil, that his act had been a very noble and voluntary act and she appreciated it and she wanted to make that codicil and present it to him, which she did."

Q. Did she at the same time tell you that within a few weeks, or probably sixty days after her marriage, Judge Bingham had gotten from her $50,000 to pay himself out of debt with?

A. No, sir; she didn't tell me that. She said she had helped him considerably and that she was very glad to do it. She went that far. She said she helped him very considerably.

Q. Do you know the facts otherwise than from her statements, that he did get $50,000 from her, say, within sixty days after her marriage?

A. I have heard it since she died.

Bruce shifts the line of questioning, asking those questions only Ravitch can properly answer. Nevertheless, he puts them to Davies.

"When did Dr. Ravitch go out there and begin spending his nights out there regularly?"

Davies replies coldly, "About a week, as I say, before she died, Dr. Ravitch was there at that time, but what night he went I could not tell you."

Q. Do you know how long he had been staying there at night prior to that time?

A. No, sir; I could not tell. I was not there myself and could not know.

Q. Did he have any assistant staying there?

A. Yes, sir; he had an assistant staying out there.

Q. Who was that?

A. Dr. Steinberg.

Q. Do you know how long he had been staying there?

A. No, sir; I do not. I think he was there about a week before Mrs. Bingham died, but how long he had been there I do not know.

Stymied, Bruce returns to the signing of the codicil, to which Davies was a witness.

"When was this paper, which is signed by Mrs. Bingham, the codicil, written?—This identical paper?"

A. On the day when she signed it—about one o'clock on the nineteenth of June.

Q. Did you copy it from a paper that you had previously prepared?

A. I did not because it is practically what the tentative copy showed. I did not have the tentative copy with me at the time. That was in my office there in my desk.

Q. Who first mentioned it to you, the idea of a codicil?

A. She did herself.

Q. Where?

A. At her own house.

Q. When?

A. Several days, I should say three or four days.

Q. Who was present when you were drawing those tentative drafts?

A. I was alone and my stenographer copied them.

Q. Were you staying out at Judge Bingham's house at that time—were you spending your nights out there?

A. No. I think during that time—during I should say, the week prior to that, I spent probably two nights out there, but was not staying there regularly.

It will be noted that Davies has sidestepped any claim to have written the final codicil. He only admits to having prepared the drafts.

Again Bruce returns to the activities of Ravitch, asking questions that can only be answered by the doctor.

Mary Lily Kenan, a pensive thirty-six-year-old, shown here wearing the intricately detailed lace gown she sported at a *bal poudré* during the 1903–04 season. The *bals*, at which guests donned powdered wigs and clothing reminiscent of another era, were highlights of the Palm Beach social season. (*From* The Kenan Family *by Alvaretta Kenan Register; with the permission of J. Shields Kenan II, Statesboro, Georgia*)

Mary Lily Flagler, in a March 1903 portrait by Mrs. Leslie Cotton, posed wearing her wedding present from husband Henry M. Flagler—an impressive strand of pearls valued at $1 million—and her ruby engagement ring. The portrait now hangs in the music room of the Henry Morrison Flagler Museum in Palm Beach. (*North Carolina Collection, UNC Library at Chapel Hill*)

Robert Worth Bingham, in an 1889 group photo of his classmates at the University of North Carolina. (*North Carolina Collection, UNC Library at Chapel Hill*)

William Watkins Davies, called "Dave" by his friend and partner Robert Worth Bingham, was a classmate of Bingham's at the University of North Carolina. (*North Carolina Collection, UNC Library at Chapel Hill*)

Colonel Robert Bingham, shown in his uniform in this undated photo, was a persistent defender of the South in his teachings and writings. (*North Carolina Collection, UNC Library at Chapel Hill*)

Dr. Hugh Young, shown here in his Johns Hopkins office in 1906, was a medical pioneer, inventor, and friend of Robert Worth Bingham, serving as best man at Bingham's marriage to Mary Lily Kenan Flagler. (*Courtesy of the Alan Mason Chesney Medical Archives of the Johns Hopkins Medical Institutions, Baltimore, Maryland*)

Dr. M. L. Ravitch, in a photograph that appeared in his 1937 book *The Romance of Russian Medicine*, was the doctor Robert Worth Bingham called upon to treat his wife, Mary Lily, when she fell ill. Ravitch, who began his career in Louisville after studying in his native Russia and at a medical college in St. Joseph, Missouri, was a dermatologist and a friend of Bingham's.

Mary Lily and Henry Flagler on an informal outing around wintertime 1909–10 in Palm Beach. Arthur Spalding, a young organist hired for the 1909–10 season at Whitehall, kept a collection of photos and reminiscences of activities in which he participated during that period. (*A. C. Spalding Collection, Henry Morrison Flagler Museum, Palm Beach, Florida*)

Mary Lily Bingham and her future father-in-law, Colonel Robert Bingham, in Palm Beach, February 1916. (*The Henry Morrison Flagler Museum, Palm Beach, Florida*)

Mary Lily Kenan Flagler told her husband Henry Morrison Flagler that she wanted a marble palace. He responded by building her Whitehall, shown here in the winter of 1901. The cost of its construction was $3 million. (*The Henry Morrison Flagler Museum, Palm Beach, Florida*)

In the outdoorsy tweed garb he favored, Ambassador Robert Worth Bingham is pictured here in London with an unidentified companion. (*Sallie Bingham*)

Ambassador Robert Worth Bingham, *left,* was present at Paddington Station in London when American General John Pershing arrived to attend the coronation of King George VI in spring 1937. (*Wide World Photos*)

Melcombe Bingham, the Bingham home on River Road east of Louisville, was named by Robert Worth Bingham after an ancestral home in Great Britain. Shown here in 1966, the estate includes two homes and an outdoor theater. (*Courier-Journal/Louisville Times*)

Moustachioed Barry Bingham, Jr., was editor and publisher of the *Courier-Journal* and the *Louisville Times* until family wrangling prompted his father to sell the newspapers in 1986. (*Courier-Journal/Louisville Times*)

Young Henrietta Worth Bingham, here astride "Billy Bow," was to become a noted horsewoman and a member of London literary circles. She died in 1968 in New York City. (*Courier-Journal/Louisville Times*)

Actresses Carrie Nye, *left,* and Tammy Grimes flank playwright and novelist Sallie Bingham in New York, celebrating Bingham's play *Paducah.* Bingham, granddaughter of Robert Worth Bingham, returned to Louisville in the late 1970s, her writing career stalled, and began her attempt to become involved in the family business. (*Courier-Journal/Louisville Times*)

Eleanor Bingham Miller, youngest of the grandchildren of Robert Worth Bingham, returned to Louisville around the same time as her sister, Sallie Bingham, and eventually joined in Sallie's fight to become involved in the family businesses. She was negotiating a proposal to divide control and ownership of the broadcast and newspaper companies between Barry Bingham, Jr., and herself before the decision of their father, Barry Bingham, Sr., to sell.

(*Courier-Journal/Louisville Times*)

Barry Bingham, Sr., decided to sell the family businesses to end arguing and to assure financial stability for the coming generations of the Bingham family.

(*Courier-Journal/Louisville Times*)

"Was Dr. Ravitch staying out at the Bingham house at the time this paper was drawn?"

The question is sloppy. On the eve of the signing, Ravitch attended a meeting at Lincliffe but on the day the paper was drawn he was staying in town. Davies easily slips through the loophole.

"No, sir; he was not."

Bruce tries to recover, asking, "He subsequently went out there and stayed continuously, did he not?"

"When her condition became quite critical," said Davies, "Dr. Ravitch went out there and stayed a good deal, he and the other doctor stayed there a good deal."

Q. Who was the other doctor?
A. Dr. Boggess.
Q. Did Dr. Boggess ever spend the night out there?
A. Yes, sir.
Q. How many?
A. While I was there, I remember of his spending two nights, while I was there. How many others I could not say.
Q. While you were there, do you mean the last week of her life?
A. Yes, sir; the last week.

Shifting directions again, Bruce attempted to show that Bingham had taken everything he could get from Mary Lily prior to her death. That Robert Bingham was the sort of man who might drug or coerce her into signing the codicil. A review of the testimony shows that the questions would have been far more devastating had they been directed at Bingham instead of Davies.

Q. Didn't she say that within two or three months after the marriage, in the month of February 1917, he had gotten from her securities of the listed value of $696,500 which are now paying to him an income of more than $50,000 a year?
A. She told me she had—she didn't tell me that she had but she told me in the winter when she was here that she was setting aside property or securities for her husband Rob, as she called him, that ought to give him an income of about $50,000 a year.
Q. Did she say how she was setting that aside?
A. No, sir; she did not give me the details. She stated just what I have said.

Q. Did you learn from her or from any source, Judge Bingham or otherwise, the fact that she had offered to set aside securities upon which he should receive the income and that he had objected and insisted upon being given the securities themselves?

A. No, sir; I have heard nothing about that. I heard no discussion of that. She stated just what I have said, that she was setting aside securities that ought to give him an income of about $50,000 a year. That was in the winter.

Bruce next tried to show that Mary Lily wanted the securities reverted to her should Bingham precede her in death.

Q. Did she say anything to you about having made a request of him to give her a writing to the effect that these securities should come back to her estate at his death?

A. She did not discuss that with me at all—no.

Q. Is the phraseology of this codicil yours or hers?

A. It is my phraseology at her suggestion. The first part of it she suggested herself.

And now Davies firmly plants the testimony which will seal the case: the reasons why Mary Lily wanted the codicil kept secret and why she didn't use her own lawyers.

"If you want," said Davies artfully, "I can tell you what she said when she suggested the phraseology."

Bruce went for the bait.

Q. Well, what did she say?

A. She said to me—she says, I am—I have a will, as you know, in existence and I am going on East in the late summer or early fall to make some changes in it—or to make some codicils to my will and I want this codicil so that nothing I do with my will will affect this. I want this to be independent of the will if need be, it is not revoked by anything I do with the will. That is the reason of the phraseology you will find there in the first part of the codicil.

Q. You mean there was an attempt to make this so that she could not revoke this if she wanted to?

A. No, sir; as a lawyer I did not think anybody could make a codicil that could not be revoked but she asked me about this at our first conference. She told me she wanted this independent of her will and it was under what she said that I drew the first part of that codicil.

Q. Did you advise her that a codicil could be independent of a will?

A. I followed her dictation. I did what she wanted me to do although I knew that a codicil, as a will, could be revoked but at the same time she said, "I want it a part of my will but any working over or changes in my will I do not want to affect that codicil, that is an independent thing."

Q. Was she under the impression that it was irrevocable?

A. She was not and I told her—I said anybody can make a will and revoke another will or will and codicil or as many codicils that it may have.

And thus it was done. Davies had established a reasonable basis for Mary Lily's actions, and simultaneously explained that as an attorney he had not misled her.

Although he had firmly impaled himself upon Davies' sword, Bruce was not yet ready to surrender. Thrashing about wildly, he began to repeat himself, trying to tie Davies, Bingham, and Ravitch together in a conspiracy.

Blatantly, as we shall see, Davies lied his way through the questioning.

Q. Had you ever discussed with Judge Bingham the idea of a codicil to his wife's will?

A. I had not.

Q. Never up to the time it was finally signed?

A. I had not.

Q. Do you know what conferences she had, if any, with Judge Bingham?

A. What conferences she had with Judge Bingham?

Q. Yes.

A. No, I do not know about that—no.

Q. What was done with this paper immediately after it was signed?

A. She gave it to me and after the second or third day, she asked me to return it to her that she might herself present it to Judge Bingham, and she did present it to him.

Q. Then what was done with it?

A. Judge Bingham kept it because some few days after that I saw it in his possession.

Q. And where did it remain from that time until her death?

A. Judge Bingham had possession of it and it remained, I suppose, in his safety vault box.

Once again Bruce had run into the wall of the defense. Only Robert Bingham could testify as to how and why he had obtained the codicil. But Robert Bingham was not in the courtroom. With futile desperation, Bruce turned back to Davies.

"Do you know why it was not placed by Mrs. Bingham with her original will and the preceding codicil to her original will—why it was left in Judge Bingham's possession?"

"No," replied Davies with cool patience. "She said she wanted to make it a gift to her husband herself."

Q. I know, but my question is this: You knew she had an existing will, did you not?

A. Yes, sir; she told me she had one.

Q. You knew she did not have that in her possession, did you not?

A. I did.

Q. Why was this codicil to the will not placed with the original will—why was it left in Judge Bingham's possession?

A. During one of our conversations she laughingly said she didn't want to go to my office or any lawyer's office, that she was a woman of great wealth and more or less in the public eye and that she preferred to let this matter remain in secrecy. That was a part of her wish.

Q. Did I understand you to say, Mr. Davies, a moment ago, that you kept the codicil first?

A. Yes, sir; I kept it and after the second or third day she asked me to bring it to her and said she wanted to present it to Judge Bingham herself.

Q. You took it out to the house to her?

A. Yes, sir.

Having asked Davies the questions that only Bingham could answer, Bruce proceeded to ask the questions which only Ravitch could answer.

"Mr. Davies, what was she going to Dr. Ravitch's office for?"

"I don't know," said Davies. "That is a medical matter I wouldn't know very much about."

Q. Do you know whether or not any medicine or any drug of any kind had been administered to her on the day of this codicil either hypodermically or otherwise?

A. I do not know anything about Dr. Ravitch's treatment, but she had nothing in her manner that would indicate any such thing. That is the only way I could judge.

Q. Do you know how long she had been going to Dr. Ravitch's office?

A. No, sir; I don't know how long she had been going there. I think Dr. Ravitch had been attending to her for some time.

Q. Have you any idea how long?

A. I could not tell you. Very likely I think he visited before she went away from here to Palm Beach—along after Christmas. I think he attended her then because I remember she mentioned having been there when she had some sickness or indisposition of some sort.

It will be noted that throughout his testimony under oath, Davies was careful to avoid mention of Mary Lily having any "heart" condition or problem. He was consistently vague as to her "indisposition" and "sickness." It seems that Davies had doubts about the cause of her death and was distancing himself from any connection to it.

Q. Do you know whether or not she had for any material length of time prior to the date of this codicil been a regular visitor at Dr. Ravitch's office?

A. No, I do not know how regularly she had visited Dr. Ravitch. I am quite sure she had had treatments there. How many, I do not know and how regularly I do not know.

Q. Did you ever hear her speak of receiving hypodermic injections from Dr. Ravitch?

A. I have not.

Q. You know nothing about that?

A. No, I know nothing about that. That is entirely out of my department and I do not know anything about that.

Bruce was nearly exhausted, worn out by Davies' skillful denials, evasions, and lack of knowledge. Frustrated, Bruce turned to yet another flank, hoping to find a crack in the Bingham defense. He wanted to show that a severe rift existed between Mary Lily and Bingham just prior to the signing of the codicil, an estrangement which would have made it unlikely that she had signed the codicil of her own free will.

Bruce introduced the fact that in the spring before Mary Lily's death she and her husband were at Palm Beach and had quarreled when he insisted upon leaving her in order that he might go to Louisville to pass the Easter holidays with his children.

"Mr. Davies," asked Bruce, "did you not know it to be a fact that what Mrs. Bingham termed the improper treatment of herself by Mr. Bingham's children and their lack of appreciation of what she had done for them had given her very great pain and the pain had gone to such an extent in the latter part of her life that she told Judge Bingham that his children could not come into her house?"

Bingham's counsel jumped to his feet with an objection that the quarrel over the children wasn't germane to the case.

Judge Greene agreed, saying, "It does not seem to me it should go that far."

Bruce countered that he wanted "to ascertain all the conditions there just before and after the making of this will."

Smiling indulgently, Humphrey responded that "we have allowed very great latitude because we have absolutely nothing to conceal in the matter, but I am bound to object at this time when Mr. Bruce attempts to bring Judge Bingham's children in here."

The court agreed. "Let the objection be sustained to that question."

Bruce returned to his main case, but this time he kept to questions Davies could not easily sidestep—namely Davies' own actions in preparing the codicil.

Q. Mr. Davies, you spoke of drawing tentative drafts of the codicil?
A. Yes, sir.
Q. This is a very short codicil. What was the occasion, if you recall, of so many drafts of a simple paper like this?
A. The first copy—the tentative copy—that I drew, I drew after my conference with her and she stated that she wanted me to embody in that codicil something about the amenities of life as between husband and wife, so I did it. It was something of a meteorical finish, I think. I thought so at the time. She wanted that in the codicil. I submitted that to her and she told me, she said, "This is my property and I am dealing with it myself and I think that clause sounds a little apologetic to my relatives and my trustees and so on, it is my property and I have a right to do with it as I please, cut that out." . . . I did. The second one she had told me she wanted a clause in the draft enjoining secrecy as to the existence of the codicil for the same reason, her family and so on, and so I told her at the time that would not make it any stronger so far as secrecy was concerned, but she wanted it there, and when it was there she read it over and I reassured her that it didn't make it any stronger and she told me to take it out, which I

did, and so it left the codicil just about in that form and that was the final rough draft that was made, and when I went to Dr. Ravitch's office I did not take that with me, not being summoned there on anything but a social errand as I thought, so that was drawn.

Astonishingly, Davies said that he did not keep copies of the draft versions, nor did he have any other evidence to support his version of events.

Q. Have you those drafts?

A. I have not. I destroyed them because she enjoined secrecy about the whole matter. They were of no more use and I tore them up and threw them away.

Q. Did you ever draw any other papers for Mrs. Bingham?

A. No, I never drew any other papers for her. That is the only one except those tentative drafts.

Q. Did you ever act in any other capacity for Mrs. Bingham?

A. No, sir; I never did. That was the only occasion.

Q. You have been the lifelong friend of Judge Bingham?

A. I have.

Q. You and he were former partners?

A. Yes, sir.

Q. How long were you and Mrs. Bingham at Dr. Ravitch's office the day this instrument was signed?

A. I suppose we were there—I should say about three-quarters of an hour.

Q. Was anybody else in [Ravitch's office] at the time?

A. Dr. Ravitch's secretary or stenographer I am quite sure was there as she generally is and there may have been a patient or two waiting. I do not know. I am not certain about that.

Q. Did you leave there with them—with Mrs. Bingham—I mean when she left Dr. Ravitch's office?

A. Yes, I left with Mrs. Bingham and I put her in the automobile and said goodbye to her and she went away in the machine.

Bruce now played his final card. He had been informed by the private detectives that Bingham, Ravitch, and Davies had met at Davies' house the night prior to the signing of the codicil, possibly to draw it up for Mary Lily to sign the next day.

"Mr. Davies," asked Bruce, "did Judge Bingham and Dr. Ravitch spend the night with you at your house at any time the last two or three months of Mrs. Bingham's life?"

Unaware that the Kenans had such information, Davies was caught by surprise. Nevertheless, he recovered quickly.

"I was ill one night, quite ill. My family was out of town and I sent for Judge Bingham and he came and spent the night with me. I had a case of indigestion, a very bad case of indigestion and was very sick and he came and spent the night with me. That was the only night he spent there I am sure."

Q. Was Dr. Ravitch there?
A. He visited me professionally on that occasion but he spent the night after that. I have forgotten what night it was.
Q. Dr. Ravitch did?
A. Yes, sir; his family was out of town.
Q. When was it that Judge Bingham spent a night with you?
A. I cannot remember the date. It was when I was ill some time within the last two or three months.
Q. You cannot approximate it any better than that?
A. No, let us see. Well, I should say it was since the beginning of the summer, probably some time in June.
Q. Was it before or after this codicil was written?
A. I do not remember. I could not say about that.

During the entire eight days of testimony, it was the only time that Davies was shaken.

Belatedly, Judge Humphrey interceded to protect his witness.

"I do not see what that has to do with the matter, Your Honor, please . . ."

But Davies wanted to say more, interrupting Humphrey to make a point.

"I will say this though," he shouted at Bruce. "Judge Bingham during his life has spent many hundreds of nights at my house and so have I at his."

Smelling blood, Bruce struck for the throat.

"Did you ever discuss with Judge Bingham prior to the execution of this codicil the question of what he was to get or what he would get or what he expected to get?"

"No, sir," shouted Davies, jumping to his feet. "I did not. It was a delicate matter and I remained entirely away from that and so did Judge Bingham."

Bruce riposted quickly. "Where did you say Judge Bingham was when this codicil was written?"

"He was out of Kentucky. He was down in North Carolina."

"Do you know where in North Carolina?"

"I heard that he was at Asheville, North Carolina."

Pounding his gavel, Judge Greene interrupted to order both men to speak more calmly. Tensely, Davies lowered himself back into the witness chair. Bruce returned to his place behind the plaintiffs' table and sipped some water before resuming.

"Did I understand you to say," he said calmly to Davies, "that you had never heard Mrs. Bingham speak of treatment hypodermically from Dr. Ravitch?"

"No sir," replied Davies. "I never heard her speak of that— no."

"I believe that is all," said Bruce, ending the cross-examination.

The hearing was in recess, but the case was just about to begin.

Exhumation

IN NEW YORK CITY, on Monday morning, September 17, 1917, a secret conference was held in a private room at 26 Broadway, stronghold of the Standard Oil Company. Present were William H. Beardsley, president of the Florida East Coast Railway; William Rand Kenan, president of the Flagler System; and Judge William Blount, legal counsel for both. Under the Henry Flagler will, the three men were the trustees of the Flagler commercial properties which had been bequeathed to Mary Lily. Dating from May 1913, the will gave them control for five years and, thus, they had more than six months yet to serve.

While the meeting was in progress, a *New York Herald* reporter walked into Beardsley's office seeking details of the contest over the codicil.

The reporter was admitted to the conference chamber by Mr. Beardsley and to all three gentlemen he outlined the information in the *Herald's* possession, suggesting that . . . publicity was inevitable. . . . Mr. Kenan, acting as spokesman for the associates, requested that the reporter retire to an adjoining room . . . after about five minutes . . . Mr. Kenan said, "We are sorry that we cannot give the *Herald* a story, but it has been decided that it is best at the present time that we should make no comment nor explanation whatever." [1]

In fact, the purpose of the meeting was to consider the most expeditious means to ascertain if drugs played any sinister part in Mary Lily's death.

Following the meeting, events moved rapidly.

That afternoon in Wilmington, North Carolina, 500 miles to the south, Mary Lily's lawyer, cousin Graham Kenan, posted guards at the cemetery after he received word from a grounds keeper that several strange men in an automobile had visited the grave and were seen to poke about the sod with their canes.

In the evening, the local New Hanover County Board of Health issued a permit granting undertaker James F. Woolvin permission:

to exhume the body of Mrs. Mary Lily Bingham now buried in Oakdale Cemetery for the purpose of examining this body with a view to determining the cause of death. This examination is desired by the members of the family of Mrs. Bingham, the permit for this exhumation having been requested by Mr. Graham Keenan [sic] a near relative. . . .[2]

Immediately following the signing of the permit, Graham and Will Kenan led a team of doctors, local officials, and cemetery workers to Mary Lily's grave.

Using shovels, spades, and mining picks, the workers dug down 6 feet where they encountered the concrete slabs protecting her casket. As darkness fell, they erected a tripod with ropes and pulleys above the hole, intending to winch up the concrete cover. Three times they laboriously tried to hoist the slab. Three times it broke the tripod.

It was about nine o'clock at night when they gave up on the tripod idea. One man descended into the grave, using a pick to break up the cover. The work continued until midnight before the casket was finally hoisted up from the grave.

Placed ignominiously on a single-axle gardener's cart, it was wheeled to the cemetery lodge where the casket was opened and the body removed.[3]

There was little decomposition and Mary Lily's dress seemed as crisp as the day she had been buried five weeks earlier. She was so lifelike that the Kenans left the room.

A team of six physicians and pathologists began their grisly work. The lead pathologist, Dr. Charles Norris, director of the Bellevue Hospital Laboratories in New York City, began passing slices of the liver, kidneys, intestines, and other vital organs under his microscope.[4] A Bellevue chemist, Dr. Alexander Gettler, sub-jected other slices to chemical tests.

It was 3:00 A.M. before they reached their conclusions.

The doctors went to the main lobby of the lodge and informed the Kenans that Mary Lily's body had been subjected to morphine for many months, possibly longer. One described the amounts of morphine in her body as "enormous."[5] Also found were traces of injected adrenaline, and some heavy metal poisons, such as arse-nic and possibly mercury.[6]

Norris cautioned that while the presence of morphine was certain, the findings on the poisons needed to be verified with the more elaborate equipment he had at the Bellevue lab.

Taking the organs with them, Norris and Gettler returned to New York. They told the Kenans they would have results by the end of the month. All this would be kept secret. Only the Kenans and the doctors would know.

Within forty-eight hours, however, rumors of the graveside autopsy had leaked to Bingham's attorneys and probably through Bellevue hospital contacts, to the New York press. The *American* reported in banner 72-point type:

MRS. BINGHAM WAS DRUGGED

The story said an exhumation had occurred and the Kenan family had received information that "Mrs. Bingham was placed under the influence of drugs on several occasions."[7]

So many rumors of suspicious circumstances gained credence recently that members of the family are determined either to dissipate or sub-stantiate them.

At the time of the probate hearing, Helm Bruce, attorney for the heirs opposing the codicil, examined W. W. Davies, who for years was a partner of Judge Bingham, and the man who drew the document. He was exhaustively questioned along lines that Mrs. Bingham was under the influence of drugs at the time the codicil was drawn and at various other times. Mr. Davies was also closely questioned as to his relations with Judge and Mrs. Bingham. . . .

It was freely gossiped in New York that Mr. and Mrs. Bingham were not happy. Mr. Bingham's three children, the oldest, Robert Jr., being twenty, were mentioned in this connection. . . .

It has been made plain that, despite statements from Louisville, Ky., the Kenan family is not concerned over the $5 million bequeathed by Mrs. Bingham to her husband in a codicil to her will. They merely wish to forever clear away any suspicions that might linger in the minds of friends and relatives as to the actual circumstances of Mrs. Bingham's death. . . .

Mrs. Bingham died after an illness of several weeks. For days preceding death, her condition was very grave, although reassuring telegrams were sent by Mr. Bingham to his wife's relatives in North Carolina. . . .

The cause of death was described by her doctors as "acute heart disturbance." This in itself is considered by physicians to be out of the ordinary as it does not carry a positive statement concerning the nature of the "disturbance." It leaves wide open grounds for conjecture and serves to heighten suspicion.

It was pointed out that such a record could cover a multitude of definite causes for death. When their attention was called to it tonight, local health authorities wondered that they had overlooked this ambiguous statement. . . .[8]

The *Sun* correspondent in Louisville reported:

A theory widely held here is that the Kenans contested the bequest to Bingham but when they couldn't shake Davies on the stand they made the midnight exhumation in a last effort to get something upon which a contest might be based and the $5 million diverted to the Kenans. . . .

[A] feature of the case which is attracting attention is that neither Graham Kenan nor any of the other Kenans saw fit to advise Helm Bruce, Scott Bullitt or E. J. McDermott, their Louisville attorneys, of the exhumation. . . .[9]

The press speculations grew to such a furor that Graham Kenan found it necessary to issue a public explanation.

He said six physicians were present at the autopsy, but refused to give their names. He said the facts and circumstances relating to the illness and death that were disclosed to the family justified them and made it their duty to consult physicians who advised the autopsy. He said the autopsy was performed "in the regular and usual way on the advice of leading physicians." The autopsy was warranted. He explained:

All interested may be assured that any investigation which has been or may be made has been and will be conducted in a proper and legitimate manner and with absolute fairness to all parties concerned. The feelings of the family naturally made them desire to have as little publicity as possible given the matter. I hope the public will be fair enough not to jump at any conclusions based on the facts now in their possession.[10]

The *Herald* reported that "relatives of Mrs. Bingham . . . assert that the dead woman had been placed under the influence of drugs on several occasions." New York's leading newspaper of the era then speculated that a grand jury might be called in either Kentucky or North Carolina: "Rumors that death was caused from other than natural causes can lead to demand for an inquiry."[11]

The exhumation occupied front-page headlines for a week. The *World* reported that special security measures were being taken in Wilmington to protect Mary Lily's grave.

Guarded by day by the superintendent and his force and by night by two special officers, there is no chance of the grave of Mrs. Bingham being entered by other than authorized persons. Instructions have been given that no one be allowed on the plot, under penalty of indictment of trespass. Fresh flowers are placed on the grave of Mrs. Bingham every day by a local florist upon instructions from the family. . . .

The autopsy was performed in the presence of a detective of national reputation and some of the vital organs removed and sent to New York. . . .[12]

In Louisville, attorneys for Bingham issued a statement of indignation, which included their version of the facts surrounding the "midnight exhumation."

It appears that the autopsy was performed in the presence of William J. Burns and several physicians; that vital parts of the body were removed and that these parts were turned over to someone and taken to New York. It is needless to say that all of this was surreptitious and this was a secret closely guarded until the object was accomplished. It is presumed that the disinterred body was reburied. It was then that the supposed necessity arose of jealously protecting the grave from violations. . . .[13]

Neither Judge Bingham nor any of his friends knew anything whatever about [the exhumation]. . . . On Thursday, July 12, two weeks before her death, Mrs. Bingham had a severe attack. Her brother William R. Kenan was summoned by Judge Bingham and came. He conferred fully with Dr. Ravitch concerning Mrs. Bingham's condition and approved everything that was being done. On Sunday, July 23, Mrs. Bingham's condition was such that Judge Bingham wrote her sisters that he thought that they should come. Responsive to this her sister, Mrs. Wise, came, arriving Wednesday evening, July 25. Mrs. Bingham was then fully conscious and remained so until Thursday night. Mrs. Wise remained with her until the end came on Friday. There were two trained nurses. Their official charts and records are in the custody of Dr. Boggess. These records will be kept in a secure place and produced when a proper occasion arises. . . .

It belongs to the public to form its opinion of this ghastly drama. . . .[14]

The Kentucky correspondent for the *New York Evening Journal* filed a story from his home base in Lexington reporting that, "information received here is that general sympathy is in favor of Judge Bingham in the controversy."[15]

Bingham announced that he had hired his own prestigious New York pathologist, Dr. Otto Schultze, to verify any findings made by Norris and Gettler. He added that he had offered the "bedside notes of the three doctors who attended Mrs. Bingham," only to have the Kenans demand the originals instead of copies. Bingham backed off from that, saying he would retain the originals.[16]

The announcement was made by Bingham's New York counsel, Almuth C. Vandiver of the firm of O'Gorman, Battle & Vandiver.

We have engaged Dr. Otto H. Schultze.

Let me state clearly the position of Mr. Bingham. He has not engaged our services to interrupt, interfere with, block, prevent, or in any way retard the analysis. Quite naturally, he wants protection. He feels he has been the victim of malignant reports and influence.

We have not planned any legal action to recover the vital organs now under analysis. We have been told the laws of North Carolina make it unlawful to exhume a body without the consent of the husband.

As to the analysis, we regard Dr. Norris, with the possible exception of Dr. Schultze, as the best pathologist in the entire country. We are sure he is fair and honest. And Dr. Schultze thinks Dr. Norris will find nothing.[17]

Vandiver stressed the Bingham position that Mary Lily died of heart disease, and tried to argue down any rumors to the contrary. "According to our information," said Vandiver, "the Kenans are a long-lived family. Mrs. Bingham was in the prime of life and she certainly did appear to be strong and healthy. But persons who especially devote themselves to active outdoor pursuits are frequently victims of heart trouble."[18]

Dr. Schultze defended the diagnosis of heart disease saying that the symptoms had been overlooked by Mary Lily's physician-cousin, Dr. Owen Hill Kenan.[19] "Although Mrs. Bingham was often attended by [Dr. Kenan], it is entirely possible that even he did not detect the symptoms of endocarditis, which eventually caused her demise."[20]

Buried in that sentence is an important clue to the cause of Mary Lily's death. It is the word *endocarditis,* or inflammation of the heart lining, and it is being used in this case for the first time. Its significance is that endocarditis is the first specific diagnosis given in the death of Mary Lily. The previously announced causes were vague catchalls: "oedema of the brain," a swelling which could derive from a variety of causes including heart disease, liver disease, kidney failure, or a virtual medical dictionary full of other problems; "myocarditis," which in those years meant basically heart disease without further definition of the type of heart disease; and "acute heart disturbance," which as the Kenan reports pointed out means virtually nothing. Drinking too much brandy too quickly can cause heart disturbance. So can having the "vapors."

It is obvious that Schultze, an expert pathologist, called together the Ravitch medical team and wrung from them enough information to identify a precise cause of Mary Lily's death.

Schultze dismissed the morphine reports with some condescension, noting that "morphine may have been administered during those last few days of pain and it will be mighty difficult for Dr. Norris, noted specialist that he is, to extablish any effect that may have had upon her death.[21]

In a separate interview, Bellevue chemist Gettler partially confirmed the presence of the poisons, but said the report about them was "entirely unauthorized."

"Whether the report is made public," he added, "depends on the family of Mrs. Bingham." [22]

The poison theory gained further impetus when the *New York World* reported, in a story datelined Louisville, that a person close to the Bingham family said Mary Lily "frequently felt ill without apparently having any special malady." [23]

□

Meanwhile, on the night of September 19, some sixty hours after the trustees' meeting in New York, two men in downtown Louisville quietly emerged from their hiding place in a basement storeroom of the Atherton Building.

They had hidden there in the afternoon, provisioned with briefcases containing lock picks, a crowbar, flashlights, ham sandwiches, and two bottles of beer. They waited until midnight, then quietly moved up the service stairwells to the fourth floor.

They had no difficulty entering the office. Both were former policemen. Now they were burglars, working under the license of the William J. Burns Agency. They worked silently, removing records from the filing cabinets, ransacking the desk drawers.

They had legitimately sought the same records earlier in the day at the T. P. Taylor and Newman & Co. drugstore downstairs. They had been refused. When they asked for the names of employees who filled the prescriptions of Dr. Ravitch, they were again refused. When threats of subpoena proved futile, the detectives tried a long shot. They approached Drs. Boggess and Steinberg with money, seeking narcotics records, not perjury. Once again, they were rebuffed.

It was after that they decided to obtain the records directly from Ravitch's office.

Now, in the dark, working steathily by flashlight, they were again stymied. The last filing cabinet had been searched. The last desk drawer pried open. There was nothing of interest. Ravitch either kept no records on drugs, or he had hidden them too well for the detectives to find. Then one of them noticed a painting on the wall. It hung straight, while all the other wall pictures were slightly tilted, this way and that, by the natural vibrations of the building.

The painting, hung on hinges, swung easily aside. As the operatives studied the wall safe by flashlight, smiles spread across their faces. It was a flimsy box, easy to jimmy open with the crowbar.

Minutes later they had what they sought, records of the narcotics prescriptions for Mary Lily.

They left the Atherton building elated. They had what they had been told to find and that was their victory. The mistake was that they had been instructed to look for the wrong thing. They should have sought her medical records, the documents showing the diagnosis of her condition and the descriptions of her treatment. It was the medical records which would have made a case against Ravitch. Those records, too, had been in the wall safe, but the detectives had passed them over. That had been their defeat. They had focused on the trees and missed seing the forest.

The following morning, when the robbery was discovered, Ravitch called a press conference and announced with scarcely concealed glee that he had been burglarized.

He reported, accurately, that narcotic records were the only things of value taken, adding that the burglary followed an attempt to secure records from the drug company showing the quantities of narcotics purchased on his orders for patients under his care.

"The drugstore refused to furnish the records, and also refused to give the names of employees who filled the orders." [24]

He refused to state whether the stolen records involved Mrs. Bingham or whether he had ever administered any drug to her.

Because of the involvement of drugs, federal authorities took jurisdiction and Ravitch filed an affidavit with the Internal Revenue Department setting forth the facts of the robbery and detailing the narcotics records which were lost.

In further interviews, Ravitch said he knew of the attempted bribery of two physicians and a nurse. He laid the whole plot to Standard Oil, saying the giant corporation was scheming against

Bingham in order to keep the entire $150 million Flagler estate intact.[25]

The news hit the street with headlines running across the top of page one.

EXTRA! EXTRA!

Hearing the shouts of the newsboys through the open windows of his office, Dave Davies went down to the street. He grabbed a paper, read the story, and blanched.

He did not walk but ran, ran all five blocks to Ravitch's office. Reporters were already there, gathered for more news. Who were the bribed doctors? they wanted to know. Who was the nurse? Who were the detectives offering bribes? What did they hope to obtain? Was there truth to a rumor that Ravitch had been paid $50,000 and a new car by Bingham?

Pushing his way through, Davies got inside Ravitch's suite of rooms and found the doctor in the very back office. There was some shouting, all of it by Davies, and half an hour later he emerged. Ravitch was muzzled.

Returning to the crowded hallway, Davies told reporters that henceforth he and Bingham would be the spokesmen.

W. W. Davies, counsel for Judge Bingham, stated last night that no report on the perpetrators of the burglary had been received as yet and none was expected until some time today. Dr. Ravitch refused to discuss the case in any way, but a statement by Mr. Davies failed to bear out the remarks attributed to the doctor yesterday that two doctors had been approached with bribes by private detectives. Mr. Davies did say that a nurse who attended Mrs. Bingham had been approached and questioned in such a way as to indicate that "she was being used to testify to things that were not true." . . .

The statement made by Mr. Davies yesterday follows:

"The facts in regard to that robbery have been slightly misunderstood. The detective operators, whoever they may be and by whom employed, who have in this matter clearly proven themselves criminals, broke into Dr. Ravitch's office with the evident intention of stealing papers connected in some way with the last illness of Mrs. Bingham. It has been stated that what the thieves stole were copies of prescriptions for narcotics issued by Dr. Ravitch. . . . What happened at Dr. Ravitch's office was that the thieves, clearly acting under a concerted programme, tore out of Dr. Ravitch's book the records showing what narcotics the doctor had secured for use among his patients. . . . I know nothing of any attempt to influence a physician. I think I am in a position to say that we can prove when the time comes, if it does come, that a nurse who waited upon Mrs. Bingham was interviewed in such a way as to make it appear that she was being used to testify to certain things which were not true. However, that can be met at the proper time." [26]

To cover the other aspect of the publicity problem, Bingham called a press conference to deny payment of a $50,000 fee to Ravitch.

It was reported in one of the newspapers some time ago that Dr. Ravitch, who, with Dr. Boggess, attended Mrs. Bingham in her last illness, had received since her death a present or fee of $50,000 and an automobile. Both of these statements are entirely incorrect, as Dr. Ravitch has at no time recieved for his services in treating Mrs. Bingham anything other than the ordinary fees charged by physicians. . . .[27]

As to the truth of the $50,000 fee, Bingham's financial records for the period have vanished. There is no direct evidence that the fee was paid. However, within the coming year, Ravitch's life-style improved dramatically, as will be seen in later chapters. As for the burglary, Louisville police showed a marked lack of interest: "Nothing was missing but the narcotic reports required by the Government, and when I found the matter had been reported to the Federal authorities my men were withdrawn," said Captain Charles Carney.[28]

Following the first round of newspaper interviews, Davies proceeded to turn the burglary to Bingham's advantage. Speaking on the record earlier, he had denied any approaches to the doctors. Now, speaking off the record, he told reporters that the bribe offers had been made to Drs. Boggess and Steinberg and to nurses Eva Mueller and Elizabeth Wise.[29]

He had thus compromised any testimony by the doctors or nurses. Anything they might say which could be harmful was darkened by the hint of bribery.

Once again the Bingham team had totally out maneuvered the Kenans. The narcotics records, obtained by burglary, were legally useless. And Davies' hints of bribes had tainted any possible testimony from the previously cooperative nurses.

□

While Davies controlled the scandal and played point man for the press, Bingham managed to remain aloof. Concentrating on his county commissioner campaign, he conducted "politics as usual," organizing committees, making speeches, living at Lincliffe while Mary Lily's estate paid the rent, and financing his campaign with the money she had given him before her death.

It was all for nought. In the November elections, the public in its wisdom voted down the entire Democratic machine, including Bingham. Republican George Weissinger Smith was elected mayor after a campaign against corruption, which charged that the machine openly protected gambling and prostitution. An officer at the U.S. Army's Camp Taylor, asserted that in forty years of service he had "never seen a city anywhere in the world where vice is more open than it is in your city."[30] Louisville voters had memories and to them Robert Worth Bingham was not the white-hat crusader portrayed by New York newspapers.

□

The September 30 date for public release of the autopsy report had come and gone. In the first week of October, New York papers reported that the Kenan family had received the report and, based on the autopsy information, planned a court fight to break the codicil.[31]

Helm Bruce was invited to New York to meet with the family and trustees at the Florida East Coast Railway offices in the Standard Oil building.[32]

Upon Bruce's return to Kentucky, he filed a suit protesting the administration of the estate. On November 3, Judge Charles Ray of the Jefferson County Chancery Court ordered briefs.[33] On November 14, Judge Ray ruled in favor of Bingham.

The Kenans were unconcerned about the verdict. They introduced no evidence to Judge Ray. There was no mention of the autopsy report. And there was no testimony. Their strategy seems to have been to get the case out of the unfriendly courtrooms of

Louisville and into a state appeals court in Lexington. If they lost there, they would go into federal court.

On November 26, Judge Ray granted the Kenan motion for appeal and the case was sent to the Kentucky Court of Appeals.

It never went further.

In early April 1918, attorneys for Louise Wise Lewis informed Bingham that there would be no further contest of the will and that Bingham would receive his $5 million on July 27.

No explanation was given.

Some seventy years later, family historian Thomas S. Kenan III said the suit was "dropped because its chief instigator, Graham Kenan, died of flu in the New York influenza epidemic that year. Nobody else wanted to push it." [34]

Graham Kenan, Mary Lily's first cousin and brother-in-law, did indeed die of influenza at the age of thirty-seven. [35] The death, however, was in February 1920, nearly two years after the suit was dropped. Therefore, the reason for abandoning the suit remains unexplained, and the question still exists: *Why?*

The Publisher

FOUR MONTHS would elapse before Bingham would receive his money and begin assembling his baronial estate. During that time, the Kenans fought tenaciously to reduce the inheritance taxes on their own empire.

The tax litigation was held in April and May at Lexington, where a reporter was moved to observe, "at times during the hearing, a feeling arose that Henry Flagler and his widow were really 'poor little rich folks' and that to be possessed of nearly a hundred millions is a pretty tough proposition."

He added that the Flagler trustees, William Kenan and Judge William Blount, did everything except complain that "the Kenans didn't know where their next meal is coming from." [1]

Perhaps the most surprising testimony given, from the standpoint of human interest, was a statement by Judge Blount, who at the time was president of the American Bar Association. He said he had never known Henry Flagler.

"How long did you know Henry Flagler?" he was asked.

"I never knew him," he replied. [2]

This surprised knowledgeable people because Judge Blount was not only being paid $50,000 annually as executor of the Flagler estate, but he was the man who drew the divorce bill that enabled Flagler to divorce his wife and marry Mary Lily Kenan.

The evasion was possibly a technical splitting of hairs rather than a perjury. Although there was correspondence between Judge Blount and Flagler, it is possible the two never met face-to-face.

Blount was undoubtedly anxious to keep the door closed on any possible discussion concerning Flagler's divorce. There is no indication, let alone evidence, that he was involved in the briberies, but he was certainly aware of the rumors. As a smart lawyer, he decided to steer discussion away from that can of worms.

□

None of the Kenans could or would explain the disappearance of the $1 million pearl necklace. But it was revealed that the estate owed Tiffany's $228,000 for a string of 111 pearls bought by Mrs. Bingham in February 1917, and that when she died, Mary Lily had a previously undiscovered checking account of $1,070,000 in the Guaranty Trust Company of New York City.

The Fidelity & Columbia Trust's inventory also had overlooked two Packard automobiles which Mrs. Bingham had bought in Louisville, the executors explaining she had so many that they had "lost track of them." [3]

□

Stites, president of the Louisville Trust Company, testified that the estate's proper evaluation ranged from $130 million to $150 million and said he had been showed the $1 million necklace but was baffled as to why it wasn't included in the inventory of the estate.

Initially, he declined to name the person who showed him the necklace, but threatened with contempt of court, he revealed that it was Davies.

□

In Louisville, Bingham was given a friendly interrogation by Kentucky State Revenue Agent Walter Byars. When Byars asked about the necklace, Bingham cavalierly dismissed it as fantasy: "The talk about Mrs. Bingham having a string of pearls valued at $1 million is mere gossip without any basis in fact whatever." [4]

Byars' involvement in the case is a good example of how birds of prey lurk within the government looking for private advantage. Not only was Mary Lily's fortune sought by Bingham, her family, and the tax collectors, but its charms also fascinated a money-hungry bevy of crooked revenue agents and lawyers.

The assignment of Byars as agent-in-charge defied good sense and was a testament to his powers of manipulation. He had already been exposed for accepting a "gratuity" a few years earlier in the handling of the Kentucky portion of the Harkness family estate. In that matter, Byars had first written and then approved a compromise judgment in the Harkness tax case that deprived the state and Fayette County of $7 million in taxes. Following the settlement, Byars received a $5,000 check from the Harkness family.[5]

Ironically, this was a branch of the same family which had been related to Henry Flagler by marriage. It was the Harknesses, indeed, who had secretly provided the $100,000 seed money to start Standard Oil. Indirectly, this was part of the same fortune which Bingham and the Kenans were seeking to inherit.

Was Byars' assignment to Mary Lily's case a coincidence? Not likely. Byars, through his influence in the Kentucky State Revenue Department, had contrived to take over the handling of the two largest estate claims ever probated in Kentucky. His goodwill was especially important to the Kenan family because Byars' evaluation would set the foundation for all inheritance taxes whether they be local, federal, or the taxes imposed by the various states, including New York, Florida, and Kentucky. Bingham, who received his $5 million bequest off the top, was not involved in any payment of inheritance taxes.

Helm Bruce later revealed that on four different occasions, beginning in the fall of 1917, Byars had offered settlements which would involve "compensation" to Byars and to Kentucky tax lawyers who were handling the case.

For example, said Bruce, just prior to the Lexington litigation, Byars requested a conference with Bruce and Judge Blount at Blount's home in Pensacola at which Byars suggested "all claims for counsel fees and penalties could be settled. He spoke of the fees that he believed the special counsel for the state would insist upon . . . that this was a matter which could be adjusted."[6]

It was estimated that total taxes—local, federal, and the various states—would amount to 10 percent.

Byars was willing to settle on a taxable estate of $68 million—somewhere between a half and two-thirds of what Mary Lily's estate was believed to be worth. Bruce flatly turned down the offer. Rebuffed, Byars caused the evaluation to go up and up over the next two years, ultimately assessing the estate's taxable value at $100 million.[7] At the original offer, the Kenans would have paid slightly less than $7 million in taxes. When Byars' final assessment came in, it appeared that Bruce's honesty had cost the Kenans approximately $3 million in additional taxes.

More litigation ensued and ultimately, in December 1921, a Kentucky appellate judge ruled that the Kenans needed to pay taxes on only $68.4 million of the estate.[8]

□

Bingham, following settlement of his share of the estate in the spring of 1918, reorganized his law partnership, with himself becoming senior partner in the firm of Bingham, S. E. Sloss, George Cary Tabb, Arthur H. Mann, and Emanuel Levi.[9]

Meanwhile, the courtroom battles over taxes revealed an incredible dependence by Bingham on Mary Lily's money. Since Mary Lily's death, her estate had been paying his expenses at Lincliffe—everything from food, wine, and rent to coal for heating and the salary of servants.

When she died, Bingham was apparently broke, despite having received nearly $1 million in cash, securities, and other gifts from Mary Lily in the ten months of their engagement and marriage. And despite having paid cash for a new Packard. Where did the rest of the money go? The financial records are missing, but there are two reasonable possibilities: (1) he had used it to pay off debts, including those incurred before he courted Mary Lily; and (2) it had been posted as security in his planned purchase of the newspapers.

A third scenario is that Bingham was simply continuing his

vengeful pattern of making Mary Lily, even though dead, pay for everything.

Indeed, he did not move out of Lincliffe until six weeks after the settlement, nearly a year after Mary Lily's death, when he temporarily took a home at Cherokee Park, a development of 409 acres in eastern Louisville which was watered by a winding creek fed by springs from limestone cliffs overlooking the subdivision.

Until then, incredibly, in death as in life, Mary Lily paid every dime, every dollar spent at Lincliffe including:

Rent	$ 950
Coal for heating	285
Electricity	256
Servants	1,710
Burglary and fire insurance	126
Telephone	121
Louisville Gas & Electric Company	136
Louisville Meat Market	637
Stewart Dry Goods Company	1,242
Security deposit paid to Belknap	250
Liquor	334

And some $3,000 for other household expenses incurred while Bingham was a resident at the house.[10]

□

Bingham even billed her estate for flowers he sent to her funeral ($85.55).[11]

If one wonders why the Kenans were so generous toward the man suspected of murdering their kinswoman, it should be pointed out that the payments were made by Bingham's bankers, the Fidelity & Columbia Trust Company, which was in charge of administering Mary Lily's estate until all tax and personal matters were settled. The Kenans were presented only with an accounting of the expenditures after the fact. They could have challenged them, but it would have involved another court fight and they seemed weary of that.

The estate also paid for Mary Lily's funeral, in the amount of $1,614 to "Lee E. Cralle for funeral expenses," paid on August 30, 1917.

The payment was discovered some three weeks later by William Rand Kenan, who had assumed his sister's funeral costs had been paid by her husband. Incredulous and outraged, Kenan promptly reimbursed the estate for the full costs.

A month later, however, Bingham—either prodded by Kenan or fearing a scandal—paid the funeral costs and had the funeral director reimburse Will Kenan.[12]

□

On July 28, 1918, Bingham received his full $5 million, virtually all of it in cash, from the estate. The remainder was divided among the heirs as originally specified by Mary Lily's will.

In the meantime, Bingham's friend Dr. Michael Ravitch was faring well. Following Mary Lily's death and the rumored but never proved receipt of a $50,000 bribe from Bingham, Ravitch exhibited a more expensive style of life—reducing his medical practice and moving his family from their modest home in the Aragon Apartments, 1508 South First Street, to the luxurious Weissinger-Gaubert Apartments, at Third and Broadway in downtown Louisville.[13] He, his wife, Betty, and his daughter, Helen, remained in Louisville until 1921 when they moved to Chicago. He resumed his dermatology practice in that city in 1923.[14]

(Ravitch's prosperity, however, was only of brief duration. The year 1924 saw him returning to the daily grind by taking a job on the staff of a Chicago hospital. While in Chicago, his daughter, Helen, developed movie ambitions and—while it is unclear whether they were assisting Helen or following her—Ravitch and his wife and Helen were living in Hollywood, California, by 1931. The following year, he resumed a desultory private practice. In 1936 at the age of sixty-seven, he retired and moved to New York City where he died eleven years later of a heart attack.)

□

Bingham now turned to his heart's desire, the purchase of the *Courier-Journal* and the *Louisville Times.*

On August 6, 1918, slightly more than a week after receiving his bequest, Bingham signed a check for $1 million and bought two-thirds interest in the papers. He would purchase the remaining interest over the next two years.[15]

He had bought himself some winners.

The *Courier-Journal* dated back to 1868 when Walter Haldeman and Henry Watterson had merged their two papers, the *Courier* and the *Journal.* They added the *Times* in 1884. The *Times* was little more than a pleasant metropolitan daily intended for a local readership. But the *Courier-Journal,* which had been the Democratic voice of the entire region since Reconstruction, considered itself and was considered by others to be *the* newspaper for all of Kentucky.[16]

Among his first coups was to retain Henry Watterson, possibly the most prestigious newspaper editor in the South. Watterson, who had won a Pulitzer prize for his editorials some three months prior to Bingham's ownership, agreed to stay with the paper as editor emeritus at his old salary of $10,000 a year.[17]

Shortly after the purchase, Bingham had a bronze plaque installed in the front lobby of the newspaper building reading:

I have always regarded the newspapers owned by me as a public trust and have endeavored so to conduct them as to render the greatest public service.

By 1920, women shared beats with men and Arthur Krock, later to move to the *New York Times,* was named editor-in-chief. Shortly afterward, the *Courier-Journal* won its first Pulitzer under Bingham's direction, the prize going to reporter William Burk Miller for his interviews of the trapped Floyd Collins deep inside Kentucky's Sand Cave.[18]

□

Bingham had changed.

He would prove far more successful in newspaper publishing than he had been in law or politics. Under Bingham, the reputation, value, and accomplishments of the two papers multiplied beyond imagination. As a publisher, he was tough but fair, courageous but compassionate. He consistently advocated more freedom—more freedom for women, more freedom for blacks, more freedom for the poor.

The one-time ruthless opportunist soon found himself a place among the nation's most thoughtful and effective liberals. He readily took on, as a duty, unpopular views, such as his ardent support of the League of Nations.

For example Bingham had a dispute with editor Watterson, who was an opponent of the League of Nations. Bingham regretted that a man of Watterson's influence had chosen to fight against the League and asked him to reconsider. Watterson, however, would not.[19]

Bingham, the conniving, lying, and deadly political hack, changed almost overnight into something akin to an ideal journalist. His loyalty was to the public, to the reader who put down three cents, a nickel, a dime, or a quarter for his papers. The perception of ultimate loyalty to the reader was certainly not unique. It had been the ethical foundation of American newspapers since 1733 when immigrant Peter Zenger began his *New York Weekly Journal* to defend the public against government policies and was imprisoned for his effort.[20]

Bingham carried on the Zenger tradition and established a newspaper ethic which would be carried on by his son and grandson over the ensuing decades when other newspapers would abandon the philosophy of public service.

But he was not so changed that he stepped entirely away from politics. Beginning with a contribution of $5,000 to the Democratic National party in November 1918, Bingham became a regular and open-handed contributor at the national level.[21] Still, apart from comments on the editorial pages, he disengaged himself from local politics. To prove his point, he declined his party's nomination for the U.S. Senate, stating that newspaper publishers should not hold public office.[22] It must have stunned his former political associates to see the once ruthlessly ambitious county attorney turn away from the state's most prized political plum, an almost certain seat in the Senate.

Bingham kept his eye focused on journalism. In 1920, he witnessed the establishment of the world's first commercial radio station, KDKA in Pittsburgh, Pennsylvania. Within two years, Bingham had his own radio station on the air, WHAS of Louisville.[23]

He personally received his radio broadcasting license in April 1922 from mining engineer Herbert Hoover, then secretary of commerce in the Warren Harding administration and later, of course, President of the United States.

In accepting the license, Bingham stated a populist philosophy which he would increasingly embrace during the remainder of his public life:

I want a radio station which will reach into the farthest confines of the state, where a man may string an aerial from his cabin to the nearest pine tree, and sitting before the fire . . . have a pew in a church, a seat at the opera, a desk at the university.[24]

WHAS went on the air with the announcement, "This is WHAS, the radio-telephone broadcasting station of the *Courier-Journal* and the *Louisville Times* in Louisville, Kentucky." [25]

Radio broadcasting was then a very personal matter, bristling with the unexpected from minute to minute, heavy with excitement. And among the pioneers in bringing to the radio audience news, weather, and artistic and popular entertainment was WHAS. Programs were put on from four to five every afternoon and from seven-thirty to nine o'clock on weekday nights. The studio was an airless, padded room, supposedly soundproof, which caused acute discomfort to those inside.

On opening night, July 18, 1922, the weather was stifling and the actors and the announcer himself very nearly passed out. Listeners 1,000 miles away were asked to wire collect "if they heard or not," a bit of early broadcast humor.[26]

The only hitch on the opening program was that when the assembled notables were introduced over the air they merely bowed instead of responding, which was not so satisfactory to the thousands whose ears were glued to the phones of their crystal sets.

Advertising programs were first tried out in 1925 when a cigar manufacturer offered to purchase time for $400 an hour and to send three cigars to each person writing in.[27]

☐

In June 1921, Bingham's one-time nemesis, seventy-year-old Judge William A. Blount, died of cancer at Johns Hopkins Hospital in Baltimore, Maryland.[28] Although Bingham was unaware of any portent at the time, it was a curious presage of his own fate. Bingham himself, with Hugh Young at his side, would die of a cancer in the same hospital some sixteen and a half years later.

☐

By the early 1920s, Bingham had established himself as a regional leader and had become the guest of presidents and future presidents. Although a Democrat, he was appointed to presidential committees by Republican presidents Harding and Coolidge.

And his interest in agriculture triggered an even more important friendship.

In 1921, the price of burley tobacco, an important ingredient in American cigarettes, dropped ruinously. To rescue an important Kentucky industry, Bingham organized the Burley Tobacco Growers Cooperative Association, modeled along the lines of the thriving California agricultural cooperatives he had seen on a marketing trip. By pooling marketing, the Burley Cooperative successfully stabilized prices. In January 1922, through his efforts, the War Finance Corporation agreed to lend the Burley Cooperative $10 million as startup money. Bingham pledged a million and he announced that the National Bank of Kentucky would not only lend the bank's limit but would rediscount a million and a half dollars' worth of country bank paper as well.[29]

It was during his work with the Burley Cooperative that he became friends with Franklin Delano Roosevelt, a rising politician who, while eleven years younger than Bingham, was a leader of the reform liberal wing of the national Democratic party, the party's vice presidential nominee in 1920, and the future governor of New York State (1928–32) and four-term President of the United States (1932–45).

"They shared a mutual interest in agricultural conservation," recalled Bingham's son Barry.[30]

Bingham's newspaper support of the League of Nations also led to a close friendship with Cordell Hull, a powerful Tennessee congressman and later Roosevelt's secretary of state.[31]

□

Bingham's business powers also increased. He sat on many boards of directors, including those of the Louisville & Nashville Railroad and the Liberty Bank and Trust Company. He became president of the Associated Press.

□

And he became a friend of black people; for example, he provided time, money, and contacts to the son of a waiter at Louisville's Pendennis Club. The youth was Roland Hayes, the first black singer in America to obtain recognition as a serious artist. Later, Hayes said that he never would have had a national and international career without Bingham's help.[32]

As a leading stockholder and member of the Kentucky Jockey Club, which controlled Churchill Downs racetrack, Bingham appeared before the 1922 legislature to oppose efforts to kill the pari-mutuel law, which would have sounded the death knell for horse racing in Kentucky. He thus saved, among other things, America's most prestigious horse-racing event, the Kentucky Derby. Not long afterward, however, Bingham disposed of his holdings in the Jockey Club and through his newspapers condemned the tactics of the organization in wielding power over Kentucky's government.[33]

He had come a long way from the hungry, ambitious attorney who had run on his hands and knees to the L&N railroad seeking cases.

□

In that same year, 1922, Bingham's friend and stockbroker, Byron Hilliard, died, leaving his widow Aleen and two children, James Byron Hilliard and Alice Lithgow Hilliard. After a period of mourning, Bingham began seeing Aleen.

He enjoyed playing the organ and the cello, but more and more often his leisure time was spent at a newly purchased 300,000-acre Georgia plantation which he named "Pinelands Lodge."

He spent much of the winter there with his bird dogs. He built a charming stone-and-timber lodge and erected kennels for his seventy-five pedigreed setters.

"The shooting was wonderfully organized," said his friend Hugh Young. "We would start off in the morning with Bob driving a station wagon to some prearranged spot two or three miles distant. There in waiting was [caretaker] Uncle John with a dog wagon, in the back of which were six fine setters, and in the front three cocker spaniels."[34]

Bingham family photographs of Pinelands, as it was called informally, show it to be a marvelous woodlands escape. But his enjoyment of it wasn't total. Beginning in 1924, he was harassed by a seven-year feud in which local prosecutors and game wardens claimed he was baiting his fields with seed to attract and shoot doves illegally. Indicted twice, tried once, Bingham was eventually exonerated.

In 1924, while on a trip to England, Bingham and Aleen Hilliard married. The ceremony was performed in London, under special license granted by the Archbishop of Canterbury.[35] The marriage included an agreement that Aleen would have no claim on Bingham's estate following his death.[36]

They honeymooned at Bingham's magnificent rented Scottish estate, Guthrie Castle, where Bingham had all the rights and titles of lord of the manor.

He adored Scotland, calling it the "loveliest country" he had ever seen and crediting Scotland with introducing "a touch of romance into my family, for my eldest son has just had the good fortune to marry a Scotch girl."[37]

His son Robert had married the former Dorothy Phyllis Fell Clark of Argyllshire, Scotland. She was a cousin of Wallis Warfield, the American for whom King Edward VIII, later the Duke of Windsor, would give up his throne.

"They and Henrietta Bingham, Bob's lovely daughter, were close friends of the Prince of Wales and frequently went on parties with him and had him at the embassy," recalled Hugh Young.[38]

Bingham sometimes described England as his "second favorite country" after his native America. Many Americans, however, thought he was one count short on his preferences.

For example, the *Chicago Tribune* regularly accused Bingham of toadying to England. On August 31, 1927, Bingham made the front page:

JUDGE BINGHAM TELLS ENGLAND HE APOLOGIZES FOR THE UNITED STATES

□

Makes Speech as Lord of the Manor of Guthrie Castle, Saying He Regrets Failure of American Delegates at Geneva to Appreciate England's Necessities; Speaks in Scotch Church of America's "Faults and Failings."

□

London, Aug. 30—Judge R. W. Bingham of Louisville, Ky., who has achieved fame as an "apologetic American," has been busy again.

Last Sunday night he occupied the pulpit of the John Knox United Free Church at Arbroath, a town in Scotland, near Guthrie Castle, where he is a summer tenant, and took advantage of the occasion to belittle his own country. His subject was "British Relationships with the United States." . . .[39]

Closer to home, the once friendly *Louisville Post* scolded, "he is known in Europe as the 'champion ashamed American' . . . and has praised England as the 'loveliest country in the world' and said that 'never in his life had he met with such kindness and hospitality.' "

The *Lexington Herald* lectured that "Judge Bingham should make his criticisms at home, not on foreign soil . . . for years he has deserted the state on the eve of every important election and while in the security and peaceful contentment of a Scottish castle, allowed others to direct the newspapers."

Bingham, the internationalist, was a personal target of *Tribune* publisher Robert McCormick, an isolationist who vehemently attacked the participation of the United States in world affairs. McCormick himself often wrote the fiery *Tribune* editorials which so roundly damned Bingham:

Speaking as lord of the manor of Guthrie Castle, he says he regrets failure of American delegates at Geneva to appreciate England's necessities; he speaks in a Scotch church of America's "faults and failings." . . . He is gaining fame as the "apologetic American" and has been busy again. He now deplores the failure of the U.S. to enter the League of Nations.[40]

The accusations of pro-English bias would pursue him throughout his career. A year later, the *New York American* published a memorable editorial denouncing Bingham as a "fatuous" servant of English interests. The editorial was entitled, "Who Put the Ass in Amb-Ass-Ador?"[41]

Bingham indeed loved the English life-style, taking thoroughly to the English lust for killing wildlife.

While in England, he was invited more and more to take part in shoots: grouse in August, partridges and pheasants in the fall.

His wonderful marksmanship gave him a great reputation. At one shoot, he bagged on the first day 129 pheasants, on the second day 220, and on the third day about 250. With eight guns present, he had killed about a third of the birds.

Bingham was amazed at the wonderful amount of game he found all over Great Britain. A neighbor of his was economist Bernard Baruch and they often killed 10,000 brace of grouse in a season. King George V, one of England's greatest shots, was reported to have killed over 1,200 grouse himself in one day's shoot nearby.[42]

□

Despite his Anglomania and contrary to the editorial complaints of his critics, Bingham did not neglect his home interests. At the beginning of the Great Depression, when the statewide

First National Bank of Kentucky went under in 1930, Bingham personally guaranteed 50 percent of the Christmas savings fund deposits so families would have funds for the holidays.[43]

His charities became even more grand during the Great Louisville Flood of 1937 when he rushed home from England to personally direct emergency operations, such as emergency communications and the provision of food, shelter, and heating.

Floods were nothing new to the city, having hit with particular severity in 1847, 1859, 1877, 1884, 1913, and 1933.

But the monster of 1937 was to its predecessors like the Himalayas to foothills. It struck in mid-January, and by the end of the month 60 percent of residential Louisville was underwater. There was no drinking water, no public transportation, electricity only at limited times, and National Guardsmen boated through the streets to patrol against looters. Whole sections of the city were abandoned.

Bingham, through the broadcast facilities of WHAS, played a leading role in the rescue and relief work, and for decades afterward the station was "peculiarly enshrined in the hearts of Louisvillians."[44]

The Ambassador

IN FEBRUARY 1933, Bingham was summoned to New York City for a secret meeting with President-elect Franklin Delano Roosevelt. There, with the two men peering at each other over their pince-nez, Roosevelt asked Bingham if he would accept appointment as America's ambassador to Great Britain.[1] Stunned, Bingham could not speak. He only nodded yes. It was a dream post which fulfilled his most ultimate social fantasies. He would be the premier diplomat representing the United States in his beloved England—the companion and counselor of kings, princes, and ministers.[2]

His years of support had paid off in a totally unexpected way. There is no indication in historical record that Bingham ever sought or even expected to receive a position in the Roosevelt administration prior to the February meeting. And then he received not only a position but the chair of honor:

Washington, Feb. 23, (AP)—It was learned in official circles here today that Kentucky newspaper publisher Robert Worth Bingham of Louisville definitely has been chosen by President-elect Franklin D. Roosevelt to be ambassador to London, succeeding Andrew Mellon.

After conferences with Mr. Roosevelt in New York, Judge Bingham was in Washington today, and it was understood he talked over with Cordell Hull, the secretary of state–designate, the war debts and other problems which will come to the early attention of the embassy in London.

The ambassadorship is ranked at the head of the list of diplomatic appointments. . . .

Usually Democratic in his leanings, especially in national politics, he was elected years ago as circuit judge in Louisville on the Republican ticket, and after he acquired control of Louisville's two largest newspapers there were occasions when they supported Republican candidates or stood aside and criticised candidates of both parties.

Bingham's papers are classed as independent in politics, but both ardently supported Roosevelt from the start. . . .[3]

Roosevelt's campaign for the Democratic presidential nomination had begun secretly the morning after his landslide victory in the 1930 New York gubernatorial election. The New York governor faced a bumper crop of competing Democratic rivals. Looming large was Al Smith, four times governor of New York State and the Democratic presidential nominee in 1928; John Nance Garner of Texas, the "beetle-browed, cigar chewing" speaker of the House of Representatives; Governor William Murray, known to his fellow Oklahomans as "Alfalfa Bill," who hoped that agricultural discontent would swing the nomination his way; and Senator Harry Byrd of Virginia.[4]

Early in 1931, Roosevelt's campaign managers officially threw the hat in the ring by launching the "Friends of Roosevelt" as an umbrella organization for the campaign.

Money is always a problem in political campaigns. It was particularly acute for Democrats in the Great Depression. The Republicans had been in power at the White House since Warren Harding's election in 1920. Accordingly, they had locked up the industrialist and big-business financing that traditionally backs the Republican party. In addition, they had IOUs to collect on nearly twelve years of presidential patronage.

In an innovative move to capture new money, the Roosevelt group decided to tap a source of dissatisfied millionaires and use them as nonprofessional fund-raisers.

The squad of blue-ribbon dissidents included Joseph E. Davies, husband of Post cereal heiress Marjorie Post; William H. Woodin, a New York industrialist and former Republican; Henry Morgenthau, Sr., a prominent financier and diplomat who had been Woodrow Wilson's chief fund-raiser; Herbert H. Lehman, banker and lieutenant governor of New York; Joseph Kennedy, Boston liquor importer and investor; and Robert Worth Bingham.

Those men not only recruited money from other sources, but put up big bucks themselves. The dollar amounts pale in the light of contributions made after World War II, but at the time they were considered heavy. Two of the biggest spenders were Kennedy, who put at least $20,000 to the campaign, and Bingham, who contributed more than $50,000.[5]

Bingham's value to the campaign also came from his newspapers, Roosevelt's group feeling that their man needed particular help in the South, the political fulcrum point for FDR, says Roosevelt biographer Nathan Miller:

Roosevelt, like Woodrow Wilson, was the hand-selected presidential choice of Eastern machine Democrats. It was not so much that they liked him but that they thought he could win. The previous Democratic candidate, Al Smith of New York, the first Roman Catholic nominated by a major party, had lost heavily in the Protestant South. It was felt that Roosevelt could bring the South back in the fold. Roosevelt was to do better than that. Like Wilson, he was to make the South the very foundation of his political base.[6]

Cordell Hull of Tennessee headed Roosevelt's Southern strategy. In meetings with Bingham and other Southern leaders, Hull stressed Roosevelt's patrician background, his part-time residency in Georgia, his commitment to do something about the depression, and most of all his potential for carrying the Democrats into control of the Congress and the White House.[7] At the time, seniority determined the committee chairmanships of both the House and Senate and with a majority in both houses, Southern interests would gain enormous national power.[8]

Roosevelt's Southern strategy worked marvelously well.

When the New Deal took office in March 1933, it had Tennessean Cordell Hull as secretary of state, the Virginian Claude Swanson as secretary of the navy, and South Carolina's Dan Roper as secretary of commerce. Furthermore, Senator James Byrnes of South Carolina was one of Roosevelt's most influential advisers, and the top diplomatic assignment went to Robert Worth Bingham.[9]

□

From the day Bingham's announcement was leaked, prominent news organizations such as the Associated Press, the United Press, the International News Service, and the *New York Times* began weaving a biography of Bingham that only partly touched on the truth. He was painted as a lifelong millionaire and virtual socialite:

He is widely known socially in New York, Chicago and London and is looked upon as one of the leading citizens of Kentucky. . . .[10]

His wealth, estimated at several million dollars, enabled him to act independently in politics, and save for serving as county attorney, mayor and later as chancellor of circuit court in Louisville more than 20 years ago, he has always declined to seek political office. . . .

He went to Louisville as a young man and engaged in the practice of law, building up a small fortune which he later extended. . . .[11]

He was described as a graduate of three universities who was a gentleman farmer and a preserver of wildlife:

A graduate of the Bingham School of Asheville, N.C., and the University of North Carolina, Mr. Bingham holds degrees also from the University of Virginia and the University of Louisville law school. . . .[12]

He has a plantation of about 300,000 acres south of Albany, Ga., in which is included a large game preserve where he spends several months each winter. Preservation of quail is one of his hobbies, and one of his chief recreations is quail hunting. Although 61 years old, Judge Bingham is noted for the vigor with which he follows his fine bird dogs. Pinelands plantation, adjoining the game preserve, is devoted largely to growing sweet potatoes, and also contains his winter lodge. North of Albany, he owns extensive pecan groves.[13]

The various press profiles, laundered until Bingham glowed like a shining Galahad, did not unduly impress the Senate Foreign Relations Committee.

Presidential nominations must be approved by the Senate, and hearings on the ambassadorial posts opened on March 16 before the Senate Foreign Relations Committee, which, in effect, would approve or disapprove Roosevelt's nominees.

The body quickly approved Bingham's friend, fellow newspaper publisher and North Carolinian Josephus Daniels as ambassador to Mexico. Just as promptly approved was Jesse Straus of New York as ambassador to France. But the committee balked at the next name on the list, Robert Worth Bingham.

Several senators, including nonmembers of the committee, raised objections over what they perceived as Bingham's pro-British attitudes.

Republican committee member Arthur Raymond Robinson of Indiana argued that "in times like these, when Britain is trying to cancel her war debts, we need a man over there to stand up for American traditions." [14]

A subcommittee consisting of a Republican and a Democrat was appointed to investigate. They were apparently swayed by Senator Alben Barkley of Kentucky, who appeared before them with an explanation that he looked upon Bingham's statements as "being remarks any visitor to a foreign country would have made" in praising their institutions in an effort to "make them feel good." [15]

Barkley's defense, weak but believable, was good enough. Bingham's appointment was confirmed on March 22 by unanimous vote of not only the committee but the entire Senate.

Bingham took up the duties of ambassador at a time when more than fifty nations were preparing to attend an economic conference in London which hoped to solve problems of the worldwide economic depression. As the premier American diplomat, he also would be an important voice in the international arena where Nazi Germany and militarized Japan were becoming increasingly hostile to Anglo-American interests. The United States and Great Britain were in common opposition to Hitler's rearmament and the invasion of Chinese Manchuria by the Japanese army.

Bingham also was to be the point man for Roosevelt and Hull in discussions aimed at reducing Anglo-American trade barriers in exchange for readjustment of British debts to the United States incurred during World War I.

Prior to Bingham's departure, he was given a grand send-off by the Louisville establishment. Despite his transformation in other areas, Bingham's ego was as big as ever, as was demonstrated on April 6, 1933, when his own newspaper, the *Courier-Journal*, ran a five-column picture at the top of page one showing a banquet and headlined:

LOUISVILLE AND KENTUCKY BID AMBASSADOR GOODBYE, GOOD LUCK

□

There were 700 persons in the crystal ballroom of the Brown Hotel. The professions, the scholars, the clergy were represented as the congratulations poured out simply and spontaneously. But the scrub woman and the bootblack and [public] were represented too. The childhood of Kentucky was represented by a group of little charges of the Kentucky Children's Home Society, which with song and flowers expressed Godspeed and good wishes for the man who, it was pointed out, has worked for its wards' welfare for twenty-seven years. . . .

Judge Bingham was given an ovation as he entered the ballroom with the speakers. The big room was decorated simply. Two flags only. Old Glory and the Union Jack, symbolical of the friendship of two great nations. . . .[16]

Not to be outdone by his publicity mill, Bingham added his own polish to the legend, telling the assembly:

I came to Louisville not by accident, but by deliberation.

Very early, there came to me a realization that my forebears had given me something which I had not earned and which I would not take—the Bingham family estates. So I looked about the country to find a new home, to begin life independent and on my own. To find a place where I could stand on my own two feet.

And in 1896, out of this whole country, I found the place and I made the choice:

Louisville.[17]

Bingham himself was the desired choice of the British. On May 24, after a transatlantic voyage with his wife and children, he was given an exceptional signal of honor by being picked up at the American embassy by the Royal Carriage manned by three scarlet-coated coachmen and other attendants. A second and third state landau brought other members of the embassy staff.[18]

At the palace, he presented his credentials to King George V. For those of us unfamiliar with the language between heads and princes of state, the letter from Roosevelt to the king is remarkably interesting for its tone of empire and glory.

To His Majesty George V, of Great Britain, Ireland and the British Dominions beyond the Seas, King, Emperor of India, etc., etc., etc. Great and Good Friend: I have made choice of Robert Worth Bingham, a distinguished citizen of the United States, to reside near the Government of Your Majesty in the quality of Ambassador Extraordinary and Plenipotentiary of the United States of America. He is well informed of the relative interests of the two countries. . . . My knowledge of his high character and ability gives me entire confidence that he will constantly endeavor to advance the interests and prosperity of both Governments and so render himself acceptable to Your Majesty.

I therefore request Your Majesty to receive him favorably and to give full credence to what he shall say on the part of the United States. . . . May God have Your Majesty in His wise Keeping,
    Your Good Friend, Franklin D. Roosevelt.[19]

Bingham himself disclaimed any interest in pomp and circumstance. In his first press interview in London, he said he intended to conform to court etiquette at the diplomatic functions. "I am now one of an international band and what the other members do I will conform to." But "you can say," he told reporters, "that I will not wear the knee breeches," which were common attire at such functions.[20]

A month later, at a presentation to the king at the "royal court," Bingham wore the breeches. The occasion was the introduction of his wife and daughter to the British aristocracy. The ceremonial glitter must have made Bingham's knees weak.

London, June 23—The last of the season's five courts at Buckingham Palace tonight was the most brilliant of all. King George was present for the first time this year.

The attack of rheumatism which prevented his Majesty from attending the earlier courts has yielded to treatment and the Monarch wore the full-dress uniform of Colonel-in-Chief of the Scots Guards. Queen Mary was a lovely figure in a gown of gold lamé embroidered in diamante and a train of Irish lace.

The list of American presentations was unusually long. After Mrs. Robert Worth Bingham, wife of the new United States ambassador, made her own curtsey, she sponsored 13 Americans, including her daughter, Miss Henrietta Worth Bingham.

The gold and white throne room provided a glittering background for the beautiful gowns of the debutantes and uniforms of the diplomatic corps. . . .

Miss Henrietta Bingham appeared in a gown of rose petal crinkled crepe in graceful lines and of extreme simplicity. . . .[21]

Although Bingham lacked previous diplomatic experience, he proved a capable and successful ambassador. His enjoyment of fishing, yachting, and hunting made him an easy favorite among the British leaders. He and his wife were often overnight or weekend guests of the king and queen at Windsor Castle.[22]

A *New York Times* profile done several months after his arrival in London described him as having:

a properly English reverence for a fine stretch of countryside with ancestors under the turf and pheasants in the hedge rows. . . . He has the English eye for a good dog and the English preference for English servants. He plays the cello and the organ, but no golf, no tennis and no bridge; and he takes a hand at poker only when he feels like losing. He dislikes hard liquor and chews rather than smokes an occasional cigar. More often he takes a puff or two of a cigarette and throws the rest away. His real sports are shooting, fishing and yachting. Long before the war, when he was studying art in Munich, he overheard a Prussian officer becoming offensive on the subject of the United States. He took the recognized course by slapping the officer and accepting an immediate challenge to a duel.

"Perhaps it is only fair to tell you that I am a crack shot," he told the officer's seconds. Practicing the next morning at a Munich shooting gallery, he found the two seconds watching him. An hour later the officer left town and the duel never came off. . . .

The Binghams belong to an old Dorsetshire family. The manor house at Melcombe Bingham was sold out of the family in 1895 but a painting of Sir George Bingham, who commanded the British garrison on St. Helena during Napoleon's exile, still hangs above the dining room fireplace. Sir George did not belong to the American Bingham line, for the founder of that line was the Elizabethan soldier, Sir Richard Byngham who left Dorsetshire for Ireland in 1560. It was one of his descendants who sailed for the States in 1790. . . .[23]

It will be noted in the above profile that the image-polishing has really hit high gear. Bingham "dislikes hard liquor" and his trips to Europe were not family vacations but aesthetic missions to study "art in Munich." The family ancestry also has been romanticized into sort of a Sir Walter Scott story, with the American line taking on the dimensions of *Ivanhoe,* commencing with an "Elizabethan soldier, Sir Richard Byngham." It is a dubious claim at best. The story of the aborted duel may be true, but careful research has failed to locate a trace of the tale elsewhere. Bingham, after all, was a newspaperman, a convivial drinker, a bon vivant, and he knew how to spice his stories.

Another writer, young Jessie Clark of the Junior League in America, found Bingham, "appearing ten years younger than his 61 years," to have a reputation as a raconteur:

He is slender, erect and faultlessly dressed always. A man of action and energy, he is keen and alert mentally as well as physically. A born diplomat, he is a brilliant public speaker and an able writer. Firm of purpose and quick at decisions, whatever the issue in question . . . aristocratic yet democratic, genial with a ready wit. His intelligence, his versatility, his fame as a raconteur have made him tremendously popular with young and old alike.[24]

As ambassador, he chaired several conferences in London on world wheat control; played a major role in the American response to the Italian invasion of Ethiopia, the outbreak of the Spanish Civil War, and the Japanese invasion of China. He was a steadfast supporter of Anglo-American unity and this frequently got him into hot water with the American press.

Bingham, of course, was only carrying out Roosevelt's policies, but Roosevelt's support often came in peculiar ways.

Biographer James MacGregor Burns cites an example where a reporter had asked Roosevelt about a statement by Ambassador Bingham in London urging closer relations between the United

States and Britain. If Roosevelt had done the natural thing of publicly backing Bingham, the newspapers would have made headlines of the president's statement, with likely ill effect on naval conversations then under way with Japan. If he had said "no comment," he would have sounded critical of Bingham. So he simply said he had not seen Bingham's statement—although in fact he had approved it.[25]

In another example of Roosevelt's charming duplicity, Eleanor Roosevelt once recalled a party where she was asked if "her husband consulted her on all important matters."

She said that wasn't "quite the way it worked," and cited the appointment of Bingham. The president, she said, "discussed" with her the instructions he planned to give Bingham, and she made some suggestions. The next day Bingham came to tea at the White House and, she purred, she heard FDR passing on virtually all of her suggestions. Then he looked at Mrs. Roosevelt, bade Bingham goodbye, and left the room.

It seemed to her that her husband wanted her to know he was taking her advice but didn't care to say so directly.[26]

Bingham was ambassador to three kings of Great Britain. He was present at the Court of St. James's in 1936 when George V died and was succeeded by his son, King Edward VIII. As the Prince of Wales, Edward had been a friend of Bingham's, and his American mistress, Mrs. Wallis Warfield Simpson, was a relative of Bingham's Scottish daughter-in-law.[27]

In December 1936, when Edward VIII announced he would abdicate the throne in order to marry Mrs. Simpson, Bingham and his family skillfully avoided any acts or utterances that might have been construed as interfering in the matter.[28]

At the coronation of Edward's successor, King George VI, in May 1937, Bingham again bowed to convention and showed up in a white waistcoat, white tie, and black knee breeches with black buckles at the knees and shoes.

Bingham's social ties to both Roosevelt and the kings of England definitely helped strengthen relations between the countries. He often served as Roosevelt's interpreter, to make the British understand who and what Roosevelt was:

From the moment that his inaugural address went out to the whole listening American nation, the somber clouds of despair began to lift, paralysis of fear was replaced with hope and courage, and with uplifted minds and hearts the whole people accepted a leadership bold, wise, statesmenlike and inspiring.[29]

His communications with Roosevelt were on the personal level and usually bypassed the State Department chain of command. A typical example is a letter written by Roosevelt in November 1933 congratulating Bingham on his performance and asking him to deliver a packet of stamped envelopes to George V.

Dear Bob:
　　Week after week I have been meaning to write to you, but because of the enormous pressure here I have kept putting it off. Nevertheless, I feel as if I had been in fairly close touch with you, for I have not only seen the dispatches but have talked with many people, including Dr. Young and my boy Jimmie. . . .
　　Everybody praises your work most highly and this comes not only from the British but also from our own people who have been passing through London. . . .
　　All goes well here, though some of the inevitable sniping has commenced. . . . The point is that employment continues on a much higher basis, and in spite of certain pessimists I think we shall get through the winter much better than I had expected. . . .
　　I have sent you a longhand note to the King and with it a little package of rather amusing envelopes addressed to me by His Majesty's subjects in many parts of the world. There is no hurry about the delivery of these. You can do it whenever occasion best offers. . . .[30]

It was a habit of Roosevelt to enlist correspondents as friendly spies who would bypass the bureaucracies and report directly to the president. Bingham was no exception:

Do write me and tell me how you think things are going on the other side. I am, of course, concerned about this German situation and the many repercussions it will have. Walter Lippmann made the interesting suggestion the other day that 92 per cent of the population of the world is ready for peace in permanent form and for progressive disarmament to support that peace. Eight percent of the world population, made up of the Germans and the Japanese, seem to be blocking an otherwise unanimous desire.[31]

The bulk of the correspondence between Roosevelt and Bingham combined the personal with the professional. Roosevelt frequently asked Bingham's advice on a variety of matters, partly because the wily president was seeking to flatter his ambassador. Bingham responded with equal flattery. In a letter dated October 15, 1937, Bingham responded to two Roosevelt inquiries, one concerning finance, the other the Hawaiian Islands:

I was told on what seems to be good authority that a margin of 55 per cent is required in buying stocks, but a margin of only 10 per cent is required in selling stocks. . . .

[As for Hawaii], I feel that the drive for statehood for the Hawaiian Islands, if successful, would be a serious menace to this country, as I understand there are 180,000 Japanese in the islands, most of whom were born there. No doubt, however, you have this in mind. . . .[32]

The biggest furor in Bingham's ambassadorship came after a July 4, 1937, speech in England wherein he thoroughly lashed the Nazi dictatorship in Germany. "If dictatorships are better to prepare for war, democracies are better to finish war," he warned.

The words were particularly strong from the leading ambassador of an allegedly neutral country.

The German regime responded promptly with a note of protest to Roosevelt, and Hitler's newspaper, *Voelkischer Beobachter*, responded with articles denouncing Bingham's speech as an "arrogant and ignorant attempt to tell foreign nations how to manage their own affairs . . . [inciting] the so-called democracies against the so-called dictatorships in almost unbelievable fashion."[33]

In fact, the speech had been prompted by Roosevelt, who had invited British Prime Minister Neville Chamberlain to formulate a joint diplomatic policy. Chamberlain refused because he preferred to negotiate with Hitler by himself. The result was the Munich conference of 1938 between Chamberlain and Hitler, which virtually guaranteed World War II.

□

In August of 1937 rumors began to circulate that Bingham might resign because of the flap with Germany.

Both Bingham and Roosevelt denied the resignation rumors, but in fact both knew such a resignation was due. The cause, however, was not Bingham's performance as ambassador but his health.

In early December 1937, ill with cancer, Bingham checked into John Hopkins Hospital in Baltimore. On December 8, he submitted his resignation to Roosevelt, saying only that he had a curable "fever."

I want to thank you first and very heartily for the great honor you conferred on me in appointing me American Ambassador to Great Britain. It has been a great and interesting experience, and one I shall think of always with interest and pleasure. The time has come now when I feel I must ask you to accept my resignation, deeply as I appreciate your request for me to carry on there. I have had a peculiar recurrent periodic form of fever, which my doctors assure me that they can cure in time, but they are entirely unable to predict how long it will take to do so. In these circumstances, with the very important work which this post involves, I do not think it is fair to you or to our country to remain at this post when it will be months before I could return to it. I feel I am doing my necessary duty to you and to the country to ask you, in the circumstances, to accept my resignation. As soon as I am able to work, although I could not accept any other official position, it is in my desire and intention to put everything possible into the effort to support you and your ideals.[34]

He died ten days later.

In January 1938, Joseph Kennedy, father of future president John F. Kennedy, succeeded Bingham as ambassador.

President Roosevelt regarded Bingham as "truly an old personal friend. . . ."[35]

As ambassador, he was often in international headlines. For example, in October 1934, in an address at the University of Edinburgh, he proposed the mutual stabilization of the dollar and the pound, a Roosevelt-endorsed speech which helped prepare the way for Anglo-American cooperation in World War II. In a Fourth of July speech, he condemned Nazism and defended democracy with unaccustomed vigor for the times.

In a front-page obituary, the *New York Times* of December 19, 1937, said, "Mr. Bingham showed great independence as pub-

lisher of his two newspapers in Louisville and on many occasions
he was a thorn in the side of his political enemies. . . . He created
much enthusiasm when he advocated lower tarrifs. 'For years,' he
said, 'the majority of the American people have belied that the
higher the tariff, the higher the wages and the general level of
prosperity in the country would be. Now they have learned the
grim lesson that with the highest tariff the country has ever had
more than 13 million have no wages at all . . .' Of exceptionally
fine physical appearance, Mr. Bingham looked much younger
than his age, wore knee breeches at the coronation and shot
grouse in Scotland."

The impoverished Louisville lawyer had risen rapidly and
high since the death of Mary Lily. Knight of the Round Table.
Confidant of English kings. Representative of America in its most
important diplomatic posting. A truly fine newspaper publisher.
A symbol of the best in Southern liberal gentility. Once he
achieved his inheritance, you can search his life closely and not
find a hint of villainy. Why the change?

There is a piece of writing, a philosophical comment done at
the turn of the century, quoting a fictional Chicago street philoso-
pher named Mr. Dooley, which is applicable not specifically to
Bingham, but to the greedy of the world.

Did He or Didn't He?

A S THE TITLE of this chapter reflects, we have come full circle in the lives of Robert Worth Bingham and Mary Lily Kenan without directly addressing that central question. It is time, therefore, to summon the suspects to the drawing room.

Like all proper detective stories, the closing interrogations begin with a synopsis of events leading to the crime:

The unhappy couple was married in November 1916, and for the next five months they spent their time almost entirely at the Seelbach in Louisville, relieved by occasional visits to Washington, D.C., and stays at Whitehall in Palm Beach and the Plaza in New York.

While at the Seelbach in late December 1916 or early January 1917, Mary Lily began to receive treatments for unspecified problems from Dr. Michael Leo Ravitch, a Louisville dermatologist and longtime personal friend of Bob Bingham. She is not known to have been treated by any physician other than Ravitch despite the availability of first-rate medical care in New York, Washington, Baltimore, and Palm Beach.

In this same time period, the Binghams rented the mansion Lincliffe, with Mary Lily picking up all the bills.

In those first few months of engagement and marriage, Mary Lily gave Bingham nearly $700,000 in stocks and bonds to provide him an income, another $50,000 in cash, and allegedly another $1 million to clear up his premarriage debts—debts he had mostly incurred through poor stock market investments.

During her last year of life, Mary Lily changed her will four times. The September 1916 document was drawn up after consultation with her heirs and the Flagler trustees and written by Flagler System lawyers.

The December 1916 will appears to have been drawn up in part by the Flagler trustees and in part by Mary Lily's father-in-law, Colonel Robert Bingham, who persuaded her to write in bequests to the University of North Carolina and establish the Kenan Professorship Fund.[1] The will was then routinely witnessed by members of Bingham's law firm, lawyer Stanley E. Sloss and secretary Emily A. Overman, neither of whom took time to read the document.[2]

The March 1917 codicil, which benefited some local Florida institutions, appears to have been drawn up entirely by the Flagler trustees and witnessed by Mary Lily's Palm Beach lawyers.

In each of those wills, either directly or by implication, it was affirmed that Bingham would not share in her estate.

Then came the veiled events of the June 1917 codicil.

□

In early May 1917, Lincliffe was ready for occupancy and Mary Lily and Bob moved into a private and secluded world. From that point onward, Mary Lily became a recluse—hermetically sealed off from the world. Why?

Since girlhood, she had been a socially active creature. In New York and Palm Beach, she was among the nation's social leaders. But in Louisville and at Lincliffe she vanished from the scene, not responding to invitations and hosting only one entertainment of her own—the garden party of June 9, where she seems to have made only a brief appearance.[3]

It is likely that the lack of social activity was caused either by an unknown illness, or by the effects of morphine. We know from a variety of sources that at least from the time she moved into Lincliffe, Mary Lily was receiving morphine injections from Dr. Ravitch.[4]

Ten days following the garden party, she performs most curiously. Bypassing the Flagler trustees, she has a shadowy third party draw up an "unbreakable" new codicil.

Although she called upon Davies for draft copies and advice, he testified he didn't execute the final document.[5]

Furthermore, during the private detective investigation, the Kenan family had hired a handwriting expert to inspect the document. The expert, in effect, confirmed Davies' testimony, saying that the codicil had been written by someone other than the signing witnesses, Davies and Ravitch. He also ruled out Mary Lily and Robert Worth Bingham.[6]

He did not, however, compare the document to the handwriting of Mary Lily's father-in-law, Colonel Robert Bingham, who was a house guest at Lincliffe at the time. The *Courier-Journal* reports that the Colonel was in Asheville until about June 13, then came to Louisville "to visit his son," apparently leaving the night of June 19 or the following morning.[7]

Although not known to have an active practice, the Colonel was a lawyer, having received his doctor of law degree in 1890 from the University of North Carolina at the age of fifty-two.[8]

Given the Colonel's participation in Mary Lily's earlier will, his legal training, and his presence at Lincliffe, it is reasonable to assume he was the mysterious writer of the codicil which so benefited his son. Once the codicil was written, the Colonel left town, preceded by his son.

Davies was kept in the dark. The less he knew, the better. Such a sequence of events would have allowed Davies to sidestep any testimony on Bob Bingham's involvement in the codicil. We may recall that at the September 1917 hearings, Davies testified:

HELM BRUCE. Who mentioned it to you, the idea of a codicil?
DAVIES. She did herself.
Q. Where?
A. At her own house.
Q. When?
A. Several days, I should say three or four days, before that [the codicil] was written.
Q. Did you discuss the matter with Judge Bingham?

A. Judge Bingham was out of the city for those three or four days in North Carolina.

Q. Had you ever discussed with Judge Bingham the idea of a codicil to his wife's will?

A. I had not.[9]

On June 19, Mary Lily met with Davies at Ravitch's office in downtown Louisville. At Ravitch's instruction, the nurses and receptionist were dismissed and, with only Davies and the doctor as witnesses, she signed the prepared codicil. It gave Bingham $5 million off the top of her estate.

Following the signing, Ravitch moved into Lincliffe, probably to keep Mary Lily under sedation.[10]

Three to four weeks later, Mary Lily suffered a severe heart attack. This may have occurred in her afternoon bath where she was "loaded with bourbon and laudanum," according to Sallie Bingham. Bedridden, she died some two to three weeks afterward, on July 27, 1917. Death was attributed to heart failure. During those last weeks of her life, she was visited often by her brother and two sisters. They were assured and reassured that she was receiving the best possible medical care. Her physician in earlier years had been her cousin Owen Kenan. But in July 1917 he was serving with the U.S. Army Medical Corps in France.[11]

For about two weeks, the "death by natural causes" was accepted by all concerned. At first, there were no suspicions. But after returning to North Carolina, her family began to hear rumors. She had a penchant for laudanum and had died because of it.

Then the family received a letter from one of Ravitch's nurses saying Mary Lily had been drugged. There were other riddles. Why was she suddenly depending upon attorneys close to her husband when she had her own attorneys in Louisville, in New York, and in Palm Beach? They were among the best in the nation and included Judge Blount, president of the American Bar Association. Given that abundance of legal talent, why did she draft a secret codicil and sign it at a secret meeting held in the office of a dermatologist? Why, after excluding Bingham from her estate in three wills written in the previous ten months, did she reverse herself?

Furthermore, why was she in Louisville that summer? Her summers, all twenty-four of them since she met Flagler in 1891, had been spent in cool climates: seaside Mamaroneck on Long Island Sound; forested Asheville, or Bretton Woods in New Hampshire; the oceanfront at Newport, Rhode Island. She had the access and wherewithal to live anywhere, go anyplace. It wasn't difficult. All she or Bob needed to do was order up her private car and have it towed in the desired direction. No explanation has ever been offered as to why Mary Lily spent June and July of 1917 as a shut-in confined to a secluded house on the steamy banks of the Ohio River.

One hypothesis is drugs.

After hiring the William Burns Detective Agency, the Kenans learned that four successive nurses attending Mary Lily had been fired by Ravitch after objecting that he was giving the patient too much morphine.

Subsequently, the Kenan family caused two autopsies to be held, the first of which established that she had large amounts of morphine in her system and traces of arsenic. Ultimately, their New York pathologist said that while he could not attribute the death to murder, he likewise could not attribute it to "natural causes." [12]

Despite threats to publicize the autopsies and break the codicil, the Kenan family instead kept the medical reports secret and in April 1918 agreed to hand over the $5 million to Bingham.

The money was no concern, the heirs could easily afford a settlement, even one as high as $5 million. But they had not been pursuing the money. Their stated interest all along was (1) whether their kinsman had been drugged into signing the codicil; and (2) whether she had been murdered, either as a result of the morphine or by poisoning with arsenic. They invested large amounts of time, money, and emotional currency in pursuing those questions. Then, eight months after the death, six months after receiving the final Bellevue autopsy report, the Kenans dropped their investigation. Bingham is paid off. Ravitch becomes inexplicably affluent. Why?

The circumstances under which Mary Lily signed the codicil and under which she died remain a mystery to this day.

These are the major questions of her riddle:

1. Why did she sign the codicil?
2. Why was Ravitch, a dermatologist, called in initially instead of a heart specialist?
3. Why didn't Mary Lily use her own doctors for medical care?
4. Why didn't Mary Lily use her own lawyers to draw up the codicil?
5. Why did she sign the codicil under such strange conditions in Ravitch's office?
6. Why did the Kenans settle?
7. Why has the Kenan family withheld the medical reports for nearly seventy years?

Without more information, it is difficult but not impossible to formulate a hypothesis which answers all or even most of the above questions. What is missing is a clearer picture of her medical record, the original medical files apparently having disappeared from the possession of the Bingham family, and other records being kept secret by the Kenan family.

Nevertheless, there are certain facts which can be applied concerning her condition and death, namely:

- She was fifty years old at the time of death, stood about 5 feet 1 inch and weighed between 115 and 130 pounds. She was, thus, voluptuously overweight, as was the style of her girl-hood. Nevertheless, at the age of fifty, in the hot summer of Louisville, it could contribute to a heart attack.
- Records at the Flagler Museum in Palm Beach, however, reflect no instance of heart attacks or any other such incidents during her marriage to Henry Flagler, 1901–13.
- There is no family history of heart disease or early death. Mary Lily's brother and sisters were all in their nineties when they died, none of heart disease. This lack of history obviously troubled Bingham's team of doctors and lawyers. It will be recalled that Bingham's New York counsel, Almuth C. Vandiver, went out of his way to minimize that aspect:

The Kenans are a long-lived family. Mrs. Bingham was in the prime of life and she certainly did appear to be strong and healthy. But persons who especially devote themselves to active outdoor pursuits are frequently victims of heart trouble.[13]

Why does he plant the idea that Mary Lily devoted herself to active outdoor pursuits? From all accounts, she was a salon-type woman, rarely lifting anything heavier than a demitasse spoon. In her more than twelve years at Whitehall, her activities were regularly recorded and while she took the occasional outing on a yacht or drive to a picnic, there is no report of her riding horses or swimming in the sea or bashing a tennis ball. Vandiver was clumsily using a false argument.

□

- Some two weeks prior to Mary Lily's demise, she was felled by a heart attack, possibly while in her bath and probably while under the influence of bourbon and an opiate such as laudanum or morphine.
- She was bedridden thereafter.
- She was experiencing hallucinations in her final days. Through family sources we learn that the hallucinations may have begun as early as three weeks before her death.
- There was blood in her urine in the final days.
- Each of four nurses complained about the amounts of morphine used by Ravitch and each in turn was relieved.
- During the last months of her life, Mary Lily's doctors were Ravitch, a dermatologist; Boggess, a pediatrician; and Steinberg, a laboratory pathologist. For a heart disease patient, it was a strangely ill-equipped team. Louisville, a city of nearly 250,000 population, had more than 600 practicing physicians of whom approximately fifty specialized in heart care.[14]

□

Omitted from this list is the cause of death as stated on the death certificate signed by Boggess and Steinberg. According to the certificate, she died of "Oedema of the brain," her body bloating because her failing heart was unable to move the fluids. The secondary cause listed on the certificate was myocarditis.[15]

In modern medicine, myocarditis is a specific diagnosis meaning inflammation of the heart muscle. In 1917, however, it was a catchall term for many types of heart disease.[16] It was apparently placed on the death certificate as an expediency.

Accordingly, as the time approached for the release of the Kenan/Bellevue autopsy, the Bingham team needed a more precise and scientific diagnosis. This was done by Bingham's expert pathologist, Dr. Otto H. Schultze of New York. After consultation with Drs. Boggess and Steinberg, Schultze declared that death was caused by endocarditis, an inflammation of the heart lining.[17]

So firm was the diagnosis that the Bingham team announced that Schultze would conduct his own autopsy "should the report by [Kenan pathologist] Dr. Norris show any finding other than that of death due to endocarditis."[18]

According to standard medical texts, endocarditis is the inflammation and infection of the lining and usually the valves of the heart by bacteria which reach the heart through the bloodstream. The bacteria usually originates in another part of the body. The original infection can come from a variety of traumas to the body, including injection of a syringe or catheter, from strep throat or impetigo, and from the irritation of rectal or genital lesions and sores. Usually, the skin infection comes first and the bacteria spreads through the bloodstream to infect the heart. Sometimes, however, the reverse happens with the heart infection spreading outward and manifesting itself in skin lesions.[19]

In modern times, drug abusers who use contaminated equipment or drugs are frequent victims of endocarditis. They are cured with relative ease, however, with antibiotics.

In 1917, there were no antibiotics to reverse the infection, and endocarditis was nearly 100 percent fatal. The accepted treatment of the time was morphine, for relief of pain, and adrenaline, for stimulation of the heart. Bingham's medical team confirmed that they had been using such treatment. "The narcotics administered to her during her final illness were similar to those administered to patients in like cases where suffering can be alleviated and heart action stimulated," said Dr. Ravitch in a press interview.[20]

It is possible that Mary Lily contracted the disease from contaminated morphine injections being given her by Dr. Ravitch.

But in 1917 there was another, more scandalous, common

cause of endocarditis. It was the disease, little known then or now, called "tertiary syphilis," or late syphilis. It is a syphilis which doesn't become apparent until ten to thirty or more years after the initial contract. It is a syphilis which lives with a man or woman "for years in harmony until something disturbs the balance." [21]

It is called tertiary because the disease runs like this:

- "Early syphilis," which has two stages: primary and secondary.
- "Late syphilis," which has one stage: late, or tertiary.

□

The first symptoms of *early syphilis* are chancres, or ulcerous sores, at the point the disease enters the body. In many cases, because of the way they are built, women do not see these chancres. They are the breeding places, however, of a spiral-shaped bacteria or spirochete. The member of the spirochete group that causes syphilis is called *Treponema pallidum.*

Even without treatment, the chancre slowly heals in several weeks; the spirochetes, however, spread throughout the body.

Early on, the spirochete settles in the heart, although it does no immediate damage. The sores eventually go away and the first stage of syphilis is usually cured either through medicine or natural immunities.

Primary syphilis is evident almost immediately after the initial infection.

Secondary syphilis, on the other hand, doesn't develop until two to six months after infection. Its symptoms are characterized mainly by fever, swollen glands, and a painless, nonitching rash over most of the body, including the genital tract, the mouth, and the palms and soles. Lesions also form in the mouth and around the vagina and anus, and these are highly contagious.

As a rule, the sores of this stage are not destructive and heal without scar formation. Secondary syphilis may linger in the body for up to two years, capable at anytime of erupting into all its dreadful symptoms. Eventually, these symptoms resolve and the disease enters its latent, or tertiary, phase.

The sores and other symptoms of *tertiary syphilis* do not appear until some ten to thirty or more years after initial infection.[22]

It is among nature's most lethal and dreadful surprises. People can have contracted the disease in their youth, passed through the first two stages without any apparent symptoms, then in middle age be struck dead by its power.

□

In 1917, a common treatment for all forms of syphilis was arsenic medicine, traces of which were found in Mary Lily's body. The main problem with arsenicals, however, was that they often had the side effect of attacking and damaging the kidneys. In the same press interview in which Ravitch confirmed that Mary Lily had been treated with drugs to allow her suffering to "be alleviated and heart action stimulated," Dr. Boggess said that a contributing cause to Mary Lily's death was kidney failure.[23]

It is shocking to contemplate, but the probable reason Mary Lily saw Dr. Ravitch in January 1917 was that she had, or suspected she had, tertiary syphilis.

In 1917, indeed until 1960, syphilis was treated primarily by dermatologists, the doctors of dermatology operating under the supervision and training of the College of Dermatology and Syphilisology, which was also known as the College of Dermatology and Venerealogy.[24]

To a lesser degree, venereal disease was also treated by urologists. The cooperation of the two disciplines was recognized by a common medical journal, the *American Journal of Dermatology and Urology.*[25]

As a hypothesis, the syphilis scenario explains why Mary Lily was treated by a dermatologist and not a heart specialist, why arsenic was found in her blood, why she had kidney failure, and why she had endocarditis.

It does not explain, however, why her husband didn't call in heart specialists once the endocarditis was diagnosed, nor move her away from the Louisville summer heat.

Those explanations died with Robert Worth Bingham. However, it is reasonable to assume that once Ravitch was brought in to treat syphilis, he was kept on to administer morphine and make Mary Lily helpless. So helpless that within a few months she was unable to break out of her prison at Lincliffe. He would keep her so compliant she would ultimately change her will.

Bingham and Ravitch must have been alarmed when her heart reacted badly to the overdosage. Her illness was so severe it was beyond Ravitch's abilities. To save her life and avoid murder charges, they had to bring in other physicians. But it was necessary that the new help be friendly. Neither Bingham nor Ravitch could afford independent specialists, who would inform the authorities of the overdosage. So they looked for cooperative doctors and the best they could find were a pediatrician and a laboratory researcher.

If the syphilis hypothesis is correct, Mary Lily almost certainly contracted it from either Henry Flagler or Robert Worth Bingham, her only known lovers. Chances of being infected by means other than sexual intercourse are minuscule.

It probably wasn't Flagler. There is not the slightest hint of such a disease in his history. But there are some strong suggestions in the past of Robert Bingham. First, although neither was a celibate, Bingham was far more of a womanizer than Flagler. Second, Bingham had some hidden reason for abruptly quitting college in 1891 and secluding himself in Asheville for the next three years. Third, under the referral of urologist Hugh Young, Bingham underwent a series of confidential medical treatments in 1900.[26] Fourth, Hugh Young indicates that Bingham had a near obsession with venereal disease, teasing him that "you really are considerably medical in your makeup, particularly when it comes to problems of social hygiene."[27] Fifth, twice in 1905 and possibly in other years, Bingham was treated for some disease by dermatologist Ravitch.[28] There is no question that Ravitch was experienced in the treatment of venereal disease. During World War I he was consultant on such cases to the U.S. Army at Camp Zachary Taylor, Kentucky.[29]

□

So where does this information leave us in regard to the death of Mary Lily? At this point, the facts and speculations support five possible scenarios:

- *Natural Causes.* No syphilis. No victims. No villains. No excessive drugs. She signed the codicil out of love and generosity. She stayed in Louisville to be with her husband. She had a heart attack, possibly provoked by drinking bourbon in the July heat. She was bedridden for an unspecified time, and died of natural causes.
- *Syphilis/Natural Causes.* Mary Lily had syphilis, but Robert was a caring husband. There were no excessive drugs, no coercion to signing the codicil, and death was natural. He remained silent to protect her from scandal.
- *Syphilis/Conspiracy.* Mary Lily had syphilis and that enabled her husband and Ravitch to enter a morphine conspiracy and coerce her into signing the codicil. When her health deteriorated, they called in cooperative physicians but it was too late. She died a victim of the conspiracy.
- *Morphine/Conspiracy.* Mary Lily did not have syphilis but was treated by Ravitch for some other cause and thus became a victim of the morphine conspiracy.
- *Malpractice.* Mary Lily, suffering from heart disease, syphilis, or some third cause, was unintentionally killed by Dr. Ravitch, who was unaware of the effects of morphine on heart disease.

□

Of the above hypotheses, the Natural Causes scenario answers the fewest of the seven basic questions. The only scenario which answers all the questions is the Syphilis/Conspiracy hypothesis (see chart that follows).

Thus on the basis of the best available evidence, the most probable sequence of events is that Mary Lily was a victim of tertiary syphilis, most likely picked up from her schooldays lover, Robert Worth Bingham. The disease lay dormant, however, for some twenty-five years.

SCENARIO	QUESTION #1	QUESTION #2	QUESTION #3	QUESTION #4	QUESTION #5	QUESTION #6	QUESTION #7
Natural Causes	Generosity	Mistaken diagnosis	?	?	?	?	?
Syphilis: Natural Causes	Generosity/ Blackmail/ Guilt	Syphilis	Fear of scandal	?	?	Fear of scandal	Fear of scandal
Syphilis: Conspiracy	Blackmail/ Drugged	Syphilis	Blackmail/ Drugged	Blackmail/ Drugged	Blackmail/ Drugged	Fear of scandal	Fear of scandal
Morphine Conspiracy	Drugged	To do the drugging	Drugged and helpless	Drugged/ Davies was discreet	Drugged	Be rid of nuisance	?
Malpractice	Generosity	Mistaken diagnosis	?	?	?	?	?

SCENARIOS

- *Natural Causes.* No syphilis. No victims. No villains. No excessive drugs. Mary Lily signed the codicil out of love and generosity and died of natural causes.

- *Syphilis: Natural Causes.* Mary Lily had syphilis, but Robert was a caring husband. Death was natural. He remained silent to protect her from scandal.

- *Syphilis Conspiracy.* Syphilis enabled her husband and Dr. Ravitch to enter a morphine conspiracy and coerce her into signing the codicil. When her health deteriorated, they called in cooperative physicians but it was too late.

- *Morphine Conspiracy.* No syphilis, but she was treated by Dr. Ravitch for some other cause and thus became a victim of the morphine conspiracy.

- *Malpractice.* Mary Lily, suffering from heart disease, syphilis, or some third cause, was unintentionally killed by Dr. Ravitch's incompetency.

QUESTIONS

1. Why did she sign the codicil?

2. Why was Ravitch, a dermatologist, called in initially instead of a heart specialist?

3. Why didn't Mary Lily use her own doctors for medical care?

4. Why didn't Mary Lily use her own lawyers to draw up the codicil?

5. Why did she sign the codicil under such strange conditions in Ravitch's office?

6. Why did the Kenans settle?

7. Why has the Kenan family withheld the medical reports for nearly seventy years?

It is a thought-provoking piece of irony that it apparently broke out when she and Robert were wed. Was some subconscious guilt within Mary Lily punishing her for returning to Bob Bingham? Equally strange phenomenon have been triggered by the unconscious: Science cannot explain what allows firewalkers to tread barefoot across red-hot embers without pain nor can it explain the "placebo effect," the mysterious process by which a sugar pill acts like a powerful drug just because the user believes the pill will cure.

Symptoms seem to have first appeared in January 1917, by which time it had thoroughly infected her heart, causing endocarditis.

At that juncture, Bingham could and should have called in expert medical help, either by tapping the substantial resources available in Louisville or by moving her to medical centers in New York, Washington, or Baltimore.

He took none of those steps.

Instead, the preponderance of evidence leads us to believe that he entered into a conspiracy with Ravitch to addict his wife to morphine and eventually reduce her to a state of utter helplessness. Inexorably, step by step, she was led to her death.[30]

In the court hearings which followed, Bingham remained remarkably confident. And why not? In the game against the Kenans, he had the hole card which would win the game anytime he played it: *Mary Lily was a victim of syphilis.* It was a scandal too horrible for the Kenans to face.

It is unclear when the Kenans found out. Probably it was after the second autopsy. Such a finding would explain why the autopsy report was suppressed then and has remained suppressed for the seventy years since.

It is clear that after receiving the autopsy report, the Kenans folded their tents. There was no more challenge of the codicil. Things were allowed to drift. And in April 1918, probably after a prod from Bingham, they settled.

Their kinswoman, the source of their future fortunes, had indeed been drugged by her husband.

He may not have been guilty of murder, but one could certainly make a case for it: he had motive, and he had opportunity.

The circumstantial evidence is certainly convincing, too: he needed money quickly to buy his newspapers, and he had written Hugh Young's wife in May that his financial picture was about to change. Simply by withholding proper medical attention he was murdering his wife as surely and swiftly as if he had spooned arsenic down her throat.

But let's not call it a murder. There was a very similar case in the 1980s involving Claus von Bulow, a European businessman who had married an American heiress, Martha "Sunny" von Auersperg.

In 1980, after twelve years of a boozy but apparently tranquil marriage, Sunny was found collapsed and near death in her Newport mansion. Her life was saved but she entered an apparently permanent coma. Two years later, while Sunny lay unconscious in a hospital, her husband was tried and convicted in a Rhode Island court of attempting to murder her by giving her injections of insulin.

After the trial, jurors said that a primary consideration in his conviction was: (1) motive, he stood to inherit $12 million in cash and securities plus Mrs. von Bulow's Newport mansion and her New York apartment upon her death; and (2) opportunity, he was alone in the house at the time of her collapse and insulin and hypodermic needles were on the premises.[31]

The verdict was overturned by the Rhode Island Supreme Court, partly on the basis of improper evidence presented to jurors.

At a second trial in the spring of 1985, von Bulow was acquitted of the same charge. The difference between the two trials was that the second barred evidence of motive.

It was the elimination of testimony concerning motive that allowed von Bulow to go free, said Sunny's twenty-seven-year-old daughter, Princess Annie-Laurie Kneissl.

If the financial testimony had come in by the banker . . . [as] to what my stepfather had to gain from trying to murder my mother . . . that would have made everything clear. It certainly did make everything clear during the first trial, and it's facts and figures which tell the true story, not opinion.[32]

Thus, on the basis of much weaker evidence than in the Bingham case, we find one jury convicting von Bulow and a second acquitting him.

In Bingham's case, both motive and opportunity were clearly present. Also he did not need to personally make the injections to cause her death. During Mary Lily's last seven months, he could have at any point taken steps to save her. He didn't. And while that may not be a 100 percent murder, it is certainly a 100 percent killing.

Love

WHAT are we to make of the life of Robert Worth Bingham? Does it contain some instruction for us? Is there some hint of a truth that might help make sense of what happens around us?

Here is a man who for the first forty-five years of his life was a classic knave—an unprincipled but charming rogue, a desultory student, an incorrigible womanizer, a snob, a lawyer who tried to swindle his relatives, a hack politician, and an absentee father. Search his life up to that age. Be as charitable as you can. And it is still hard to find redeeming social factors. The few which do exist are mostly negative virtues: He didn't carve graven images. He didn't adulterate food. That sort of thing.

There are only a few positive assets.

He was a dutiful son.

He was considerate of his first wife, although one can hunt through man-high stacks of papers, letters, memos, bills, and other surviving documents and find few signs of affection.

He was generous.

He was discreet in his affairs and never, from as far as we can tell, allowed Eleanor or the family to be beset by want or embarrassment. And, although he preferred to have his children not only out of sight but out of town, he stashed them in quality places—good schools and the spalike homes of Asheville relatives.

And that's about it for saying good things about the young Robert Worth Bingham. His brief stint as the touted "reform" mayor of Louisville was in fact a sham, as we have seen. And the title of "judge," which he carried for the rest of his life, was a minor, short-term political appointment characterized by an absolutely blank record of accomplishment.

Then came the seduction, the drugging and the killing of Mary Lily Kenan, descendant of a family which for nearly 150 years had eclipsed the Binghams in status, fortune, and influence.

However, once the crime was done, once Robert Worth Bingham had his millions and bought his power, he became a different man. Suddenly, overnight, he was a leader of liberal causes, a philanthropist, a Southern patrician who became an accomplished diplomat. And there was more. He became the founder of a communications dynasty characterized by community service, philanthropy, and enormous wealth. He became the head of a family which, though cursed with tragic deaths, would for two-thirds of a century reign as the mandarins of Kentucky.

Robert Worth Bingham died an honored man with eulogies from both sides of the Atlantic—from the king and Parliament of Great Britain; from President Franklin Roosevelt, who called him "not only an old personal friend," but one of the "foremost citizens" of the nation; from congressmen and senators and from Bingham's successor in office, Joseph Kennedy, who described the Judge as a "great public servant at home and abroad."[1]

There was a great outpouring of such sentiment and, of course, it is in the nature of eulogies to speak only good of the dead. But the point is he was honored, and he was remembered, for the job he did as Roosevelt's premier ambassador, for his hard work at rescuing banks and bank accounts, for saving the Kentucky tobacco industry, and for the relief work of the Louisville flood.

That all of this could happen to a ruthless egocentric like Robert Worth Bingham, a man who ascended by coldly destroying his wife, suggests that life isn't fair and justice doesn't prevail. And that's not surprising either, is it? Any of us who have been weaned from our mother's skirts have learned that lesson time and time again.

But perhaps there is some justice after all. Perhaps the ghost of Mary Lily was heard, some fifty years after Robert Worth Bingham's death. If it was indeed justice which struck in the 1980s, then the hammer was Bingham's granddaughter, a stiff-spined playwright and novelist named Sallie who did not know when she was whipped.

But the story begins not with her, but in the 1920s when her father and Robert Worth Bingham's other two children came to their maturity.

□

The symbol of family prestige was Melcombe, the large, Georgian brick mansion east of Louisville which Bingham had purchased in 1919 from Charles Ballard of the Ballard Mills flour fortune.[2] Originally named "Bushy Park," Bingham retitled the holdings "Melcombe Bingham," after the country estate in Dorset where Binghams had lived during the twelfth century. The Judge took over the manor house. There was another house built on the estate, which, though spacious was smaller than the mansion and came to be called the "Little House."

Perched high above the Ohio River with a view of the low hills of Indiana in the distance, the estate was a work of art and the Bingham seat of power. When the prominent and powerful visited Louisville, they called at or stayed in Melcombe.[3]

The houses sat at the top of a hill overlooking rolling landscaped lawns which swept down to the ancient River Road and the banks of the deep, blue waters of the broad Ohio. There were kennels, a tennis court, and gardens secluded by screens of conifers and other trees, framed by walls of brick and hedges. The Louisville Melcombe was an English park embracing woods, pools, and a classic Greek theater. The kitchen was equipped to prepare meals for 150. There was a lot of marble and oak in the place, and a grand staircase at the end of an immense entrance hall. There was a pond near the barn, and a pen full of geese and ducks that set up an incredible din when people came near. Gardeners grew much of the produce for the house. They also cultivated grapes and made wine.[4]

Despite the beauties and comforts of the estate, however, only one of Bingham's three children made it their home. Of the three only Barry was willing to take up the burdens of the Bingham businesses, values, and style which his father paid so much to obtain.[5]

It was Barry who took up the family business while his siblings fled from responsibility. And he acquitted his duties remarkably well, building one of the nation's finest newspapers, expanding the radio operation, opening a television station, and all the while maintaining a position of duty and responsibility to his community and family.

It was Barry who lived in the Little House, and when the Judge died he moved into the mansion.

Both of Barry's siblings walked away from the burdens of the family business. Neither his sister, Henrietta, nor his older brother, Robert, had interest in the business or in Louisville. They were the flappers and flower children of their time.

Robert had a great fondness for travel and drink and lived much of his adult life in Scotland.[6] He was twice married, the first in 1925 to Scotswoman Dorothy Phyllis Fell Clark and the second in 1944 to Felice Desmit. He and his second wife spent the last several years of their life in the ski-resort community of Aspen, Colorado, where he died in 1965 at the age of sixty-eight.

Henrietta, too, spent years in England and was a fringe member of the "Bloomsbury Group," a literary and social clique known for its snobbishness, which included Lytton Strachey, Virginia Woolf, E. M. Forster, and John Maynard Keynes.[7] Henrietta established a certain notoriety for the variety of her conquests, male and female, including a long affair with thespian John Houseman and another with a "famous female tennis champion."[8] She returned to the United States and to Louisville in 1936 purchasing a horse farm in Goshen, Kentucky. She later married Benjamin McKenzie, but they were divorced in 1954.

Both Henrietta and her brother were left sufficient money in the Judge's will to maintain their life-styles. Neither had children. Henrietta died in a lonely New York apartment in 1968. She was sixty-seven.

Like his brother and sister, Barry—born George Barry Bingham in 1906—was given a chance to find himself. In his youth, he wanted to be a novelist. After he graduated magna cum laude from Harvard in 1928, his father financed a year's sabbatical for him to travel and to write. He did produce a novel which he later described as "extremely long and very dreary," and which, "thank God, was never published." A manuscript still exists, "but under very heavy lock and key."[9]

In June 1931, he married Mary Caperton of the highly social Richmond, Virginia, Capertons. They had met in Boston in the 1920s when Barry was at Harvard and Mary was at Radcliffe. They would have five children. Their daughters Sallie and Eleanor recalled that their mother was not much impressed by the Bingham family style when she arrived in Louisville. Said Eleanor: "My mother talked about marrying my father and coming down here to what was for her, a Richmond belle, a real jungle, heathen, with dogs sleeping on the furniture. It was like a hunting camp, with boots steaming by the fire." And, added Sallie, "a monkey and a dog which sat up in a high chair. It was very much a man's place."[10]

Barry began work on the papers as a police reporter in 1930 and became acting publisher upon his father's appointment as ambassador. With the death of his father in 1937, he became publisher. Other businesses he ran included Standard Gravure, which would eventually print most of the nation's newspaper Sunday magazines and was a sort of gold mine, often supporting other Bingham enterprises. Barry also upgraded the radio station into one of the nation's finest and took an early leap into television, opening station WHAS in 1950.

Under his leadership, the newspapers became one of the fine journalistic institutions of America, enjoying statewide influence and national prominence.[11] He ran them autocratically, in the style of the Judge. "My father felt that newspapers have to be run by a single person," Barry has explained.[12]

His liberal positions put him in frequent conflict with his readership and with the essentially conservative Kentucky constituency, most dramatically during the civil rights era of the 1960s. Under Barry's stewardship, the papers took the lead on a variety of causes, ranging from child labor laws and rural electrification to public education and a bitter, decade-long fight in the 1960s against strip-mining companies which were turning the beautiful Kentucky landscape into something looking like the moon. The papers also took other major controversial stands in the sixties and seventies, opposing the Vietnam War and supporting the civil rights movement.

In 1975, when the newspapers supported a local plan to bus students to integrate the schools move, a mob police estimated to be in the thousands gathered outside the newspaper building and smashed windows with bricks and rocks. Barry and his editorial policies, however, held fast.

Under the Binghams' aggressive direction, the newspapers were the watchdogs of Kentucky, uncovering corruption or setting the public agenda by focusing on such problems as strip mining. Their news columns and editorials even exposed pollution caused by their own company, Standard Gravure.

Not only was Barry the sole offspring to work seriously for a living, but he was the only one to give Robert Worth grandchildren—in sequential order: Worth, Barry Jr., Sallie, Jonathan, and Eleanor—all born between 1933 and 1946 and all raised at Melcombe.

All, it seemed, were affected by a perceived aloofness from their parents.

Sallie has said that growing up at Melcombe was a matter of being raised by servants rather than a family affair.

Looking back, I guess they [the staff] saved me because the alternative would have been isolation and chaos or being shipped off very early to boarding school. When my parents were away, they were the whole world. I got a feeling from them, which I really value, of a whole other world of rich and interesting relationships, with a pecking order, queen bee and everything. I was fascinated by that, but they also gave us a real sense of family. . . .[13]

We had Cordie Stokes, who was the cook. A wonderful cook. Ollie Madison. She was the maid. Curt Madison, her husband, was this sort of chauffeur and handyman, who took care of the furnace. He also was an absolutely brilliant carpenter. Mother still has two beautiful chests of drawers, very formal, one a French antique and one the copy Curt made. He was a silent man. Lizzie Baker, who had been my father's nurse, was the one who ran all of the others. And, of course, there was our nurse, Lucy Cummings, who was white. She was called Nursie. The women used to wear a striped cotton dress and a white apron and cap. Curt had a chauffeur's uniform that he didn't wear very often. They were all Kentucky people. They lived in the house, and it was like family. In fact, they stayed with the family until they were too old to work, and the family took care of them after that. I don't think of them as having been servants because they were there from the time I was born. I knew them well, and they were important figures to me.[14]

Sallie had no such warm memories of her own parents. "My father never told me he loved me until recently, when we had a lunch. I was forty-eight years old."

The tales of loneliness, of growing up with dark memories of cold and distant parents, are echoed by Eleanor and Barry Jr.

"For years," said Barry Jr., "the family position has been basically one of not seeing much of one another . . . we communicate basically by memo."[15]

Sallie recalls that, in the early 1980s, she wrote a memo to her father to explain why she was living with tall, strapping Tim Peters, a Louisville construction contractor, whom she eventually married. "I didn't want the family to be embarrassed in case my 'living in sin' was found out, so I sent Father a memo."[16]

□

The 1960s were a decade of great accomplishment for the Binghams but it was also a time of successive thunderstrikes of calamity. In 1964, Barry and Mary's youngest son, Jonathan, a Harvard dropout, was electrocuted while trying to connect power lines for a Cub Scout reunion at his house. He was twenty-one. The following year, Barry's older brother Robert died in Nevada. In 1968, Henrietta was found dead of a heart attack in her New York apartment. And in that same period, a freak accident killed Worth Bingham, Barry's anointed heir to leadership of the dynasty.

□

Christened Robert Worth Bingham III, Barry's firstborn was as handsome and smooth-talking as his father and grandfather. He combined some of the best talents of both. Typical of his grandfather, he was absolutely charming, being one of those rare people everyone seemed to enjoy. Typical of his father, he had a sense of duty and, when motivated, was eager for hard work.[17]

With his father's guidance, he prepared himself carefully for the future leadership of the Bingham newspapers. Following graduation from Harvard and a hitch in the U.S. Navy in the late 1950s, he served his apprenticeship as a reporter at the *Minneapolis Tribune,* writing obits, covering police, doing rewrite. He then moved to editing jobs at the *San Francisco Call-Bulletin* and the *San Francisco Chronicle.*

"He was a laid-back sort of guy who you just knew had the world in the palm of his hand," says a former *Chronicle* colleague.[18]

In 1960, he returned to Louisville where he served in a variety of positions until his death.

There was a dark side to his personality, however, more akin to the grandfather. A young rake, given to life in the fast lane and trips to Las Vegas, his losses sometimes forced him to make urgent calls to company executives asking them to replenish his bank account without informing his parents.[19]

On July 12, 1966, while driving on Nantucket with his wife and young daughter in an open car, a surf board, standing in the rear, swung around and broke his neck. He was thirty-four and dead on the spot.

□

In the opinion of some Binghams, the dissolution of the dynasty dates from the death of Worth Bingham.

The tragedy pushed his father into a bleak despair. "There were times that I wondered if I would be able to keep on," Barry Sr. told an interviewer. "Nature helps, through its healing, and I drew great strength through the church."[20] As in many other crises of his life, he depended heart and soul upon his wife.

But perhaps even more affected by the death was Worth's younger brother Barry Jr.

At Worth's funeral, recalled Sallie, "no one was more desolated than Barry. He sobbed and cried and it was absolutely heartbreaking."[21]

He may have been crying for himself as much as for Worth.

The death altered the lines of succession. Barry Jr. gave up a career in television for which he had been preparing and moved over to the newspapers. A 1956 graduate of Harvard University, Barry Jr. had worked as a management trainee for CBS in New York City until 1959, shifting to NBC to produce documentaries before joining the family business in 1962. He had planned to take control of the family's television and radio stations. Instead, following Worth's death, he agreed to prepare himself to take over as editor and publisher of the *Courier-Journal* and *Times* company.

Cold in manner and somewhat snobbish, he attaches no sentiment to the action. It was mostly a business decision, he explains.

"The family was in disarray and sorrow. I was asked if I'd be interested. Who wouldn't be interested in the job he was offering? It was an opportunity."[22]

In the beginning, Junior, as he is regularly called around the company and around the city, began learning the subaltern positions while his father continued to run the newspapers, an heroic era which saw the *Courier-Journal* win four Pulitzers.

After the string of successes, Senior retired in 1971, becoming chairman of the boards of the family companies. Barry Jr. succeeded him as chief executive officer of the companies, including publisher of the newspapers. His father moved into the Little House and Barry into the mansion.

"My father said we should move into the big house where we could do corporate entertaining," he has explained.[23]

Of the surviving Bingham children, Junior alone remained in Louisville during the 1960s and 1970s.

□

Eleanor, born in 1946, the prettiest and the youngest, has described herself as a "flower child" of the 1960s, sporadically attending a series of colleges including the University of Louisville, Columbia University, New York University, and the University of Sussex in England. During those same years, she worked as a volunteer counselor at a camp for migrant workers' children at Riverhead, Long Island, and on a kibbutz in Israel. After operating a boutique in London in the late 1960s, she returned to America and began a career of documentary filmmaking, working out of New York, Aspen, and Los Angeles. Her most successful work was a film showing the inner workings of the Ku Klux Klan that was aired on 117 public television stations in the U.S. and widely broadcast in Europe. In the late 1970s, she returned to Louisville where she married and began to raise children.

□

Her elder sister, Sallie, was likewise an absentee during much of those two decades.

Of all the Louisville Binghams, long, tall Sallie in her blond ponytail was easily the most luminous. In 1954, at the age of seventeen, she won the national first prize for a short story in the annual *Atlantic Monthly* creative writing contest. In 1957, she was the first woman to win the Dana Reed Prize, an annual award given for the best undergraduate writing to appear in a Harvard University publication. The prize was given for "Winter Term," a short story which appeared in the *Harvard Advocate,* a literary magazine for Harvard and Radcliffe, and was reprinted in *Mademoiselle* magazine.

By the time Sallie was twenty-one, she had a three-book contract with Houghton Mifflin, which resulted in publication of her novel, *After Such Knowledge,* in 1959; and two collections of stories, *The Touching Hand* (1965) and *The Way It Is Now* (1972). She also is the author of four plays; the most recent being *Paducah,* which in 1985 had a short run in New York with actresses Tammy Grimes and Carrie Nye.

Despite this record of accomplishment, achieved without direct benefit of family money, influence, or power, Sallie has said she never felt she had won the approval of her parents, a feeling that developed into a resentment which kept her away from Melcombe for most of her adult life.[24]

In 1958, she married Whitney Ellsworth, co-founder and publisher of the *New York Review of Books,* and moved to New York, with no intention of involving herself in the family business or returning to Louisville.

The union fell apart, however, and in the 1960s she married

Wall Street lawyer Michael Iovenko. When that marriage went the way of the first, she returned to Louisville, coming "home on her shield." Her failed marriages and sputtering career had propelled her into "complete demoralization."[25]

About the same time, her younger sister Eleanor likewise returned to Louisville after some ten years' absence. It was not long after that, says Sallie, that she ran into the "rampant sexism of the Bingham males" and the family feud was on.

□

When the daughters both returned in the late 1970s, Barry Sr. feared what he called the "grandchildren syndrome," a condition whereby the sheer number of third generation owners splits the family businesses apart. The family becomes too large, too diverse in interests, and too scattered geographically to maintain common interests. The children and their spouses who don't work at the family company become critical of those who do and seek to sell out. His fears were well placed. Such a syndrome had forced the sale of other family-owned companies, including such newspapers as the *Chicago Sun-Times,* the *Des Moines Register,* and the *Detroit News.*

Accordingly, to knit the family interests, Barry Sr. decided that his two daughters needed to be involved.

He made Sallie, then over forty years old, and Eleanor, in her early thirties, voting members of the boards of the family companies. Barry Sr. also appointed three other women to the board—his wife, Mary; Worth's widow, Joan; and Junior's wife, Edith.

Sallie says she and Eleanor viewed the appointments with mixed feelings, being thrilled on the one hand and insecure on the other, having always regarded the businesses with awe.

Although Barry Jr. reluctantly supported the appointments, he in fact was hostile to the new board arrangement, but powerless to prevent it.[26]

Barry has claimed that conflicts arose immediately because his mother and sisters were allowed to criticize his decisions without having to bear the burden of decision-making.

"They were not involved in the day-by-day running of the companies," he said, "and therefore did not have to run the risks of making executive decisions. It was a lot of Monday morning quarterbacking."[27]

In confirmation, his father says none of the women showed interest in management positions.

Sallie disagrees, saying both she and Eleanor would have wanted management jobs but "remarks made at board meetings made it plain that running the companies was man's work."[28]

At board meetings, Sallie says, she asked questions—sometimes pointed ones about the poor performance of the family's printing operations—but never cast a negative vote. Barry Jr., she says, "was completely silent at board meetings. He attended as a formality, then did what he wanted. We needn't worry our heads about such things."[29]

About this time, 1979, Sallie went public with some matters the family considered very private, including her resentments about the alleged sexism she saw in the Bingham companies. Her parents tried to mend the breach by urging her to join the newspaper staff as book editor, working at an entry level salary of $21,000 a year, a job her mother had once filled.

"My parents called up and said they thought it would be good if I put the Bingham name back in the book editor business again," says Sallie. She never thought about Barry's reaction to it at the time, but realized that it was a step not in keeping with the traditional management chain. "I think it bothered him because he never thought any of the women would be in that building." Plus, "I was just one of the hired hands. I was out there on the floor. I got to know people. He's always been such an isolated person."

A secretary who worked in payroll says that it was well known that Sallie was making a mere $21,000, compared to other newsroom salaries, which were roughly $10,000 to $20,000 higher.

Knowing how much they are worth, millions of dollars, I mean after one million what do you do? We would think about Sallie's paycheck but she never acted like it was too small. She was fine to be around and what she had to say about the companies being sexist was really good. It really told it like it was and we all thought about it that way. It's too bad about the fight, but families are like that.[30]

Tensions heightened when Sallie wrote a letter to the editor assailing Barry Jr.'s endorsement of a political candidate, and, according to the father, the relationship between his last surviving son and his eldest daughter came to be one of fundamental suspicion.

Barry Jr. made it clear that he was suspicious of the kind of role his sisters wanted in the companies. He thought they mostly wanted to make the news operations more responsive to their own interests and to those of their friends and to ease criticism they got at cocktail parties. When he wouldn't let them do that, he said, they sought to undermine him and ultimately succeeded. Executive editor Paul Janensch said it is "bullshit, pure bullshit" that Sallie has seen the conflict as a feminist issue. The real problem, he said, is that the sisters behaved like "Southern belles," expecting the hired hands to do their bidding. "I just don't see it that way. I don't work on a plantation."[31]

Eleanor seemed a little puzzled that there was controversy over her and her sister's conduct: "This ain't no General Motors, honey. I mean this is a local communications outlet, and we all live in Louisville, and we all go to cocktail parties and get pinned to the wall about why in the name of God was this in that article, or this in that editorial, or this in that political cartoon. So obviously we need to converse with Barry about it."[32]

The breaking point came in 1980. To ease the pain of having the women on the board, Junior insisted each board member sign a "buy-back" agreement which stipulated that should they receive an outside offer to sell their stock the Bingham companies would have sixty days to match the offer.

It was, of course, a legitimate and somewhat standard business procedure against takeovers, but Sallie bristled and refused to sign. All sides agree that is when the fight began.

"Her refusal was an indication of something," complained Barry Jr. with a dark, suspicious look on his face.[33]

Sallie countered that the buy-back agreement was sprung on her and the board "out of the blue."

I told him that since he didn't trust me, a piece of paper wouldn't make it any better. In addition, the buy-back sort of let Barry set the purchase price. It was done at one of the meetings held at Melcombe. They put papers in front of us. I said, "What is this? I think I should have my lawyer look at this." My mother said, "The room is full of lawyers." I wondered how is this to my advantage? If they don't trust me, how is this going to fix it?[34]

Barry Jr. explains, "It was intended to ward off unfriendly offers and takeovers. Every other member of the family signed. As far as I'm concerned, that's where the problem began."[35]

☐

Three years passed with bitterness. Then, a few days before Thanksgiving 1983, Barry Sr. summoned his daughters to the Little House. He told them that Barry Jr. had issued an ultimatum: Either the women family members left the boards of the companies or Barry Jr. would resign.

The elder Binghams, the sisters, Worth's widow, Joan, and the nonfamily management staff such as Executive Editor Janensch beseeched Junior not to insist on the women's removal. But Junior wouldn't be budged. The women, he said, were making no contribution. They had to go to make room for experienced professionals.

"There were board meetings when my wife was doing needlepoint, one sister was addressing Christmas cards, and one sister didn't bother to attend," Barry Jr. complained, adding that the idea to get rid of the women on the board was initiated by consultant Leon Danco of Cleveland, who specializes in family-owned businesses.

Danco said, "You need a professional board of directors and that generally doesn't include family members with no business experience." I thought it was good advice. I made the suggestion, but it was not something that just came out of my head. I was not going to kiss them goodbye. You have to keep them informed on business. We were going to have four quarterly meetings of family members at the same time as the four quarterly board meetings. They were not going to never hear anything again. The other members of the family left the board without problems, including my wife, sister and mother. Sallie was the only one who refused to leave.[36]

The fight was on. The question put before the family was whether the women would resign peacefully, or would more drastic action be needed?

Sallie, for one, was not prepared to go. She dug in her heels:

The sexism, then and now, was really obvious. The attitude of management never changed from the day I arrived on the board.

At the board meetings, we'd have to listen to bra jokes—jokes about the size of women's breasts. It was like going back to the fifties. There were so many women at the lower levels unhappy and the affirmative action plan had run aground. Although Barry employed some women in management positions, essentially women were there as window dressing. He certainly couldn't handle women at his level. At meetings, everything was wonderful, but "don't ask to see the figures." . . . The *Courier-Journal* had the first woman managing editor in the United States—for a year. Then they kicked her out of upper management and made her an ombudsman.[37]

The experience galvanized an already latent feminism in Sallie.

I was really a feminist in the fifties when I wrote *After Such Knowledge.* But I didn't know what to call it then. And in the sixties, I was too afraid of belonging to what seemed to me then a far-out bunch. That doesn't bother me anymore. . . . When I first came back, people would ask, "Which one are you? Are you Eleanor?" The suggestion that all the women in the family were indistinguishable infuriated me.[38]

She recalls with a laugh that her efforts to raise the aspirations of women in Louisville became a local joke. "They called it Sallie's 'take-a-lesbian-to-lunch' program."[39]

The decision to resist was a turning point in her life.

"My mother has a tongue that just will take your skin off," Sallie told the *New York Times,* recalling that her mother accused her of "trying to destroy your brother."

"But I wasn't about to back down. They made me feel guilty, they shunned me, but finally at the age of forty-seven I was able to stand my ground."[40]

To Barry Sr. it seemed clear that Junior's move, ostensibly aimed at all the women, was in fact done expressly to purge Sallie from the boards, not so much for what she had done, but for what

Barry Jr. was convinced she would do. "He felt she would be very critical of him. He strongly suspected she would undermine him."[41]

Confronted with that argument, Barry Jr. offered a compromise. He would turn over management of the companies to a group of nonfamily professional managers. His father scornfully refused, saying that the companies might as well be sold if Binghams were not going to manage them.

"He just communicated desperation," Sallie says of Barry Jr. "He looked like someone pleading to be let off somehow."[42]

Ultimately, Barry Sr. and his wife ruled in favor of their son, who *was* after all the chief executive officer of the companies. Like it or not, the women had to resign from the boards as a demonstration of support for Barry Jr., who bore the burden of management on their behalf. Nevertheless, Sallie defiantly refused to resign.

She shocked the family, not to mention much of Louisville, by publicly announcing she would sell her stock to outside bidders.

The disintegration of the dynasty had begun.

Ironically, the dynasty she accused of sexism had a strong tradition of public service and liberal causes.[43] But there is little doubt that Junior stubbornly objected to sharing power with his two younger sisters.

Like it or not, as Barry had said, Sallie was voted off the boards at the shareholders meeting in March 1984. It wasn't even close. It was unanimous, except for her. Deeply humiliated, she sat at the end of the long conference table all by herself and watched the women of the family vote against her one by one— her mother, her sister, and Barry Jr.'s wife, Edith. Following the vote, the other three women resigned.

It began a split between Sallie and her mother that may never be resolved.

"She has called two or three times to say let's go to a movie or have lunch, but I told her I just couldn't see my way to do it," says Sallie.[44]

Barry Sr. mournfully endorsed the removal of the women. "It was my son's initiative but I agreed because it was a reasonable argument. I expected there might be trouble, but not as much as came. It, however, wasn't just disagreements between Sallie and Barry. I had to think of the larger family, nine grandchildren, [ranging] three months to twenty-four years of age."

He anticipated problems, "but not to the point it reached."[45]

□

In July 1984, seeking to ease the feud, Sallie drew back from her offer to sell to outsiders. Instead, she would sell her 15 percent of the family businesses to the family. It was agreed that Lehman Brothers, an investment banking firm which handled family business, would appraise the companies to determine their market value and the value of her stock. Lehman Brothers eventually said her shares were worth between $22 million and $26.3 million.

Suspecting that her shares were worth more, Sallie hired her own appraisers, Henry Ansbacher Inc., a New York investment banking firm specializing in the sale of communications companies. They estimated the value of her holdings at more than $80 million—nearly four times the Lehman estimate.

Accordingly, in December 1984, she resumed her plan to sell to outsiders.

□

In the meantime, relations also worsened between Barry Jr. and Eleanor, who had attempted a nearly impossible feat: remaining friendly with Sallie while supporting her parents and brother with her corporate votes. In February 1985, Eleanor sent Barry Jr. a letter in which, he said, she "told me she was disinterested in staying in any company with me as the head and her dependent on dividends."[46]

Junior responded in March 1985 with an offer to swap his stock in the television company in exchange for Eleanor's stock in the newspapers. She could run WHAS. He would run the papers. There was a condition: Eleanor needed to convince Sallie to sell at the family price. If Sallie could be bought out, the struggle for control would end.

To Sallie, the offer was not only hypocritical, "it was amusing. Barry kicked me and Eleanor off the board then all of a sudden he says Eleanor can run the TV station, okay? How do you explain Barry kicking all the women off the board because they are inept, then saying a year later, I think one of them ought to run the broadcast properties?"[47]

Eleanor eventually agreed to Junior's offer, but only if the family could reach agreement with Sallie on a price.

In an effort to achieve family peace, Sallie dropped the price to $32 million. This was in December 1985.

However, Barry Jr. was not so generous. He refused to go above $26.3 million. That's when gridlock set in and Senior decided the best way to achieve peace among his children was to sell all the companies.

On Wednesday morning, January 8, 1986, Eleanor and Barry Jr. were summoned to the Little House where they were met by their parents. Sallie ignored a call from her mother that morning and consequently missed the meeting.

Barry Jr. recalls:

We met at his house and we were told he had made a decision—a decision to sell everything . . . we were to get together the next day and each of us would have our press statements. I wanted to pursue the newspaper option, the stock swap, but he said no. The Thursday statements expressed my feelings at the time. Father said he was going to sell the companies, no matter what. . . . I didn't see the justification of it.[48]

The Binghams of Louisville were breaking up.

The public announcement came the following day, on January 9.

The first to hear were the managers of the Bingham companies, summoned to a meeting room at the newspaper. Editor Janensch says that despite the shock, newspaper tradition was upheld.

Just as Barry Junior mentioned the enormity of it, the managing editor of the *Louisville Times* said, "Hold it. We can still make the paper with this." He stopped the presses, ordered a replate and directly dictated a new page one as the words tumbled out of Barry Junior's mouth and the reactions swept the staff.[49]

In Barry's press statement, he shocked many by calling his father's decision "irrational" and a "betrayal." Months later, still angry, in words sounding much like those of Sallie, he refused to back down. "I had to explain my feelings at the time. At some point in life, you've got to say what you think. And that's what I think. Do I still feel my father's decision was irrational? Yes. I don't understand the justification for it."[50]

To dramatize his objection, Junior resigned in a fury and summoned employees to the newspaper cafeteria to say goodbye.

"In my proprietorship here," he said, "I've tried to operate these companies so that none of you would be ashamed of the man you work for."[51]

When he finished, the several hundred employees rose in a standing ovation. Many wept. But the applause was not entirely for Barry Jr. It was also for his stand against selling.

Yet not all were displeased to see the Binghams go.

For example, Congressman Carroll Hubbard of Kentucky, a conservative Democrat first elected in 1974, said the newspapers' sale was a cause for celebration.

There are tens of thousands of Kentuckians who are overjoyed that the Bingham family is selling. In fact, there are tens of thousands of constituents in my twenty-four-county western Kentucky district who look forward to the time when the Louisville newspapers are owned by a corporation or individuals who will give our portion of the state fair news coverage.[52]

In May 1986, the *Courier-Journal* and *Louisville Times* were sold to the Gannett Company for $307 million. Of that amount, Barry Bingham, Sr., and his wife were to realize $98.4 million from the sale. Barry Jr. would receive $29 million, while Sallie and Eleanor would receive approximately $40 million each. The balance of approximately $100 million went to pay off debts, claims, and other liabilities.[53]

The remaining properties, the television and radio stations and the Standard Gravure company, were sold later for about $133 million.

Financially, the Binghams did not suffer from the family feud. In the years prior to the sale, Barry Sr.'s children had been receiving about $300,000 a year in dividends from the Bingham companies, and Barry Jr. had a salary as a company officer in addition to that. A document prepared during negotiations for the stock swap projected his 1986 salary, with the swap or without it, at $167,000 a year.

Evaluations by five media analysts suggest that Sallie and Eleanor's total holdings will be worth $59.9 million each, with another $22 million apiece to come from a trust on the deaths of their parents. That comes to a total of $82 million, very close to the evaluation given to Sallie by her own advisers and more than twice what she had been offered by Junior and the family.[54]

Sallie has announced her plans for spending her share and it goes right to the heart of this morality play, where characters seem to represent abstractions like good and evil.

She has established a Mary Lily Bingham Trust Fund to aid women. With a $2 million annual budget, the fund sets up Mary Lily Bingham Scholarships to aid, says Sallie, "girls in middle school levels who aren't honor students but who are on the edge of achievement. The scholarship will follow them through college and graduation."

Her father's reaction was basically to grit his teeth. The name of Mary Lily Bingham is not a welcome one.

"But," counters Sallie, "the Bingham family has shortchanged her at best. Although she's barely mentioned in the family histories, her money is what started it all. I think it's time for a Bingham to give her some credit. It's a bit of justice for Mary Lily."

□

When this book was begun, little had been done for Mary Lily. She was killed. She was buried. Her fortune was divided among her heirs, all of whom prospered greatly.

To the few who had ever heard of her, she was the widow of Henry Morrison Flagler, without much history of her own. According to legend, she was a seamstress, the impoverished daughter of a once-grand Southern family gone into decline. Then Flagler came.

And now someone has truly come to her rescue. Her granddaughter by marriage establishes that a debt is owed to a kind and generous woman whose dark secret was entombed by Binghams long before Sallie was born.

That is good, for a terrible thing was done to Mary Lily.

Her love was turned against her.

It can happen to any of us.

EPILOGUE

Standard Oil created three great family fortunes: Rockefeller; Flagler, whose money drifted into the Kenan and Bingham heirs; and the Harkness fortune, deriving from the Stephen Harkness' investment which started Standard Oil.

The history of John D. Rockefeller is relatively well known. He had exceptionally talented sons and grandsons, highly publicized and effective philanthropies, and lived twenty-four years longer than Flagler. For those reasons, he became synonymous with Standard Oil. In the many histories and biographies written on Rockefeller and the great Standard machine, flagler has been given only a few sentences.

The Harkness money was mostly inherited by his son, Edward S. Harkness, who bestowed more than $200 million in a wide-ranging spread of philanthropies, most notably in donations to Yale University.

In this book, we have focused on the Flagler money and the manner in which it spread to the Binghams and Kenans.

Looking back through time, we can see that many lives were affected by the seemingly trivial event of pretty Mary Lily Kenan having met Flagler in St. Augustine in 1891. In the words of a University of North Carolina writer:

Had not the 24-year-old woman from Wilmington met Henry M. Flagler during that visit, just think how different things would have been for them, their families, and the University of North Carolina at Chapel Hill. In all likelihood, there would have been no Kenan Professorships which played a major role in transforming a good school into one of the South's top universities. The UNC football stadium probably would not be named Kenan. The Kenan family of Wilmington and Kenansville, one of North Carolina's oldest families, would never have become one of the state's wealthiest families with assets measuring in the hundreds of millions of dollars. Judge Robert W. Bingham of Louisville, Kentucky, probably would never have had the wherewithal to purchase the *Louisville Courier-Journal* and to become ambassador to the Court of St. James's.[1]

As Yale has benefited from the Harkness connection, so has the University of North Carolina from the Bingham and Kenan connections.

When Mary Lily died in 1917, she had placed as item eight in her will a bequest establishing the Kenan professorships fund. It stated that for twenty-one years, her trustees were to pay to the university the sum of $75,000 annually to "be perpetually used . . . for . . . paying the salaries of professors . . ." who were to be known as Kenan professors.

At the end of the period, the funds producing the annual sum were turned over to the university, to be administered by its board of trustees.

In writing about the Kenan Professorship, A. C. Howell, professor of English and secretary of the faculty, said, "This endowment, unusual if not unique among gifts to American state universities, has done more, perhaps, than any other single factor to secure for the University of North Carolina its distinguished position among institutions of higher learning in the United States."

The title of "Kenan Professor" has long been the most prestigious accolade the university can bestow upon a faculty member. Howell credited Colonel Robert Bingham with persuading his daughter-in-law to leave the money for faculty salaries instead of buildings.

In making her gift to the university, Mary Lily Kenan was following tradition on both sides of her family. Her mother's great-grandfather, Christopher Barbee, had donated a large part of the university campus, and her other great-great-grandfather, Brigadier General James Kenan, who fought in the American Revolution, was a university trustee before Chapel Hill was selected as its site. He was a contributor to a fund raised to erect Old East, the university's first building.

The university was further aided in 1926 by Mary Lily's brother, Will Kenan, when UNC alumni were seeking funds to build an adequate football stadium. When the alumni drive faltered, Kenan put up $275,000 to build the stadium and another $28,000 for the field house as a memorial to his parents. In later years, Kenan made additional contributions to enlarge the stadium. On his death in 1965, Kenan left the bulk of his $100 million estate to charity. The William R. Kenan Jr. Charitable Trust contributed further millions of dollars to the school, including a grant of $5 million to set up the William R. Kenan Jr. Professorships, which supplements the pay of twenty-five professors.

In 1973, UNC dedicated its new $4.2 million chemistry building and named it the William Rand Kenan Jr. Laboratories. The Charitable Trust also put up the money to build and endow a facility devoted to studying the free enterprise system. That facility likewise bears Kenan's name.[2]

□

Mary Lily's prospective home site across from Central Park in New York City was sold for $600,000 in October 1918. The seaside mansion at Mamaroneck, New York, was sold a year later for $293,000 to movie director D. W. Griffith.[3]

The naming by Mary of her brother, William, and her sisters, Jessie and Sarah Kenan, as her heirs had significant consequences for all of them.

Following Mary Lily's death, Will Kenan and his two sisters owned the Flagler System, which included the Florida East Coast Hotel Company, the Florida East Coast Railway Company (FEC), the Model Land Company, the Miami Electric Light Company, the West Palm Beach Water Company, various smaller land companies, the Florida East Coast Car Ferry Company, and several newspapers.

William assumed the presidency of the Flagler companies and maintained offices in St. Augustine, Florida, as well as New York City and later Lockport, New York.

During his tenure, the Florida East Coast Hotel Company shrunk in size and changed its name. It remains, however, in the hands of the Kenan family. Its properties include the Breakers Hotel in Palm Beach, two other hotel-type properties, a country

club, and a computer software firm which markets computer programs for resorts and hotel management.

A substantial portion of the FEC railroad, Flagler's Key West
Extension, was killed in a single terror-filled night on Labor Day,
September 2, 1935, when a hurricane smashed 41 miles of track,
depots, and stations into a jumble of twisted rails and washed out
roadbed. The dead included hundreds of World War I veterans
who had gone down to pick up depression wages by building a
federal parallel to the tracks. a total body count has never been
made.

As a railroad, Flagler's dream was dead.

In another form, however, it lived on. Florida persisted with
its highway, using Flagler's roadbed much of the way. Its viaducts,
bridges, and roadbed were used as the foundation of the overseas
highway. In 1938, the last broken link was closed and U.S. 1 was
open from Maine to Key West.

Will Kenan and his two sisters owned the Florida East Coast
Railway until it went bankrupt during the depression. Financial
entrepreneur Ed Ball, somewhat of a robber baron himself and in
command of the Alfred I. duPont estate, slowly bought the railroad's bonds until he acquired a controlling interest—purchasing
$26 million worth of bonds for less than $4 million.

Despite the loss of the FEC, however, the Kenan's Standard
Oil stock and their other properties continued to grow in value.

When Will Kenan died in 1965, he left a vast estate which
included $100 million in bequests for philanthropies. The two
sisters died shortly afterward, leaving estates of more than $160
million each and with similar philanthropic bequests.

For example, Sarah inaugurated a fund in honor of her husband, Graham, the Kenan Fellowship in Philosophy. She also
later endowed the Southern Historical Collection.[4]

□

Another principal heir, Louise Clisby Wise, gave liberally to
schools, churches, and hospitals. Otherwise, the quality of
Louise's life was not noticeably improved by the $40 million she
inherited from Mary Lily. From all accounts she chose carefully
and well the first time in marrying Lawrence Lewis, of Cincinnati.

They had two children, Lawrence Jr. and Mary Lily Flagler Lewis. Something was wrong in the union, however, and in 1926 she divorced him on the grounds of desertion. Her friends and his seemed to agree that the real reason was "too much money."

Her second marriage followed shortly afterward and was also to a man named Lewis—Hugh R. Lewis, no relation to the first, of Bear Creek, Pennsylvania. Hugh was in the ice business, but apparently not in a much bigger way than Flagler was in the grain business when he married. But again money talked too much and unhappiness came even sooner, followed by divorce. Louise's third husband was Frederick G. Francis, a resident of St. Augustine. A onetime professional baseball player, he was an alcoholic who often beat Louise. Following a drunken world tour in such widely varied climates as New York, Buenos Aires, Rome, Puerto Rico, Cairo, and Florida, the unhappy marriage was ended.

Louise Wise preferred Kirkside and St. Augustine to Palm Beach and consequently Whitehall was left vacant for seven years. She sold it, and in 1926 ten storys were added behind the mansion. The once proud home of Mary Lily became a luxury hotel, which it remained until 1959, when Mrs. Jean Flagler Matthews (1910–79), one of Flagler's three surviving granddaughters, purchased the property and caused it to be restored and converted into the magnificent Flagler Museum.

Ms. Wise died prematurely in 1937 at the age of thirty-nine.[5]

□

Sterling Ruffin, the youthful suitor of Mary Lily, became one of Washington's best-known physicians, practicing in the nation's capital for more than fifty years. He was one of the physicians who attended Woodrow Wilson during the former president's last illness. He died in June 1949 at the age of eighty-two.[6]

□

Henry Flagler's insane second wife, Ida Alice Flagler, survived not only her husband and her successor, but also many other players in the game. Still believing she was loved by the czar, she died in July 1930, leaving an estate of $12 million. It consisted almost entirely of Standard Oil stock; it had not only grown from the original $1 million set aside for her by Henry, but had paid for her care in a luxurious private cottage on the grounds of Dr. Charles W. Pilgrim's Sanatorium at Central Valley, New York.[7]

□

The Colonel, Robert Bingham, died in May 1927 at his Asheville residence, Bingham Heights, overlooking the French Broad River. He was eighty-nine and had been in declining health for three years.

Efforts in the community to keep the school in operation failed, and it permanently closed in 1930. The Bingham family retained possession of the property, however, and for years afterward, the Colonel's daughter, Mrs. R. T. Grinnan, made her residence in the picturesque but almost deserted old Bingham School building, as did his son-in-law, Colonel Sol R. McKee, and his nieces and nephews, Robert Bingham McKee, Miss Martha McKee, and Miss Sadie Temple McKee. Until World War II, the 250 acres of school land were cultivated and harvested by tenant farmers.

The structures of the old Bingham School still exist, owned now by Mr. and Mrs. Robert Kelly, who have "restored it into a bed and breakfast inn . . . with several of the original pieces of furniture from the nineteenth century still being used."[8]

The Grove Park Inn in Asheville, where Mary Lily and Bob Bingham were reunited, operates today as a luxurious year-round resort.

□

The outdoor theater on the grounds at Melcombe, built on the foundations of an old clubhouse by Thomas Hastings of Carrère and Hastings, is actively used for a variety of purposes, including the Louisville Ballet, which performs there about once a year.

□

Louisville's Seelbach Hotel, where Mary Lily was taken for her unhappy honeymoon, slowly faded after the stock market crash of 1929, passing through decades of decline. In the early 1980s, however, a group of developers headed by movie actor Roger Davis and financed to the tune of $24 million by Metropolitan Life restored the grand hostelry to the peak of its former aesthetics. A "modern" façade added in the 1950s was torn away. The old stone was stripped and new stone put on. The double entrance of the Hotel's original layout was restored. A cobblestone drive in front of the hotel on Fourth Avenue was added. The Georgian-style ballroom was fully renovated with Palladian windows, natural maple flooring, and Axminster area rugs. Today it is once again ranked among the nation's leading hotels.

□

As mentioned in the main text, a few years after Mary Lily's death, Dr. Ravitch moved from Louisville to Chicago. There he joined the staff of Michael Reese Hospital, where he remained until 1928. It is unclear where he was living the next several years, but he seems to have shuttled frequently between Los Angeles and New York, and he may possibly have made a trip to the Soviet Union.

A 1931 American Medical Association directory lists him in New York, but with no license to practice in that state. AMA directories of 1932 through 1934 show him practicing dermatology in Los Angeles. By 1936, the directories show that Ravitch had returned to New York and he retired that year from the active practice of medicine. He was seventy years old.

The following year, Ravitch published an informative but odd book on the medical history of Russia entitled *The Romance of Russian Medicine*.[9] Fully two-thirds of it consists of uncritical praise and adoration for Stalin and the wonders of Soviet medicine and the Soviet government. He closes the book with a quote from Stalin: "We must bring up a new generation—healthy, joyous, capable of increasing the power of our Soviet land. . . ." And some words of his own: "Russia is showing the way to a real democracy, where riches and class distinctions are banished and where life is made happier and more satisfying. . . . The Soviet

Government has awakened the latent genius of the Russians, and Russia is marching on and on!"[10]

Living out his retirement at various addresses on East Eightieth and Eighty-first streets, Ravitch died of coronary thrombosis in January 1947. He was seventy-nine.

□

Robert Worth Bingham's widow, Aleen, spent the years of World War II as a leader of the "Bundles for Britain" relief program and died at her Louisville home in 1953.

□

Following the sinking of the British liner *Lusitania* by a German submarine in 1915, W. W. "Dave" Davies wrote a brief demanding reparations from Germany for his sister, May Davies Hopkins, for the loss of her husband, Albert Lloyd Hopkins, who had been a passenger on the ship. His brief is said to have set the pattern for others submitted in behalf of *Lusitania* victims which later resulted in generous awards being made. Because of failing health and a desire to write, Davies retired from the practice of law in 1926 and left Louisville, for a time living in New York City. In 1928–29, he made a tour of the world and in 1939 he became a resident of New Canaan, Connecticut, thereafter dividing his time between his home there and a summer residence in New London, New Hampshire. As a pastime, he wrote on various semihistorical and fictional subjects; little of his work, however, was published. He died in New Canaan on March 1, 1945.

□

Hugh Young, friend of presidents, princes, and men and women of world renown, received the Distinguished Service Medal in World War I for his work on contagious diseases which resulted in the "conservation of manpower to a degree never before obtainable." In 1917, he founded the important *Journal of Urology*, which he edited for a number of years afterward. In 1929, he was appointed chairman of the Maryland State Aviation Commission and toured England, Italy, France, Holland, Ger-

many, and Switzerland to study their airplanes and airports. Ultimately, he became almost as prestigious in the world of aviation as
he had been in medicine. In 1941, he was one of four scientists to
receive the first Francis Amory award from the American Academy of Arts and Sciences. He retired in 1942 and died three years
later.

APPENDIX: THE COLONEL

William James, Bob Bingham's grandfather, operated the increasingly prestigious Bingham School from the time of his father's death in 1826. By the 1840s, Bingham's school could boast of pupils from almost every state in the Union, and its tuition, $150 per year, was supposedly the highest charged by any preparatory school in the nation. In the late 1850s, however, failing health increasingly caused him to turn over the duties to his sons: William, born in 1835, and Robert, born in 1838.[1]

Robert, the father of Bob Bingham and who throughout most of his adult life would be known as "the Colonel," would emerge—despite the setbacks of the Civil War and his own racist attitudes—to become a national authority on education, being an early advocate of women's colleges and free public education for blacks.

He and his brother, William, were the third generation of Binghams whose lives would be centered around the school, which would provide the mainstay of income into the 1920s.[2]

By July 1857, the two sons and the father had formed a partnership and renamed the school, W. J. Bingham and Sons. Upon graduation from the University of North Carolina the following year, Robert Bingham briefly toured Virginia to observe educational procedure at the University of Virginia and the more prominent secondary schools, and then returned to the University of North Carolina where he received a master of arts degree in 1860.[3] Classmates of his at the University of North Carolina included William Rand Kenan and Thomas Stephen Kenan, respectively the future father and uncle of Mary Lily Kenan.[4]

□

247

When the Civil War approached, the Bingham family met in council and declared its opposition to secession. On the motion of young Robert, however, the families resolved to support the state of North Carolina against the federal government, if war were declared.

In 1861, Robert Bingham courted and wed pretty Delphine Louise Worth of the Randolph County Worths, a family which was among the most patrician in the South. Her father, Bob Bingham's maternal grandfather, was John Milton Worth (1811–1900), who operated profitable cotton mills, held considerable mining interests, and would serve as state treasurer of North Carolina (1870–85).[5] Her uncle was Jonathan Worth, statesman and thirty-eighth governor of North Carolina.

Like the Binghams, the Worth families were opposed to secession, but when war broke out they, too, gave their loyalty to the Confederate government and acted in good faith toward it.[6]

Less than a year after his marriage to Delphine Worth, on March 8, 1862, Robert enlisted in state service and was elected captain of Company G, in the 44th North Carolina Infantry Regiment. His service during the war is the stuff of which legends are made.

□

The unit's first battle action came in central Virginia, some 20 miles north of Richmond, in the summertime greenness of June 1863.[7]

At the time, Robert E. Lee had launched his Army of Northern Virginia at Pennsylvania. The 44th North Carolina was assigned to guard railroad communications, centering at Hanover Junction, in order to protect Lee's communications with his base at nearby Richmond, the Confederate capital.

The area had been the scene of repeated fighting that year between the forces of Lee and Union general Ulysses Grant.

On June 26, Bingham's company occupied a small section of trenches some 300 yards north of the riverbank, on the Union side of the river. Bingham had placed his forty men about 2 feet apart, with strict instructions to take deliberate aim, but not to fire till ordered. Those dispositions had scarcely been made when what seemed to be half a world of General Phil Sheridan's cavalry delivered a charge right at Bingham's front.

According to the official regimental history, when the Union cavalrymen were within about 40 yards:

Company G received the order to fire, with quite a number of dead men and riderless horses as the result of Company G's marksmanship, most of whom could knock a squirrel out of the highest tree in the woods; and the enemy got to the rear faster and in worse order than they came. Two other frontal attacks with increased numbers were repulsed by Company G, with more deadly effect, as the men gained more confidence in their own skill and in the vulnerability of an enemy on horseback.

It was an incredibly heroic stand. For more than four hours, Union artillery pounded Bingham's small group and neighboring Company C. Eighty Confederate infantry withstood repeated charges by more than 1,200 cavalry.

"We had some excellent target practice while the Federals were charging up the bank of the river, emptying a good many saddles," recalled Bingham.

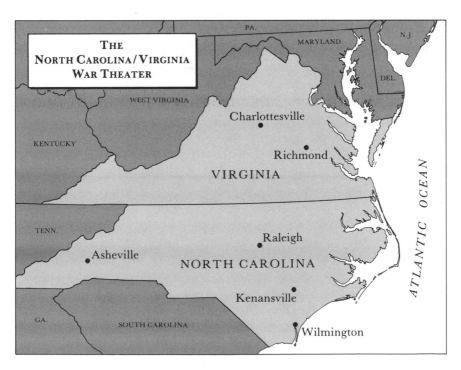

THE
NORTH CAROLINA/VIRGINIA
WAR THEATER

Part of the Southern success came because the Federals were so much in each other's way they could not shoot without hitting their own men. Finally, at the abutment of the bridge, with the odds increased to thirty to one, the fight reached its last desperate minutes—hand-to-hand fighting with saber, pistol, and bayonet. Inevitably, the Federals closed on Company G's front and rear and, encircling them with drawn pistols and carbines, demanded an immediate surrender. Further resistance being useless, Bingham ordered his men to throw down their guns. The stand at South Anna Bridge became famous and allowed Lee's army to pass onto the south side of the river and preserve its communications with Richmond.

Now began imprisonment and what Bingham in an essay would later call "our escape from the gallows." Here, in his words, is the tale:

The privates were sent to Fort Monroe and were soon exchanged; but the seven officers of the 44th and ten more from other commands were put into close confinement in Fort Norfolk to be hanged as hostages, on this wise. . . . The so-called Fort Norfolk was not a fort, but was intended only for the storage of ammunition. The seventeen prisoners of war . . . were put into close confinement in a room seventeen feet square, with only one window two and one half feet square and so heavily barred as to leave only half the space open for air and light. The pitch of the room was so low that I had to stoop to pass under the joists. There was no ceiling and there was a slate roof over us. We passed the 4th of July, 1863, in this place of torment with a temperature of 140 degrees.

They fed us on sour loaf bread, rancid pickled beef and "tea" made of the leaves of blackberry bushes, with the blackberry briers in evidence on every "tea" leaf. The heat was so great that we could not bear a stitch of clothing on us, and were all perfectly nude. The only thing which prevented the gallows from being cheated by the conditions of our confinement was an abundance of excellent cistern water. This saved our lives. . . . Our party of seventeen men was sent first to Fort Delaware, where we were guarded by Negroes, and then to Johnson's Island [in Lake Erie, near Sandusky, Ohio]. In July we endured a temperature of 140 degrees under a slate roof. In January we endured a temperature of 30 degrees below zero.[8]

Bingham won his freedom through the friendship of a young Southern woman, Miss Lida Tarring, who was living with relatives in Ohio. "She was a beautiful girl of 20 who came often into the hospital and was a ray of golden sunshine and an Angel of Mercy to the prisoners." [9]

At the time, Bingham was making dental fixtures for the prisoners and "she came almost every day to my little work bench and I made trinkets for her—inlaying rings, breastpins, earrings, etc., with Lake Erie shell showing most of the colors of the rainbow." Lida tried to pay him with money, but Bingham declined saying, "I had everything I needed but freedom." [10]

In April 1864, a group of "very sick and badly crippled" prisoners was being prepared for exchange with similar prisoners held in the South.

One Confederate captain proved too ill to go and [the doctor], at Miss Tarring's suggestion, asked if I could be ready to take the sick man's place in ten minutes. I was ready in five minutes, got to Richmond on the first of May 1864, and was exchanged in time to be in ten pitched battles during the siege of Richmond and Petersburg. [11]

Even in war, the paths of the Binghams and the Kenans crossed. Although not mentioned in Bingham's memoirs, among the seventeen officers held at Fort Norfolk as hostages and then transferred to the hell of Johnson's Island was Colonel Thomas Stephen Kenan, Mary Lily's future uncle and commander of the 43rd North Carolina Regiment. He was captured in the Battle of Gettysburg, July 3, 1863. Unlike Bingham, he was unable to obtain release and remained a prisoner of war on Johnson's Island until March 1865, when he was paroled. [12]

□

Returning to his regiment, Bingham went immediately to Lee's command where the Confederates had set up a series of fortifications and trenches stretching 25 miles from Richmond to Petersburg. The main defense line, established behind the James and Appomattox rivers, took advantage of the many natural barriers and was supplied by a major railroad running behind the front lines.

The final chapter of the war was a textbook campaign, perhaps the greatest of Lee's career, a series of faultless examples of how to use small resources to baffle overwhelming force. Grant, attempting to deal a death blow to the rebellion with his flesh and blood hammer, believing brute force to be the only way to success, was constantly thwarted by Lee, maneuvering with brilliance behind his seemingly impregnable line. Finally, in the gloomy midsummer of 1864, frustrated by the defenses and growing impatient with his generals, Grant reluctantly approved a plan to tunnel beneath the Confederate trenches and blow up a key Confederate fort at Petersburg.

As chance would have it, the defender of that fort was twenty-five-year-old Captain Robert Bingham.

The project, which would become known as the "Petersburg Crater," was proposed and carried out by a regiment of Pennsylvania coal miners. Although the miners did their job ingeniously and well, there was mismanagement by the generals.[13]

Initially, the project was deemed impossible. No such tunnel could exceed 400 feet in length, the experts said, because that was the limit at which fresh air could be provided without ventilation shafts. The proposed tunnel was projected to extend more than 511 feet. The miners, however, overcame this by devising a fireplace near the entrance which sent heated air up its brush-masked chimney, creating a draft that drew the stale air from the far end of the tunnel and pulled in fresh air.[14]

The plan called for tunneling 20 feet down and then 511 feet horizontally until the miners could reach a position beneath the fort. There they were to pack 4 tons of explosives—320 kegs of black powder, weighing 25 pounds each—among eight connected magazines, sandbagged to direct the explosion upward.

On the morning of July 30, 1864, the powder was exploded. When the blast erupted, there was "a slight tremor of the earth for a second, then the rocking as of an earthquake." An awed captain would recall:

And with a tremendous blast which rent the sleeping hills beyond, a vast column of earth and smoke shoots upward to a great height, its dark sides flashing out sparks of fire, hangs poised for a moment in mid-air, and then, hurtling down with a roaring sound, showers of stones, broken timbers and blackened human limbs, subsides—the gloomy pall of darkening smoke flushing to an angry crimson as it floats away to meet the morning sun.[15]

The explosion, the biggest of the war, was to be the signal for four divisions of Union troops to storm across the gap and forever break the Confederate lines.

When the fort blew up, however, the stormers, instead of advancing, huddled in the crater, held in awe by what they saw before them. Where the Confederate fort had stood there now was a monstrous crater, 60 feet across and nearly 200 feet wide, ranging in depth from 10 to 30 feet. To make matters worse, the frightened leader of the Union attack hid in a bomb-proof shelter in the rear.

Meanwhile, more than 10,000 men were crowded shoulder to shoulder in a steep-walled hole smaller than a football field. Bingham found before him a compact target his cannoneers could not miss. The Confederates massed around the rim of the crater and picked off the troops with artillery and rifle fire, resulting in 4,000 Federals sacrificed and no advantage gained. A furious Grant pronounced it "the saddest affair I have witnessed in this war."[16]

Bingham's men held the breach against all assaults for six weeks.

During the rest of the year and the following spring, the Federals pounded repeatedly at the Richmond-Petersburg line. Grant laid down the longest siege in American war history—nine months of ghastly pounding which cost the lives of 70,000 men. Finally, on April 7, 1865, with his best generals in the field, including Sheridan and Sherman, Grant carried the entrenchments at Petersburg. The following day, Lee evacuated Richmond, the beginning of the end.

Events moved swiftly.

Lee's ragged troops, including Bingham's unit, retreated to Appomattox station, some 90 miles west of the old Richmond-Petersburg line.

At daybreak, Palm Sunday, April 9, the starved and ragged Confederates surrendered.

About 1:30 P.M., Lee and Grant met at the house of a man named McLean. Lee was carefully dressed in a brand-new uniform. Grant wore his working clothes, the mud-spattered outfit of a private, bearing merely the shoulder straps of a lieutenant general.

□

Lee reviewed his troops for the last time, riding between solid walls of soldiers who cried out that they would fight on if he wished them to and wept as he passed.[17]

Bingham was among those troops: "I had the great honor," he recalled, "of being one of General Lee's 7,892 armed men at Appomattox Courthouse, surrounded by about 200,000 men, including Hunter's Army from Tennessee, whose presence in General Lee's front with Grant's Army in his rear and on both flanks, determined the surrender on April 9th." [18]

Elsewhere he said, "I saw the last sun rise on the army of Northern Virginia. I was one of Lee's armed men at Appomattox Courthouse, who never bowed the knee to any, but fought to the bitter end." [19]

He left the field with his horse, and the regimental flag.

"The 44th regiment which General MacRae always made the center of his brigade, never lost a flag to the enemy, and we never charged the enemy without their giving way in our front. But our first flag was so mutilated by shot and shell that it was too small to be of service as an ensign any longer, and during the winter of 1864–65 a new regimental Flag was issued." [20]

More than seventy years after the fact, Bob Bingham bitterly related his father's adventures to Margaret Mitchell, author of the novel, *Gone With the Wind*.

My father commanded the 44th North Carolina Infantry before he was twenty-four. He was a prisoner on Johnson's Island in Lake Erie, where hundreds of his fellow prisoners starved and froze to death.

He was at Appomattox, and came home, lousy, ragged, hungry and barefooted to the wreck left by Sherman. . . .

My father was hunted with bloodhounds by Kirk's raiders. When he turned his face homeward from Appomattox, he had nothing except the remnant of the battle flag of his regiment. Nine men were shot down carrying that flag in one battle. The survivors of the regiment—how few there were—met after the war and gave it to my Mother, who had nursed the sick and wounded at Petersburg. I have it to pass on to my son and my son's son.[21]

Robert Bingham returned to a devastated countryside and a reversal of the political order. On the death of his father in 1866, he became co-principal with his brother, William, of the Bingham School. Robert and Delphine took rooms at the school, by that time located in the community of Mebane, Orange County, North Carolina, just north of Chapel Hill and the university. There they began their household. They had five children, four of whom survived to maturity. On November 8, 1871, their first, a son, was born. They baptized him Robert Worth Bingham.

ACKNOWLEDGMENTS

In compiling this book, Mary Voelz Chandler and I found the people of Louisville to be extraordinarily helpful. Chronologically, the assistance and courtesies began in the summer of 1984 with Sallie Bingham, granddaughter of Judge Robert Worth Bingham, who shared information, scrapbooks, family tales, and photographs.

Initially, we also received courteous and helpful cooperation from her father, Barry Bingham, Sr. Although Mr. Bingham and we disagree on the perception of *his* father, Judge Robert Worth Bingham, he nevertheless patiently responded to every question put to him, either in personal interviews or by correspondence. In addition, he provided access to the library of the *Louisville Courier-Journal* and the *Louisville Times* where, during the difficult period when the Binghams were selling off their communications properties, we were assisted with keen competence by Berenice Franklin, manager of Library Photo Services.

The major documentary source of information on Judge Bingham, his first wife, Eleanor Long Miller, and the history of Louisville in the period prior to 1918, came from the Filson Club, a museum and library where James J. Holmberg, curator of manuscripts, expertly and patiently guided us through the thousands of documents which comprise The Bingham Papers Collection.

The major source on the career of Robert Worth Bingham after 1918 was the Library of Congress, where resides The Bingham Collection, comprised of 10,000 documents on the Judge's career, including his correspondence with President Roosevelt while Bingham was the American ambassador to Great Britain. For considerable help in navigating those waters we are indebted to Fred Pauls, chief of the government division of the Congressional Research Services.

□

The major source on the Kenan family was the Flagler Museum in Palm Beach, Florida.

Housed in the luxurious setting of the restored Whitehall mansion, over the years it has become the central repository for the various collections of letters, newspaper clippings, photographs, paintings, business records, and official documents concerning the Kenan and Flagler families. The museum's director, Charles Simmons, and curator, Joan Runkel, gave invaluable guidance through the tens of thousands of documents, artifacts, and photographs which needed to be sifted before the writing could begin.

After the original research was done, they cheerfully and patiently responded to almost weekly requests for photographs, documents, and arcane questions on every facet of the families' histories.

Much published misinformation on Mary Lily Kenan was corrected by her cousin, Thomas S. Kenan III, an authority not only on the Kenan family but also on Henry Flagler, having been a board member of the Flagler Museum.

□

In addition, we would like to thank:

Kathie Steele, Jefferson County Public Library in Evergreen, Colorado, who, using the interlibrary loan system, was able to come up with some hard-to-find books and magazine articles.

I. Donald Bowden, Wide World Photos, Associated Press, New York City.

Lewis A. Buck, North Carolina Collection, Pack Memorial Library, Asheville, North Carolina.

Jerry Cotten, photo archivist, the University of North Carolina, Chapel Hill, North Carolina.

Hotel developer Roger Davis, Louisville, Kentucky.

Herman Ashley duBois.

Milton Gustafson, chief of the diplomatic branch, National Archives, Washington, D.C.

Elizabeth M. Holsten, head of the Alumni Archives at the University of North Carolina, Chapel Hill.

J. Shields Kenan, Statesboro, Georgia.

Dr. Sherrill Redmon, archivist, the Kornhauser Health Services Library, University of Louisville.

Lynne S. Renau, curator, the Filson Club.

Attorney J. Minos Simon of Lafayette, Louisiana.

Gerard Shorb of the Alan Mason Chesney Medical Archives at Johns Hopkins University, Baltimore, Maryland.

Eric Vaughan Voelz, assistant chief, civilian reference branch, National Personnel Records Center, National Archives and Records Administration, St. Louis, Missouri.

John R. Ward, Kentucky division, Louisville Free Public Library.

Frances A. Weaver, assistant university archivist at the University of North Carolina, Chapel Hill.

☐

For assistance in analyzing the medical condition of Mary Lily, I invoked the aid of three specialists, dermatologist Larry Seitz of Cheyenne, Wyoming; dermatologist and medical historian John Wolf of Houston, Texas; and cardiologist Lawrence O'Meallie of New Orleans. All offered guidance against any glaring mistakes on my part. Any errors, large or small, are mine, not theirs.

☐

All of the above were especially generous in their time, their courtesy, and their knowledge; and a great pleasure of doing this book was the opportunity to meet or correspond with them.

DAVID CHANDLER
February 1987

NOTES

CHAPTER 1 *The Knave of Hearts*

1. Interviews by author with Sallie Bingham, May 1984 through February 1986.

2. *New York Times,* January 19, 1986.

3. Marketed under the trade name of Mercurochrome, it was an organic mercury compound that was commonly used on wounds as an antibacterial agent. Hugh Hampton Young, 1870–1945, also devised many new surgical techniques and was the inventor of several surgical instruments, including the "boomerang" needle for sewing deep incisions. He spent most of his medical career associated with the John Hopkins Hospital in Baltimore, Maryland, where he was head of urological surgery and director of the James Buchanan Brady Urological Institute, the famed Brady Clinic, endowed by James B. "Diamond Jim" Brady, one of Young's patients.

4. Hugh Young, *Hugh Young, A Surgeon's Autobiography* (New York: Harcourt, Brace and Company, 1940), page 515. Hereafter referred to as Young Autobiography.

5. For more details on Bingham's final days, see *Charlotte Observer,* July 6, 1941; *Louisville Courier-Journal,* December 19, 1937; and *New York Times,* December 19, 1937.

6. See Arthur Spalding Papers, part of the Flagler Collection, Flagler Museum, Palm Beach, Florida. Her properties included the Florida East Coast Railroad, the Florida East Coast Hotel Company, the Miami Power and Water Company (which later became the monolithic Florida Power & Light), the Model Land Company, P&O Steamship Lines, and numerous mansions and private properties.

7. There are two main families of Binghams in America. The earliest to arrive were the descendants of Thomas Bingham of Sheffield, England, who came to America in 1659 and whose line includes the Binghams of Connecticut and the Mormon Binghams of Utah. The second branch emigrated from Ireland in the eighteenth century and descendants include the Binghams of North Carolina and Kentucky. See James Barry Bingham, comp., *Descendants of James Bingham of County Down, Northern Ireland* (Baltimore, Md: Gateway Press, 1980). Hereafter referred to as Bingham Genealogy.

8. *New York Herald,* November 5, 1916.

9. After Henry Flagler's death in 1913, Mary Lily was termed by the press, "The richest woman in the world." Her closest rival, supposedly, was Mrs. Edward Henry Harriman, widow of the nineteenth-century railroad tycoon and mother of William Averill Harriman, the latter being governor of New York and prominent Democratic politician and diplomat from the Roosevelt New Deal through the Kennedy era.

10. Letter dated May 8, 1986, from Barry Bingham, Sr., to author.

11. Interview with Sallie Bingham, August 1984.

12. Interview by author, January 1986.

13. Interview by author, October 1985.

14. Sallie Bingham, private collection: Memo dated June 26, 1974, from Barry Bingham, Sr., to Barry Jr., Sallie, Eleanor, and Joan Bingham, re the Judge's illness and career.

15. Bingham Genealogy.

CHAPTER 2 *The Binghams*

1. William Bingham was one of four brothers who, in the late eighteenth century, came to America, apparently at the same time. Accounts differ as to the precise year of their arrival. A three-volume history, *The Bingham Family in America*, published privately by Theodore Alfred Bingham in the 1920s, gives the date of 1793, which seems too late because it gives William Bingham too little time to begin his educational career in North Carolina. Robert Worth Bingham, after consulting family records and professional geneal-ogists, postulated that William "came to America about 1780 and he had some brothers who came to this country also. . . ." That date seems too early, however, for several reasons: (1) it contradicts University of Glasgow sources, which place William in Ireland at the time; (2) immigration was particularly risky in 1780 and 1781, those years marking the height of the American Revolution, with sea and land battles raging up and down the Carolinas; and (3) all sources, including Robert Worth Bingham, identify William Bingham as a member of the United Irishmen, a group seeking Irish independence from England, which wasn't founded until 1791. The comprehensive Bingham Genealogy gives a date of 1785 (page 6), which seems too early because of the United Irishmen connection. However, the same genealogy records (page 8) a 1963 letter from the University of Glas-gow, which states William Bingham remained a "Presbyterian minister in his native coun-try till 1793." In context, the reference is somewhat ambiguous and may only mean that Bingham was an ordained Irish minister in 1793 but was not necessarily in Ireland. After weighing the various arguments, this author has settled on 1791 as the best estimate of William Bingham's emigration.

2. The First Congress of the United States of America convened on April 6, 1789, at Federal Hall in New York City. In 1790, the seat of government was shifted to Philadelphia where it remained until 1800, when it was moved to Washington, D.C. The man who in effect began the government of the United States under the present Constitution was Senator Richard Henry Lee of Virginia, he being the twelfth senator to present his creden-tials and thus constitute a quorum enabling the Congress to begin. Although the timing was accidental, there was a certain political symmetry in the government being delayed until Lee's arrival. He was the man who in the Second Continental Congress (1776) intro-duced the Declaration of Independence, announcing the creation of the new nation.

3. Settled by Americans but not yet officially part of the new nation was the Northwest Territory, consisting of the present states of Ohio, Indiana, Illinois, Michigan, Wisconsin, and eastern Minnesota. The territory was officially ceded to the United States by Great Britain in the Jay Treaty of 1795. The only other land east of the Mississippi not held by Americans in 1791 was the Spanish territory of Florida, comprising the present state of Florida and parts of southern Alabama and Mississippi. The Florida territory was ceded in 1819.

4. Filson Club Collection, Bingham Papers: Letter dated September 4, 1905, from Robert Worth Bingham to Solicitor R. Diamond, Belfast, Ireland. Traditional sources and Bingham family histories have given the matriculation dates as ten years later, from 1784 to 1788. Robert Worth Bingham, however, not only conducted personal research but hired genealogical investigators. Having that work at hand, plus family records and traditional sources, he concluded that his forebear attended the university from 1774 to 1778, which would have been about the right age for a lad born in 1754, the authenticated birth date of William Bingham. Robert Worth Bingham also notes that his great grandfather "matricu-lated" rather than graduated. The dates and failure to graduate are confirmed in a 1977 University of Glasgow letter reported in Bingham Genealogy, page 8.

5. Biographical sketch of William Bingham from William S. Powell, ed., *Dictionary of North Carolina Biography* (Chapel Hill: University of North Carolina Press, 1979).

6. Bingham Genealogy, page 5.

7. Ibid.

8. *Charlotte Observer,* July 6, 1941.

9. Bingham Genealogy.

10. Biographical sketch of William Bingham from Powell, *Dictionary of North Carolina Biography.*

11. According to the Bingham Genealogy (page 10), Colonel Slingsby "fell" near the end of the Revolutionary War in the Battle of Elizabethtown, which would be more than fifteen years before his daughter married William Bingham. The word *fell,* however, may indicate a wound rather than death because the same reference states that William and Annie Bingham became the principal heirs to Slingsby's English estate after at least two of their children were born, suggesting that Slingsby died in 1802 or afterward. Other sources, such as Powell's *Dictionary of North Carolina Biography,* seem to confirm that interpretation, stating that following the war Slingsby settled in the Cape Fear area of North Carolina.

12. Biographical sketch of William Bingham from Powell, *Dictionary of North Carolina Biography,* and Bingham Genealogy. Following William Bingham's death, the mother, two daughters, and a third son, physician Robert Slingsby Bingham, moved to Henry County, Tennessee. The relative impoverishment of the Tennessee Binghams is suggested by Annie Bingham's 1859 will, recorded on page 10 of the Bingham Genealogy. In it, Annie leaves her estate, including slaves, to the daughters and to Dr. Bingham, noting that her other two children, William and John, are already in comfortable circumstances.

CHAPTER 3   *The Kenans*

1. North Carolina being the site of Sir Walter Raleigh's ill-fated colony on Roanoke Island in 1587 and the birthplace of Virginia Dare, the first white child of English descent born in America. When Raleigh's relief ships returned to Roanoke Island four years later, in 1591, the colony had mysteriously vanished and the sole clue to its fate was the word *Croatan* inscribed on a tree. The fate of the colonists, including Virginia Dare, and the mystery of their disappearance haven't been solved.

2. Alvaretta Kenan Register, comp., *The Kenan Family and Some Allied Families* (privately published by James Shields Kenan II, Statesboro, Ga., 1967). Hereafter referred to as Register's Genealogy. According to Ms. Register, accounts of the dates of arrival vary from 1730 to 1735 to 1738. She hypothesizes that the brothers arrived at different times.

3. Ibid. The name Kenan is found in the Bible, fourth in Adam's line to Noah. See First Chronicles, 1st Chapter, 1st Verse.

4. Ibid.

5. Ibid.

6. The Stamp Act required the purchase of a British government stamp for all publications and legal documents in the colonies. The colonials responded with demonstrations like that of James Kenan, culminating in a Stamp Act Congress held in New York City in October 1765. The congress, the first held by American colonies, declared that, as free English citizens, they could not be taxed without representation in the British Parliament and as no such representation existed, the tax was unlawful. The Parliament, fearing a trade boycott and having no desire for colonial representation, repealed the Stamp Act in 1766.

7. One of the Atlantic Coast's principal deep-water ports, Wilmington was captured by the British in 1780 and became Cornwallis' headquarters. It was a principal port of the Confederacy and kept open until 1865 when captured by Union forces. The town, noted for its beautiful central plaza with formal gardens and walks, remains an important maritime center.

8. This original Liberty Hall appears to have been located near the present town of Turkey, North Carolina, and burned to the ground prior to 1800. A better-known Liberty Hall is a museum in Kenansville, North Carolina. It is an eleven-room Greek Revival house

built in the early 1800s and there is some dispute as to who built it. According to museum publications, it was built about 1818 by Thomas Kenan II, grandson of the Scottish immigrant. Thomas' son Owen made structural improvements resulting in the house which can be seen today. However, according to Register's Genealogy, Thomas Kenan II never lived in the house; it also states that the house was built about 1830 by Owen. Both versions agree that it was Owen who named it Liberty Hall, after the original manor house. Liberty Hall was a social center for Kenansville for a century or more and remained in the Kenan family until 1964 when Owen's grandchildren restored it and dedicated it as a memorial museum.

9. Interview with Tom Kenan III, Chapel Hill, North Carolina. Mr. Kenan is the family historian.

10. Register's Genealogy.

11. Ibid.

12. Ibid.

13. Following his release from Johnson's Island, Colonel Kenan entered politics, serving terms in the state legislature, 1865–67; as mayor of Wilson, North Carolina, 1872–76; as attorney general of North Carolina, 1876–84; and then as clerk of the North Carolina Supreme Court. For many years he was a trustee of the University of North Carolina. He died December 11, 1911, some six weeks prior to his seventy-fourth birthday.

14. Thomas S. Kenan III, *Sarah Graham Kenan Foundation* (privately printed, Chapel Hill, 1984).

15. Register's Genealogy.

16. Numerous sources comment on Mary Lily's beauty and musical talents, including Register's Genealogy and the Arthur Spalding Diaries, the latter stored at the Flagler Museum, Palm Beach, Florida.

17. Interview with Tom Kenan. Mr. Kenan obtained Mary Lily's height and weight by measuring her wedding dress, which was designed in 1901.

18. See Ruffin Papers, Flagler Collection, Flagler Museum, Palm Beach, Florida. Letter dated January 8, 1885, from Sterling Ruffin to Annie Carrie Ruffin Sims, his sister, Wilson, North Carolina. Ruffin became a medical power in Washington, D.C., and doctor to several presidents, including being private physician to President Woodrow Wilson. In his letter, Ruffin says: "About my own affair! Ha, I wish I had something to tell. Last Summer, thinking there was safety in numbers, I had three at once! The names of these pretty maids were as follows, Mena Branch, Mary Lily Kenan and May Mennimon (two years too old). May gave the go by in September. I gave it to Mary Lily. What Mena is doing I don't know. . . . [Mena] was highly indignant because she heard I wrote the same thing to three girls! I knew Mary Lily told her this, so I wrote pretending I had no idea who the originator of such a tale was for it was false, and gave her informant 'hail Columbia.' This made Mena the madder, for she and Mary Lily are one and inseparable. Accordingly, she treated me with silent contempt. . . ."

19. Although John D. Rockefeller is popularly credited with starting Standard Oil, Rockefeller shares credit with his partner, Flagler. See John D. Rockefeller, *Random Reminiscences of Men and Events* (Tarrytown, N.Y.: Sleepy Hollow Press, 1984).

20. Jones was president of the South's largest rice shipping firm, Standard Rice Company, with headquarters in Wilmington, New Orleans, and New York.

21. Noel Yancey, "The Kenan Legacy," in University of North Carolina *Spectator*, March 20, 1986.

22. David Leon Chandler, *Flagler* (New York: Macmillan Publishing, 1986).

23. The date of the first meeting is listed in Register's Genealogy and several other sources.

24. Flagler had turned sixty-one on January 2. Mary Lily would become twenty-four on June 14.

25. For a fuller description, see Julian Ralph, "Our Own Riviera," *Harper's*, vol. 86, no. 514 (March 1893).

26. John T. Flynn, *God's Gold, the Story of Rockefeller and His Times* (New York: Harcourt, Brace and Company, 1932), page 125.

27. See Chandler, *Flagler*.

CHAPTER 4   *Passions*

1. Sallie Bingham, private collection: Letter dated February 16, 1937, from Robert Worth Bingham to Margaret Mitchell. Hereafter referred to as Mitchell Letter.

2. Ibid. Melanie was the role played by actress Olivia de Havilland in the 1939 film, *Gone With the Wind*.

3. Sallie Bingham, private collection: Letter dated February 23, 1937, response from Margaret Mitchell Marsh to Robert Worth Bingham. Hereafter referred to as Mitchell Response. Mrs. Marsh's reply, written some eighteen months before her best-selling novel was made into one of Hollywood's greatest movies, is of historical interest inasmuch as it sheds light on her motives in writing the book and her view of the book's characters. Here, in part, is the text of her reply to Ambassador Bingham.

> Your letter arrived at a fortunate time. On the day it came I had been harried and upset by totally false rumors that I was in Reno divorcing my husband. Naturally, all the news services had me on the wire for a confirmation or denial of this rumor. As I have had no thought of divorcing John and was not in Reno, I was greatly disturbed. That morning I began wishing that I had never written "Gone With the Wind," because its success has disrupted the peace and quiet of my old life which was so dear to me. Then your letter arrived, and after I read it I was so very proud and so very glad that I had written a book that could call forth such a response. I felt that the years of labor that went into "Gone With the Wind" were years well spent. May I thank you for insisting to me that Melanie was beautiful? Of course, I had pictured her as a very plain little person but in my heart I thought her beautiful too. I had known so many plain-faced elderly ladies when I was a child who were beautiful from the inner glow of their lovely souls, so I am glad if the inner glow of Melanie was apparent. You could not have complimented me more than by putting Melanie in the same class with your mother. So many people, Southerners among them, have chided me for drawing "a bad woman" for my heroine and have said that I set up Scarlett as a "typical Southern woman" and thereby cast aspersions on all Southern ladies of bygone days. Of course this was not my intention and I could not help finding such remarks a trifle upsetting. I was bothered because these people fastened their eyes on Scarlett and her didoes and seemed to miss Melanie and Ellen and the stout-hearted Atlanta matrons who defied the shells and took care of the wounded and defied poverty to rebuild on their old foundations. Thank you for seeing this side of my picture. I shall long remember your phrases, "the poverty and the pride, the gentility, the gracious manners, the romance, the preservation of dignity and high and generous humanity in rags and semi-starvation." I, too, had heard those stories. I was raised upon them as a child. Visiting about the South I had seen many old ladies and gentlemen who were poor in purse and rich in everything that mattered. I wanted to write them into my story, and your letter made me feel that I had succeeded. . . ."

4. Robert Bingham, "An Ex-Slaveholder's View of the Negro Question in the South." *Harper's Monthly Magazine*, July 1900.

5. Ibid.

6. The Ku Klux Klan of the 1870s, of course, was distinct from the terrorist organization of the same name which operated in the twentieth century. The modern klans generally trace their origins to a klan founded by William Simmons in a ceremony at Stone Mountain, Georgia, in 1915.

7. The riders brought harsh retribution. In April 1871, four months before Bob was born, Congress passed the Ku Klux Klan Act, which even more greatly strengthened the hands of the national judiciary and authorized the president to suspend the habeas corpus, thus allowing people to be arrested without charges, and suppress disturbances by military force. This was in great part in reaction to klan activity in North and South Carolina. For example, in October 1871, nine counties of South Carolina were proclaimed to be in rebellion and the writ of habeas corpus was suspended. Detachments of federal troops arrested nearly a thousand persons on suspicions of rebellion. Most were held in prisons for months without charges then released. Only a very few were actually charged and

brought to trial. Even fewer were convicted. Other enforcement laws permitted the use of federal troops without reference to the Klan act and in the ordinary process of criminal justice, and at every election, the interposition of federal marshals accompanied by federal troops was a normal incident. Under cover of protecting the black voter, the control of the local electoral machinery was centralized at the state capitals, and extraordinary facilities for fraud were embodied in the laws regulating both the casting and the counting of the ballots. Every election, state or national, was attended by charges on both sides of fraud, intimidation, and outrage.

8. Bingham, "An Ex-Slaveholder's View of the Negro Question in the South."

9. Ibid.

10. Ibid.

11. By 1876, the American public had had its fill of Republican excesses. In the presidential election of that year, the two major issues were the corruption of Grant's administration and the Republican-controlled Congress' doctrine of reconstruction. After two terms, Grant was too tainted for reelection and also was blocked by a tradition, dating back to George Washington (and terminated by Franklin Roosevelt in 1940), which said no president should have three consecutive terms. Accordingly, the Grand Old Party put up Hayes, a Civil War hero and three-times governor of Ohio. Opposing Hayes was Democrat Tilden, a New York lawyer, former New York governor, and a reformer who had exposed several of the era's biggest corruption scandals, including that of the infamous Boss Tweed political machine in New York City.

The election that followed was a scandal bigger than even the Tweed Ring could imagine. Tilden won the vote, both popular and electoral, but was denied the presidency. Tilden received 250,000 more popular votes than Hayes and led in electoral votes, 184 to 163. However, returns were in dispute in four states: Oregon, Florida, South Carolina, and Louisiana.

Hayes needed all the disputed electoral votes to win and that's exactly what the Republican-ruled Congress gave him: *all* the votes. The steal was made possible by behind-the-scenes agreements with the delegates from South Carolina and Louisiana not to contest the electoral count. In return, the Republicans would remove all federal troops from the Southern states.

12. Mitchell Letter.

13. Young Autobiography, page 504.

14. Interview with Charles Mangum in the *Raleigh Daily News*, December 25, 1951.

15. General Alumni Association files, University of North Carolina. Comment by Andrews is contained in Class of 1891 photo caption.

16. Mangum interview.

17. Two memorials of the Bingham name are preserved at Chapel Hill. One is Bingham Hall, named by the trustees in honor of Colonel Bingham, which houses the School of Commerce. The other is the Bingham Prize in Debate, donated by Robert Worth Bingham in 1899. Bob Bingham won the Representative Medal in 1890 for his oration "Manifest Destiny and Manifest Duty."

18. Academic record, Robert Worth Bingham, University of North Carolina, 1888–91. In a cover letter, Frances Weaver, assistant university archivist, notes that Bingham "did not take as many courses as his college contemporaries."

19. *The Tar Heel*, July 17, 1980. Named after an alleged seventeenth-century legend of the ghostly city Gimghoul, the fraternity was formally chartered in 1899. Since 1926, it has been lodged in Gimghoul Castle, a stone replica of a Norman castle built by students and alumni and located about half a mile east of the UNC campus on Hippol Road.

20. Bingham's résumé on file with the State Department listed his graduation from the University of North Carolina; Bingham Collection, Library of Congress, Manuscript Division. According to records from the universities of North Carolina, Virginia, Michigan,

and Louisville, Bingham's academic career began with his graduation in 1888 from the Bingham School. He entered the University of North Carolina as a second-year student for the school year 1888–89, taking five subjects the first semester, four the second. As a third-year student, in 1889–90, records from University Affairs: Student Records and Faculty Reports from the UNC archives, show he took four courses during the first semester, but none during the second, and did not return as a fourth-year student. Therefore he was enrolled at UNC for four semesters but actually took classes only for the first three. In September 1890, Bingham enrolled at the University of Virginia, taking courses which included anatomy, chemistry, biology, and philosophy. He left the school in July 1891. Bingham returned to UNC to attend summer law school in July and August 1896, then transferred to the University of Louisville and attended that school's Law Department in the 1896–97 academic year, graduating in the spring of 1897. The University of Louisville associate archivist, Thomas L. Owen, notes: "Since he [Bingham] didn't appear on a 1895–96 student list, I think that it is likely that he compressed the two-session course into a single session—which appears possible according to the . . . course plan." Records from the office of the registrar at the University of Michigan show that Bingham registered for one course through the College of Literature, Science and the Arts during the summer session of 1899, but did not complete the course.

21. Davies stayed on for another year to receive a law degree, then moved to Atlanta, Georgia, where he entered a law partnership with attorney Shepard Bryan.

22. Peace Institute, now called Peace College, was founded in 1857 by William Peace, an elder of the First Presbyterian Church of Raleigh. The Bingham sisters later married, becoming Mrs. Sadie Grinnan and Mrs. Mary McKee, both of Asheville, North Carolina.

23. Ralph, "Our Own Riviera."

24. "The New South," an address by Colonel Robert Bingham of the Bingham School, Asheville, North Carolina, in the interest of National Aid to Education. Delivered February 15, 1884, in Washington, D.C., before the Superintendents' Department of the National Educational Association, and repeated in Madison, Wisconsin, before the National Association, on July 16, 1884; Pack Memorial Library, Asheville, North Carolina. Hereafter referred to as *The New South*.

25. Kenan Papers, Flagler Museum, Palm Beach, Florida.

26. After completing postgraduate work at Johns Hopkins University in 1895, Hugh Young was assistant resident surgeon at that institution during 1895–98. In the latter year he became chief of the department and professor of urology of Johns Hopkins University and Hospital and was also director of the Brady Urological Institute, Baltimore. Young's field was restricted to urological surgery, in which department of medicine he was recognized as an authority, both in this country and in Europe. He was especially noted for new operations for prostatic diseases and patients came to him from all parts of the world. His most important contribution to urologic surgery was his radical operation for cancer of the prostate, reported in 1904, which to the time of his death had been altered only in minor points. Through numerous clinical papers, Young proved to the medical world that it was possible to cure, with intravenous injections of Mercurochrome, many previously incurable infectious diseases. He also invented numerous surgical instruments, operating tables, and other surgical apparatus. He was the author of over 300 articles relating to the surgery of the prostate gland and kidneys and to the treatment of the various diseases of the genito-urinary tract. A two-volume treatise entitled *Young's Practice of Urology* was published in 1926. Young's autobiography was published in 1940.

27. Young Autobiography.

28. Ibid.

29. Ibid.

30. Many sources attribute the breakup of the romance to Kenan family objections to Bob Bingham's prospects and financial status. See *Columbus* (Ohio) *Dispatch*, November 6,

1916; *New York Herald,* November 3 and 5, 1916; *New York World,* November 5, 1916; *New York American,* November 3, 1916.

31. Bingham's friend, W. W. Davies, refers to the romance in court testimony. Davies testimony, Transcript of Record, Court of Appeals of Kentucky; Louisville Trust Company, etc., v. Robert W. Bingham and William R. Kenan and William A. Blount, Kentucky State Archives, Frankfort, case number 102869. Hereafter referred to as Codicil Hearing.

32. Young Autobiography.

33. The Colonel was the last principal of the school which had been established by William Bingham in 1795. Upon William's death in 1825, his son William II became principal, followed by his son William III in 1858. Upon his death in 1873, his brother, Colonel Robert Bingham, became head of the school. An attack of influenza complicated by pneumonia finally forced the Colonel to retire from the Bingham School in 1920. Since 1904, he had entrusted the future of the school to a board of trustees, but when he died in Asheville in 1927, it did not long survive him. In the autumn of 1928, the school closed, supposedly to carry out major new construction; it never reopened.

34. Asheville was settled as early as 1673 when traders came into the region to obtain furs from the Cherokees. By 1700, a flourishing barter trade existed. Few if any settlers ventured across the Blue Ridge, however, until after the county, named the Reverend Buncombe County, was formed in 1792. Although the reverend was by all accounts a truthful and pious man, his name, "buncome," has come to mean anything spoken, written, or done for mere show. It derives from a speech made by Congressman Felix Walker of North Carolina in 1821. After Walker had made a pointless and long-winded speech in the Congress, he was asked by one of his colleagues what he meant. Walker replied, "I was just talking for Buncombe." In 1824, the Buncombe Turnpike opened and since then Asheville has been a noted tourist and health resort.

35. Bingham Genealogy, page 47; and "Bingham School Founded in Early Days of This Nation," *Asheville Citizen,* November 19, 1931.

36. Codicil Hearing: Davies testimony.

37. Born April 30, 1872, William Rand Kenan, Jr., was a graduate of the University of North Carolina, class of 1894. His research on calcium carbide, under the direction of his chemistry professor, led to the development of industrial uses of acetylene and the modern welding industry. His research was a primary factor in the success of the Union Carbide Company.

38. Papers of Warren Smith, private secretary to Henry Flagler, Flagler Collection, Flagler Museum, Palm Beach, Florida.

CHAPTER 5 *Eleanor*

1. The 255-room manor house, done in French Renaissance–château style, was at the forefront of household technology and included many labor-saving devices which the general public didn't have for years, such as the forerunners of modern clothes washers and dryers, electric rotary spits, and electric dumbwaiters. Those were for the servants. Vanderbilt provided himself with a bowling alley, a gymnasium, and an indoor pool.

2. *New York Herald,* November 6, 1916.

3. The letter is in the Filson Club Collection. The only indication of a date is an appended note saying it was written in 1896. It was addressed, however, to both Mr. and Mrs. Samuel Miller and was therefore written sometime prior to Samuel Miller's death February 2, 1895. From the context of the letter, my best guess is that it was written in August 1894.

4. The quotation from Prince Murat (Colonel Charles Louis Napoleon Achille Murat, son of the King of Naples) is cited in Ralph, "Our Own Riviera."

5. Filson Club Collection: *Louisville Courier-Journal,* February 3, 1895; headlined, "Samuel Miller Meets Death in Asheville, N.C."

6. Ibid.

7. Henrietta Miller, born in 1842, died in 1922 at the age of eighty.

8. Filson Club Collection: Bingham financial papers. The loan was made on October 14, 1895, by Asheville attorneys Theo Davidson and Thomas Jones. It was to be paid back in one year, but three years passed before Bingham repaid the $300.

9. They were married May 20, 1896, see Jefferson County Records, Book 525; *Louisville Courier-Journal,* May 21, 1896.

CHAPTER 6 *Kentucky Home*

1. The island has long since been washed away by flood waters.

2. Now part of the McAlpine Dam complex.

3. Denis was born in Londenderry, Ireland; Matthew and John were born in Erie.

4. Filson Club Collection: Long family genealogical charts.

5. Filson Club Collection: Uncited clip.

6. Ibid.

7. National Bureau of Statistics.

8. There is a disagreement about when Eleanor Miller was born. Bingham family sources give it as July 11, 1871, see Eleanor Miller Bingham's obituary in the *Louisville Times,* April 28, 1913. The Bingham Genealogy, however, gives it as July 11, 1870.

9. Samuel W. Thomas and William Morgan, *Old Louisville: The Victorian Era* (Louisville, Ky.: Data Courier, Inc., 1975). The Miller home, located at 1236 Fourth Street, is now the site of the Puritan Apartments.

10. Isabel McLennan McMeekin, *Louisville, The Gateway City* (New York: Julian Messner Inc., 1945), pages 202–203.

11. George R. Leighton, *Five Cities, The Story of Their Youth and Old Age* (New York: Arno Press, 1974), pages 68–70.

12. *Harper's New Monthly Magazine,* vol. 77 (1888).

13. "List of Students, 1896–1897"; Law Department, University of Louisville.

14. Filson Club Collection: Folder 32, The Worth Manufacturing Company, et al., v. Robert W. Bingham and Others, United States Circuit Court of Appeals, Fourth Circuit, the western district of North Carolina; June 12, 1902 and previous dates. Hereafter referred to as Worth Inheritance Litigation.

15. See Filson Club Collection.

16. See Filson Club Collection: Letter dated October 5, 1900, from H. L. Miller to Robert Worth Bingham; and letter dated October 3, 1900, from J. W. McCulloch of Green River Distillery to Robert Worth Bingham.

17. Filson Club Collection: Letter dated August 2, 1898, from William H. Taylor to W. W. Davies, Atlanta.

18. Filson Club Collection: Letter dated August 6, 1898, from W. W. Davies to William H. Taylor. The emphasis on *particular* lady is Davies', not mine.

19. *Cyclopedia of American Biography:* Davies' original paternal American ancestor was Morgan David, a Welshman, who was in Pennsylvania prior to 1646. His great-great-great-grandfather, Samuel Davies, was the fourth president of the then College of New Jersey, later Princeton University.

20. Filson Club Collection: Letter dated March 4, 1899, from Augustus Willson to Ben Howe, Bingham, and James S. McConathy, directors of the Union Real Estate & Title Co. In the letter, Willson says he has been retained by Mr. Johnson "in regard to the controversy that has arisen in your company. It is very plain to our minds as it must be to yours on reflection, that it is not good for the company nor anybody concerned that the present condition should continue . . ." and Willson seeks a conclusion either by agreement or by intervention of the courts.

21. Filson Club Collection: Letter dated October 23 to Theo Davidson of Asheville encloses check for $325 in "payment of my note and the interest thereon."

22. Filson Club Collection: See letters dated February 21, 1900, and June 7, 1900, from Robert Worth Bingham to the respective doctors and to Mrs. Charles Platt, an Asheville innkeeper. The letters to the doctors do not specifically request confidentiality, presumably because of the privacy of doctor/patient relationships. The letter to Mrs. Platt does make such a request.

23. Filson Club Collection: Series of letters dated June 22, September 23, and October 5, 1900, from Sadie Coonley to Robert Worth Bingham.

24. It was listed in 1901 as 1326 Fourth Avenue, an address that stayed the same until 1909, when the city renumbered the streets; it then became 1236 Fourth Avenue.

25. Filson Club Collection: Folder 27, *Raleigh Observer*, "Dr. J. M. Worth Dead," April 5, 1900. The North Carolina properties were the Worth Manufacturing Company of Worthville, the Worth Manufacturing Company of Central Falls, the Cedar Falls Manufacturing Company of Cedar Falls, the Nantucket Mills of Spray, and the Bank of Randolph of Asheboro.

26. Confidential detective report concerning the death of Mary Lily Flagler, July 27, 1917. Hereafter referred to as Detective Report. The information concerning the Worth estate battle comes from the Filson Club, Worth Inheritance Litigation.

27. Worth Inheritance Litigation.

CHAPTER 7   *Politics as Usual*

1. Leighton, *Five Cities*, page 80.

2. Ibid.

3. William E. Ellis, "Robert Worth Bingham and Louisville Progressivism, 1905–1910," *Filson Club Quarterly*, vol. 5, p. 191. For a further list of clients, see various papers, Filson Club Collection.

4. Accused of being part of the assassination plot, Republican Taylor fled the state and took up residence in Indiana.

5. *New York Times*, April 2, 1932; *Who's Who*, 1932–33.

6. Filson Club Collection: Letter dated November 4, 1899, from Alfred Davis to Robert Worth Bingham.

7. *Louisville Times*, October 1910.

8. Filson Club Collection: Letter dated March 28, 1902, from Robert Worth Bingham to Irvine Hampton.

9. Commented upon in *Louisville Times*, October 1910.

10. Filson Club Collection: Letter dated September 22, 1903, from Charles Ray to Judge James Gregory. The letter is signed with the initials "CBR" rather than a full signature. Barry Bingham, Sr., maintains that the signature is that of Charles Bonnycastle Robinson, a prominent businessman who was related to Dave Davies by marriage. The author is persuaded that the signature is that of Ray.

11. *Louisville Evening Post*, October 4, 1905, and cited in Thomas D. Clark, *Helm Bruce, Public Defender* (Louisville, Ky.: The Filson Club, 1973) page 33.

12. *Louisville Courier-Journal*, November 18, 1903.

13. Ibid., May 23, 1907: reprint of the full text of Kentucky Court of Appeals Decision.

14. Filson Club Collection: Letter dated November 28, 1903, from Robert Worth Bingham to F. C. Bryan.

15. Filson Club Collection: Various financial papers.

16. Filson Club Collection: Letter dated July 6, 1904, from Robert Worth Bingham to W. W. Davies.

17. University of Louisville's Kornhauser Health Sciences Library, 36th, 37th, and 38th Annual Announcements of the Louisville Medical College, academic years 1904 through 1907.

18. Filson Club Collection: Letter dated June 24, 1905, from Robert Worth Bingham to M. L. Ravitch. Bingham had had two treatments.

19. Filson Club Collection: Letter dated August 10, 1905, from W. W. Davies to Robert Worth Bingham.

20. Ibid.

21. Ibid.

22. Filson Club Collection: Letter dated September 7, 1905, from F. R. Bishop to Robert Worth Bingham.

23. Clark, *Helm Bruce*, page 40.

24. *Louisville Courier-Journal*, May 23, 1907, text of Kentucky Court of Appeals Decision.

25. Ibid., findings of Kentucky Court of Appeals Decision.

26. *Louisville Times*, October 1910.

27. Filson Club Collection: Letter dated November 7, 1906, from Robert Worth Bingham to Mayor Paul Barth.

28. *Louisville Times*, October 1910.

29. Filson Club Collection: Letter dated February 14, 1906, from Robert Worth Bingham to Hopkins Theater Company, Louisville.

30. *Louisville Courier-Journal*, May 4, 1956.

31. All of the race material comes from the *Louisville Courier-Journal* May 4, 1956, reprint of the original race coverage.

32. Filson Club Collection: Letter dated August 22, 1906, from Robert Worth Bingham to the University of North Carolina.

33. At the commencement exercise, his father was introduced by a fellow prisoner-of-war, Colonel Thomas Stephen Kenan, Mary Lily's uncle. In his oration, Colonel Bingham protested "against our legal withdrawal from the Union being called rebellion. We protest against having our children and grandchildren taught from histories written by our military antagonists and by our sectional and our political enemies that their fathers were rebels and traitors, when our National Capital bears the name and perpetuates the fame of the 'secessionist,' 'rebel' and 'traitor' George Washington. . . ." Pack Memorial Library, Asheville, North Carolina, Collection: Address of June 3, 1907, by Col. Robert Bingham on the 50th anniversary of his graduation from the University of North Carolina, "The Fifty Years Between 1857 and 1907, and Beyond."

34. *Louisville Times*, June 28, 1907; *Louisville Courier-Journal*, June 28 and 30, 1907; *Louisville Evening Post*, June 28, 1907; *Louisville Herald*, June 28 and 29, 1907.

35. *Louisville Times*, October 1910.

36. One is reminded of the finale of the film *Casablanca* when Claude Rains, just before strolling off with Rick, scornfully tosses a bottle of Vichy water in the trash, looks at the dead Nazi chief and orders his subordinates to "round up the usual suspects."

37. Bingham's friend Hugh Young said the hospital investigation led "ultimately to the construction of a fine City Hospital and the reorganization of the Medical School." Young Autobiography, page 505.

38. Filson Club Collection: Letter dated August 1, 1907, from W. Richards to Governor J. C. W. Beckham.

39. *Louisville Evening Post*, August 17, 1907.

40. *Louisville Courier-Journal*, August 21, 23, and 25, 1907.

41. Filson Club Collection: Letter dated January 9, 1909, from Robert Worth Bingham to James West accepting the invitation.

42. Interview with Sallie Bingham.

43. Interview with Barry Bingham, Sr.

44. Ibid.

CHAPTER 8   *The Flaglers*

1. Edwin Lefevre, "Flagler and Florida." *Everybody's Magazine,* 1906.

2. Rockefeller himself is the source for this rather surprising statement. See Rockefeller, *Random Reminiscences of Men and Events,* and Chandler, *Flagler.*

3. In terms of purchasing power, the 1890 American dollar was worth about twelve times the 1987 dollar. Flagler, therefore, had the equivalent of about $600 million of personal funds to invest—untaxed, unregulated, and unanswerable to any relatives, stockholders, accountants, lawyers, or board of directors.

4. Carrère and Hastings went on to design the New York Public Library, the interior of the old Metropolitan Opera House, and the U.S. Senate Office Building in Washington, D.C. Tiffany, of course, was the famed New York jewelry designer.

5. Flagler and Ida Alice were married in 1883 and resided variously, depending on season and whim, in a New York City mansion; a summer estate at Mamaroneck, New York; and a winter home in St. Augustine, Florida. There is an unresolved dispute about whether Ida Alice was in fact the nurse of Mary Harkness Flagler. Most sources, including newspaper clips from 1900 onward and Flagler biographer Sidney Walter Martin, state that Ida Alice was a nurse to Mary Flagler, hired some months prior to her death. However, Flagler's son, Harry Harkness Flagler, who was on the scene, maintained that Miss Shourds was never a nurse to his mother. But he gave no further information. His remarks, contained in annotations to Martin's book, *Florida's Flagler,* are on file at the Flagler Museum, Palm Beach, Florida.

6. George Ward Nichols, "Six Weeks in Florida," *Harper's,* October 1870.

7. *St. Augustine Evening News,* January 16, 1890.

8. See Chandler, *Flagler.*

9. John T. Flynn, *God's Gold, the Story of Rockefeller and His Times* (New York: Harcourt, Brace and Company, 1932).

10. She died of a brain hemorrhage on July 12, 1930. By the time of Alice's death and despite the stock market crash of 1929, her estate, comprised almost entirely of Standard Oil stock, had grown to $15.2 million, which was left to two nephews and a grand niece.

11. *New York Herald,* March 30, 1902.

12. Whitehall, which now houses the Henry Flagler Museum, has been restored almost completely to its original condition and is open to visitors year-round.

13. Spalding Diaries, Flagler Museum, Palm Beach, Florida, entry for January 21, 1907.

14. Ibid., entries for January 23 and February 6, 1907.

15. Ibid., entry for February 3, 1907.

16. Ibid., entries for March 8 and 15, 1907.

17. Ibid., entry for March 18, 1907. The Reverend George Ward was Henry Flagler's pastor on Palm Beach.

18. Ibid.

19. Ibid.

CHAPTER 9   *The Agreement*

1. Flagler Museum, Palm Beach, Florida: Box 41a, Executors' Minutes Book. According to a *Miami Herald* story, "A Florida Fortune Comes to Light," April 18, 1965, Flagler sold the *Herald* "just before his death" to "Frank B. Shutts for $29,000." The executors' inventory of Flagler's estate, however, shows he still held ownership at the time of his death.

2. The original three trustees of the Flagler estate were William R. Kenan, Jr., Mary Lily's brother who was a vice president under Mr. Flagler and the consulting engineer for all the Flagler projects; James Parrott, who was president of Flagler Systems; and William H. Beardsley, treasurer and chief financial adviser to Flagler. The will further provided that Parrott remain president as long as he desired; that during the five-year trusteeship Mary Lily was to receive $100,000 annually; that Henry's son, Harry Harkness, receive 5,000 shares of Standard Oil of New Jersey stock (worth about $4.5 million at the time); that the Flagler Memorial Church in St. Augustine receive $75,000; that Hamilton College of Clinton, New York, receive $100,000, Parrott $100,000, Beardsley $50,000, plus numerous smaller requests to friends and servants. As for the main business, the Flagler System of hotels and railroads, Flagler named Parrott of Oxford, Maine, as his successor president. Parrott, however, died in his native city five months after Flagler, and William Beardsley was elected to the office. Judge William A. Blount, counsel for the Flagler Systems, replaced Parrott as trustee of the estate.

3. *New York Times*, March 20, 1915.

4. Ibid., May 14, 1915.

5. Letter dated May 8, 1986, from Barry Bingham, Sr., to author.

6. According to an interview by the author with Barry Bingham, Sr., the judge resided at least part-time during the period 1914–16 at 211 Burnett Street. City directories show it to have been the home of Bingham's insurance agent, T. G. Slaughter. Barry Sr. adds that his father maintained a summer home in Cherokee Park during that period. The Louisville City Directory for 1915 lists Bingham and son at 1048 Cherokee Road. The 1916 directory indicates yet another move for the judge, listing the Binghams as living on "Milvale avenue, north of Woodburne avenue."

7. Will of Eleanor Miller Bingham, probated July 15, 1913, in Jefferson County Court, Louisville. The will, written October 12, 1906, names her sister-in-law Sadie Bingham Grinnan as her executrix in case Bob doesn't survive. Otherwise, he is executor and is to not file an inventory of her estate. Bob received all her estate as trustee for the children and could spend as much of the principal as necessary "for their support, education and advancement in life." City directories for this period list Bingham as a partner in the law firm of Kohn, Bingham, Sloss, Spindle, Mann and Levi. However, the sparse financial records available list no income other than Eleanor's allotment.

8. Letter dated May 8, 1986, from Barry Bingham, Sr., to author.

9. Filson Club Collection: Letter dated November 2, 1914, from Robert Worth Bingham to John Barr of Fidelity Trust in which Bingham confirms that he failed to keep up premiums on a life insurance policy which secured a contract he had with Mrs. Miller.

10. Filson Club Collection: Letter dated December 1, 1914, from Mrs. Henrietta Miller to Robert Worth Bingham.

11. Filson Club Collection: Exchange of letters dated January 7 and 8, 1915, between John Barr and Robert Worth Bingham. Despite the words and tone of the correspondence involving Mrs. Miller and Robert Worth Bingham, Bingham's son Barry contends in a May 8, 1986, letter to the author that the disagreements were "entirely amicable" and had "little effect on my father's financial or professional affairs." After reviewing the documents pertaining to this quarrel, I find Barry Bingham's interpretation to be unpersuasive.

12. Interviews with Bingham family sources.

13. Ibid.

14. Interview with Thomas S. Kenan III, August 1984.

15. Interviews with Sallie Bingham, May and August 1984, November 1985, and January 1986. The specific quote comes from an interview in Louisville on January 23, 1986.

16. Letter dated May 8, 1986, from Barry Bingham, Sr., to author.

17. *New York Herald*, November 12, 1917.

18. Interview with Thomas S. Kenan III, August 1984.

19. The inn was built in 1912–13 by Dr. Edwin Wiley Grove of St. Louis, Missouri, and

is currently part of the Jack Tar Hotels system. It has had a colorful history including being the seat of the Philippine government-in-exile during World War II. During that war, it also functioned as an internment center for Axis diplomats.

20. Interview with Thomas S. Kenan III, August 1984.

21. *Palm Beach Life*, February 2, 1916.

22. Warren Smith Papers, Flagler Museum, Palm Beach, Florida. Smith was Flagler's personal secretary and stayed on in a similar position following Flagler's death.

23. A copy of the will is filed in Jefferson County Courthouse, Louisville.

CHAPTER 10 *Honeymooning*

1. *New York Evening World*, November 3, 1916.

2. After inflicting heavy damage on the British fleet in the Battle of Jutland, German warships were raiding the English coast and ravaging Allied commerce in the Atlantic.

3. *Columbus* (Ohio) *Dispatch*, November 6, 1916.

4. *New York Times*, November 4, 1916.

5. Ibid.

6. *New York Herald*, November 6, 1916.

7. *New York Times*, November 16, 1916. The lot was valued for taxation at $434,000.

8. Codicil Hearing: Davies testimony.

9. Young Autobiography. Young reports that following the wedding, Robert Bingham commissioned Claire Sheridan, the famous British sculptor, to do a bust of Young. At the unveiling ceremony, says Young, a "young woman came up and said, 'I hope you appreciate that I have come fifty miles to see your bust unveiled!' Whereupon with a bow, I said, 'I would go a thousand to see yours.' " Young entered the U.S. Army in 1917 as a major in the medical corps and at the request of John J. Pershing, commander-in-chief of the AEF, he accompanied him to Europe in May 1917 to organize a department of urology for the AEF. He was made senior consultant of the department and did much toward establishing urological clinics for both the army and civil population. He was discharged from the army in 1919 with the rank of colonel and was awarded a Distinguished Service Medal.

10. Ibid.

11. The children were away at their respective schools and the scheduling of the wedding in mid-week very likely precluded their attendance. However, had the wedding been scheduled on a weekend or closer to the Thanksgiving holiday, nine days later, they could easily have attended. A reasonable inference is that their presence either wasn't desired or wasn't considered important.

12. Filson Club Collection: Bingham financial papers.

13. *New York Times*, November 16, 1916.

14. Information regarding the hotel comes from original brochures in the possession of film actor and developer Roger Davis, who has restored the Seelbach to the peak of its historical condition.

15. Davis speculates that the Binghams would have stayed in what is now the Seelbach Suite, a marvelous ensemble with a sitting room, bedroom, and marble bath done in shades of gray and light green.

16. Seelbach Hotel brochures.

17. State archives, estate inventory of Mary Lily Bingham.

18. Will of Mary Lily Bingham, dated December 8, 1916, filed in the Jefferson County Court.

19. In an interview with the author, Barry Bingham, Sr., said the information regarding the reasons for writing the December 1916 will were reviewed and confirmed by his law firm.

20. Interviews with Kenan and Bingham family sources.

21. Codicil Hearing: Davies testimony.

22. Item Eight contains the Kenan Professorships clause. It stated that her trustees were to pay to the university the sum of $75,000 annually to "be perpetually used . . . for . . . paying the salaries of professors . . ." who were to be known as Kenan Professors. Bingham family sources say the Colonel "pestered the devil" out of Mary Lily to obtain the bequest. The Colonel himself somewhat confirms the view. In his letter to university president Edward K. Graham, marked "personal and private," Colonel Bingham remarks that he had had a "long conversation" with Mrs. Flagler and told her about the needs of the University.

23. *Louisville Courier-Journal,* December 3, 1916.

24. Guest included Byron and Alice Hilliard, son and daughter of Byron Hilliard, Sr., and Aleen Hilliard. Widowed in the 1920s, Aleen Hilliard would become the third wife of Robert Worth Bingham.

25. Bingham family sources.

26. Interview with Thomas S. Kenan III, August 1984.

27. Codicil Hearing: Davies testimony.

28. Confidential Kenan family private detective report, August and September 1917.

29. Now the Eastern State Hospital. The American Medical Directory says that he graduated from Moscow State University Faculty of Medicine in 1889 and from Central Medical College in St. Joseph, Missouri, in 1896.

30. Filson Club Collection: Letter dated January 25, 1917, from Robert Worth Bingham to John Russell Pope.

31. *Louisville Times,* January 27, 1917.

32. Jefferson probate hearings.

33. Census Bureau, *Historical Statistics of the United States,* Consumer Price Index.

34. *Palm Beach Life,* February 21, 1917.

35. Copies of the codicil can be found in the Flagler Museum, Palm Beach, Florida, and in the Jefferson County, Kentucky, courthouse.

36. *New York Herald,* September 21, 1917.

37. *Louisville Courier-Journal,* April 5, 1917.

38. Ibid., April 7, 1917.

CHAPTER 11   *The Codicil*

1. Filson Club Collection: Letter dated July 16, 1917, from Hugh Young to Robert Worth Bingham. On April 6, 1917, following a series of German provocations, the United States entered World War I. President Wilson placed his military forces under the command of General John Joseph "Blackjack" Pershing, a Missourian and cavalry officer who had more than thirty years of campaign experience against Geronimo and the Apaches, the Sioux, Spanish troops in the Spanish-American War, Philippine Moro terrorists, and most recently the Mexican bandit Pancho Villa. From those experiences, Pershing had learned about soldiers and one of his first decisions was to recruit the by now renowned Hugh Young as the medical man who would protect American troops against venereal disease. By July, Young was on the front lines.

2. Filson Club Collection: Letter dated May 27, 1917, from Bessy Mason Young to Robert Worth Bingham. Miss Mason, the daughter of a Baltimore banker, and Young were married June 4, 1901. They had four children. Traditional biographical sources spell Mrs. Young's name as "Bessie." The letter, however, is clearly signed, "Bessy." I have used that spelling here.

3. *Louisville Courier-Journal,* June 6 and 20, 1917; letter dated May 8, 1986, from Barry Bingham, Sr., to author.

4. Ravitch's presence as a house guest is mentioned in a gossip column of the *Louisville Courier-Journal,* June 15, 1917.

5. *Louisville Courier-Journal,* June 23, 1917.

6. Filson Club Collection: Letter dated June 11, 1917, from Guaranty Trust Company to Robert Worth Bingham, acknowledging the transfer of the Mary Lily/Standard Oil stock gifts to Bingham, which Guaranty had been holding for him.

7. Confidential Kenan family private detective report, August and September 1917.

8. In 1900, the drug addiction rate was one out of every 400 persons, according to the U.S. Bureau of Narcotics. In the epidemic years of 1962–82, the rate averaged one in 475, according to the Drug Enforcement Agency. In 1900, the most frequently purchased drugs were opium and morphine. These were legally obtainable in drugstores and were as popular with discreet ladies "on dope" in Biloxi, Mississippi, as with hookers in Chicago and New York. Eighty-three percent of the addicts of 1900 were women, and virtually all addicts were white. The remaining 17 percent was mostly Chinese. Hispanics and blacks were not a significant factor. Opium dens flourished openly in large cities where addicts of all races and both sexes lay in bunks, side by side.

9. Interview with Sallie Bingham, May 1984.

10. *Louisville Courier-Journal,* June 7 and 10, 1917.

11. Laudanum is a narcotic preparation in which opium is the chief ingredient. Sallie Bingham reports that Mary Lily's use of laudanum is a strong part of the family lore.

12. Confidential Kenan family private detective report, August and September 1917.

13. Ibid.

14. *New York World,* September 20, 1917; Codicil Hearing, Davies testimony.

15. Ibid.

16. Filed as part of Mary Lily Kenan Bingham's will, Jefferson County, Kentucky, District Court.

17. *New York World,* September 22, 1917.

18. The lots bought in 1917 cost $3,992. See Filson Club Collection: Letter dated July 5, 1917, from Cave Hill Cemetery Company to Robert Worth Bingham.

19. There is little dispute that Mary Lily suffered an apparent heart attack on July 12, see *New York World,* September 24, 1917. However, it is disputed as to her situation at the time of the attack. Kenan family sources say she was in bed. Bingham family sources say she was in the tub, loaded with bourbon and laudanum.

20. The statement that Mary Lily's doctors received no training in heart disease is based on research on Drs. Ravitch, Boggess, and Steinberg in various American Medical Association biographies, listings, and references.

21. Filson Club Collection: Reference entitled *History of Kentucky,* by Judge Charles Kerr, vol. 4, page 230.

22. Letter from Sherrill Redmon, archivist at the University of Louisville's Kornhauser Health Sciences Library, to author. Steinberg's "preparation for medical college was unusually good for that time and place," says Redmon.

23. Filson Club Collection: Letter dated July 16, 1917, from Hugh Young to Robert Worth Bingham.

24. Filson Club Collection: Letter dated July 19, 1917, from George Ward to Robert Worth Bingham.

25. Confidential detective report, August and September 1917.

26. *New York World,* September 24, 1917.

27. *Louisville Courier-Journal,* July 26, 1917.

28. *Louisville Courier-Journal* and *Louisville Post,* July 27, 1917.

29. *Louisville Post,* July 28, 1917.

30. The Whitehall documents are kept at the Flagler Museum, Palm Beach, Florida.

31. *New York Herald,* September 22, 1917.

32. *New York Evening World,* September 22, 1917.

CHAPTER 12 *Probate*

1. *Louisville Courier-Journal*, Mary 5, 1918. For tax purposes, the evaluation was later reduced to $99.8 million, see *Louisville Courier-Journal*, April 9, 1919. The final amount, subject to Kentucky tax, was $67 million.

2. All of the testimony cited in this chapter comes from Transcript of Record, Court of Appeals of Kentucky; Louisville Trust Company, etc., v. Robert W. Bingham and William R. Kenan and William A. Blount, Kentucky State Archives, Frankfort, case number 102869. Also cited in this and other chapters as Codicil Hearing. *Report of Fidelity & Columbia Trust Company*, February 23, 1918.

3. Codicil Hearing: Report of Louisville Trust Company, October 26, 1917.

4. Louise Clisby Wise died at age thirty-nine after three marriages and two children. Under the terms of Mary Lily's will, her inheritance was passed on to the children, Lawrence Lewis, Jr., of Richmond, Virginia, and Mary Lily Flagler Lewis of The Plains, Virginia.

5. *New York Herald*, September 4, 1917.

6. *Louisville Courier-Journal*, August 1, 1917.

7. Ibid., August 29, 1917.

8. *Louisville Evening Post*, August 27, 1917.

9. Editorial, *Louisville Evening Post*, August 27, 1917.

10. Editorial, *Louisville Courier-Journal*, September 24, 1917.

11. Editorial, *Louisville Post*, September 24, 1917.

12. *Louisville Evening Post*, August 27, 1917.

13. Obituary, *New York Times*, April 15, 1932. Burns was a member of the Bureau of Investigation, commonly called the Secret Service, from 1889 to 1906. He returned to the Bureau in 1921 at the request of President Warren Harding and served four years as the agency's head. In 1925, he rejoined his private firm.

14. *Louisville Courier-Journal*, May 5, 1918.

15. Louise Wise's two children both have declined to be interviewed. In a letter to the author dated July 31, 1986, Mr. Lewis explained, "[I]t has been our long-standing policy to avoid publicity of any kind whatever and to make absolutely no comment on what we consider to be private family matters."

16. Filson Club Collection: Invoice dated August 23, 1917, from Southern Motors Company to Robert Worth Bingham.

17. Mary Lily's four cars are listed in the various appraisals filed as part of the codicil hearings. The Filson Club Collection has copies of Bingham's bills of sale. In the purchase of the Packard "325" Roadster in August 1917, he traded in one Packard, whether his or Mary Lily's isn't explained, and received $2,000 on the trade-in. Adding $1,400 in cash, he bought the roadster.

18. Thomas De Quincey, *Murder Considered as One of the Fine Arts* (London, 1897).

19. Codicil Hearing. Legally, the probate was restricted to the simple matter of witnesses to Mary Lily's signatures on her wills and changes. The proceedings were not a formal challenge of those documents. However, the *nature* of the examination by Kenan attorney Will Bruce was a challenge, going far beyond the bounds of a simple probate hearing. The strongest evidence for the challenge interpretation is the newspaper reports of the day.

20. Ravitch's presence in Lexington is described in the *Lexington Herald*, September 20, 1917. Bingham's presence in Ohio is reported in the *New York Herald*, September 22, 1917.

CHAPTER 13 *Exhumation*

1. *New York Herald*, September 21, 1917.

2. Exhumation permit, New Hanover County court records, September 18, 1917.

3. *New York World*, September 22, 1917.

4. Bellevue Hospital, on First Avenue from Twenty-sixth Street to Thirtieth Street, is one of the oldest general hospitals in the United States. It is affiliated with Columbia, Cornell, and New York universities as a medical teaching school.

5. Confidential autopsy report.

6. The heavy metal poisons are cited in the confidential report and are also referred to in the *New York Evening Journal,* September 27, 1917.

7. *New York American,* September 21, 1917.

8. Ibid.

9. *New York Sun,* September 26, 1917.

10. *Louisville Courier-Journal,* September 25, 1917.

11. *New York Herald,* September 20 and 22, 1917.

12. *New York World,* September 24, 1917.

13. Ibid.

14. Ibid.

15. *New York Evening Journal,* September 27, 1917.

16. The present whereabouts of the bedside medical notes is a mystery. In 1917, Bingham said he had them. They are not, however, part of the Bingham Collection at the Filson Club in Louisville nor of the Bingham Papers at the Library of Congress in Washington D.C.

17. *New York Evening Journal,* September 27, 1917.

18. Ibid.

19. Kenan also was personal physician to Henry Flagler in the last decade of Flagler's life. This is the same Owen Kenan who survived the sinking of the *Lusitania.* He was awarded the French Medal of Honor for bravery while fighting for the French before the U.S. entered World War I. He remained in France after the war but also maintained homes in New York City, Wilmington, North Carolina, and Palm Beach, Florida. A lifelong bachelor, he died in 1963 and is buried in Arlington National Cemetery.

20. *New York Evening Journal,* September 27, 1917.

21. *New York World,* September 21, 1917.

22. *New York Tribune,* September 22, 1917.

23. *New York World,* September 21, 1917.

24. Ibid., September 20, 1917.

25. *New York Herald* and *Louisville Post,* September 22, 1917.

26. *Louisville Courier-Journal,* September 23, 1917.

27. Ibid., September 22, 1917.

28. Ibid., September 23, 1917.

29. No relation to Mary Lily's heir, Louise Wise.

30. George Yater, *200 Years at the Falls of the Ohio* (Louisville: Heritage Corporation of Louisville, 1979) page 170.

31. *New York Journal,* October 8, 1917.

32. Ibid.

33. *Louisville Post,* November 4, 1917.

34. Register's Genealogy, page 47.

35. Graham Kenan and his wife, Sarah, were first cousins to each other in addition to being related to Mary Lily. See Register's Genealogy.

CHAPTER 14   *The Publisher*

1. *Louisville Courier-Journal,* April 26, 1918.

2. Ibid.

3. Ibid.

4. Ibid., June 9, 1918.

5. Ibid., February 13, 1919.

6. Ibid., May 27, 1920.

7. Ibid., April 9, 1919. The precise evaluation made by the state of Kentucky was $99.8 million.

8. *Palm Beach Daily News,* December 22, 1921. Walter Lincoln, Kentucky appellate judge, overruled the previous evaluation and found the estate to be worth $77.9 million of which $68.4 million was subject to Kentucky inheritance tax.

9. Louisville City Directory of 1919.

10. Final Settlement of Accounts of Fidelity & Columbia Trust Company, Administrator in the matter of the estate of Mary Lily Flagler Bingham, December 21, 1927; Jefferson County Court. Known hereafter as Settlement of Accounts.

11. Ibid.

12. These transactions are reported in Settlement of Accounts.

13. He continued, however, to be listed in American Medical Association directories, 1918–21.

14. American Medical Association Directory, 1923.

15. *Louisville Courier-Journal,* August 6, 1918.

16. Michael Lesy, *Real Life: Louisville in the Twenties* (New York: Pantheon, 1972), pages 153 and 155.

17. Filson Club Collection: Various correspondence between Robert Worth Bingham and Henry Watterson. Watterson stayed with Bingham less than two years—until April 2, 1919, when he left because of Bingham's support of the League of Nations. Watterson opposed the league, viewing it as "a Utopian scheme to have the United States underwrite" the wars of Europe. Bingham suggested that Watterson resign, saying, "I do not wish the paper to appear as assailing its distinguished former Editor and present Editor Emeritus" in the split over the league. Watterson died December 22, 1921.

18. In May 1918, the Pulitzer was awarded to Henry Watterson for two editorials published at the beginning of World War I. In 1926, the prize went to William Burk Miller for his interviews, deep inside Sand Cave, of the trapped Floyd Collins.

19. Filson Club Collection: Letter dated April 5, 1919, from Robert Worth Bingham to Henry Watterson.

20. German immigrant Zenger (1697–1746) was defended in court by a young lawyer named Alexander Hamilton. Their joint efforts established a tradition of freedom of the press in America.

21. Filson Club Collection: Receipt dated November 12, 1918, from Democratic National Committee to Robert Worth Bingham.

22. *New York Times,* December 19, 1937.

23. As more and more radio stations came on the air, it became a convention for stations east of the Mississippi to begin their call letters with the letter *W* and for stations west of the Mississippi to begin with the letter *K.* This convention wasn't in effect, however, when KDKA launched its experiment. Under Bingham's son Barry, WHAS in 1950 became one of America's first commercial television stations.

24. *Louisville Courier-Journal,* July 18, 1962, in an article observing the fortieth anniversary of WHAS Radio.

25. Ibid.

26. McKeekin, *Louisville, The Gateway City.*

27. Ibid.

28. *New York Times,* June 16, 1921.

29. Leighton, *Five Cities,* page 90.

30. Interview with Barry Bingham, Sr., January 27, 1986.

31. Democrat Cordell Hull (1871–1955) represented his Tennessee district in Congress from 1907 to 1921 and from 1923 to 1931. He was a member of the U.S. Senate from 1931 to 1933, resigning to accept Roosevelt's offer to become secretary of state. In Congress, Hull was the author of important tax legislation, including the federal income tax law, 1913, and the federal inheritance tax law, 1916.

32. Sallie Bingham Scrapbook: Letter dated December 23, 1928, from Roland Hayes to Robert Worth Bingham.

33. *Louisville Courier-Journal,* December 19, 1937.

34. Young Autobiography, pages 510-11.

35. *New York Times,* December 13, 1937.

36. *Louisville Courier-Journal,* December 27, 1937. In his will, Robert Bingham spells out the ante-nuptial agreement he entered into in August 1924 with his third wife. She relinquished all interest in his estate, in his consideration of paying her $1 million. She received $300,000 at that time, and upon his death would receive another $700,000 in lieu of all dower and widow's rights.

37. *Louisville Courier-Journal,* August 7, 1928.

38. Young Autobiography, pages 510-11.

39. *Chicago Tribune,* August 31, 1927.

40. Ibid., August 31, 1928.

41. *New York American,* June 4, 1933. The editorial denounced Bingham and demanded he "be recalled—and without delay."

42. Young Autobiography, pages 510-11.

43. *Lexington Herald,* February 24, 1933; *Louisville Courier-Journal,* December 19, 1937.

44. McMeekin, *Louisville, The Gateway City.*

CHAPTER 15   *The Ambassador*

1. Beginning in the 1920s, photographs show Bingham wearing pince-nez on some occasions. It was an unusual fashion even then and somewhat of a coincidence that both Roosevelt and Bingham favored them.

2. Roosevelt was inaugurated as president on March 4, 1933, continuing a pattern which had been set by President George Washington's first inauguration, which was on March 4, 1789. Roosevelt was the last president to be so inaugurated. The Twentieth Amendment to the Constitution, passed in 1933, changed the inaugural date of American presidents to January 20, following the election.

3. *Lexington Herald,* February 23, 1933. The Associated Press erred in saying that Bingham had been *elected* judge. He was, of course, appointed.

4. Nathan Miller, *FDR: An Intimate History* (Garden City, N.Y.: Doubleday, 1983), pages 246–49.

5. Ibid.; James MacGregor Burns, *Roosevelt: The Lion and the Fox* (New York: Harcourt, Brace and Co., 1956), page 130; Whittlesey House, *Jim Farley's Story, The Roosevelt Years* (New York: McGraw-Hill, 1948); Frank Freidel, *Franklin D. Roosevelt: The Triumph* (Boston: Little Brown and Company, 1956).

6. Miller, *FDR: An Intimate History,* pages 246–49.

7. Ibid.

8. Congress is ruled by its committees, and originally, American presidents, acting through their party leadership in Congress, selected the committee chairmen, thus giving a president control over the legislative branch not envisioned by the Constitution. In reaction to such control, the seniority system was introduced to the Congress in 1845 by Senator John Calhoun of South Carolina. It was a procedure whereby the majority party in each house automatically selected as committee chairman the party member who had continually served longest on that particular committee. The invention was simple, ingenious, and unique among the parliamentary bodies of the world. The system has always been strong in the Senate but has waned and waxed in the House where it vanished in December 1974 when a coalition of House liberals and incoming freshmen overthrew seniority as the main basis for chairmanship.

9. Burns, *Roosevelt: The Lion and the Fox.*

10. *New York Times,* February 24, 1933.

11. Associated Press dispatch printed in the *New York Times,* February 24, 1933. The story was written by the AP correspondent in Louisville.

12. *New York Times,* February 24, 1933.

13. United Press dispatch printed in the *Boston Post,* February 24, 1933.

14. *New York Times,* March 17, 1933.

15. Ibid. Democrat Alben Barkley was a member of the U.S. House of Representatives from 1913 to 1927 and the Senate from 1927 to 1949. Commencing in 1949, he served as Harry Truman's vice president for four years and was reelected to the Senate by his Kentucky constituents in 1954.

16. *Louisville Courier-Journal,* April 6, 1933.

17. Library of Congress Collection, Bingham Papers: Speech prepared for the Louisville Board of Trade, April 5, 1933.

18. *Louisville Courier-Journal,* May 24, 1933.

19. Sallie Bingham Scrapbook: Letter dated March 25, 1933, from Franklin Roosevelt to King George V.

20. *Louisville Courier-Journal* dispatch from London, May 24, 1933.

21. *New York Times,* June 24, 1933.

22. For example, see *Louisville Courier-Journal,* April 27, 1934.

23. *New York Times,* December 31, 1933.

24. Article by Jessie Clark, *Junior League* magazine, April 1933.

25. Burns, *Roosevelt: The Lion and the Fox.*

26. *Louisville Courier-Journal,* November 8, 1963.

27. Young Autobiography.

28. *New York Times,* December 19, 1937. Edward and Mrs. Simpson became the Duke and Duchess of Windsor. Living luxurious but apparently empty lives, Edward died in 1972, his wife in 1986.

29. *New York Times,* December 19, 1937.

30. Library of Congress Collection, Bingham Papers: Letter dated November 13, 1933, from FDR to Robert Worth Bingham.

31. Ibid.

32. Ibid.: Letter dated October 15, 1937, from Robert Worth Bingham to FDR.

33. *Louisville Times,* July 6, 1937.

34. Sallie Bingham Scrapbook: Letter dated December 8, 1937, from Robert Bingham to President Roosevelt.

35. *New York Times,* December 19, 1937.

36. Finley Peter Dunne, "Mr. Dooley on Making a Will and Other Evil Necessities," from *Bartett's Familiar Quotations* (Boston: Little, Brown, 1980).

CHAPTER 16 *Did He or Didn't He?*

1. *Greensville* (N.C.) *Daily News,* May 8, 1927:

To Col. Robert W. Bingham, head of the Bingham Military School of Asheville, whose son married Mrs. Flagler, must go some of the credit for persuading his daughter-in-law to leave the money for professors' salaries instead of for buildings or general endowment. In a letter to university president Edward K. Graham, marked personal and private, Col. Bingham remarks that he had had a long conversation with Mrs. Flagler and told her about the needs of the University, that "the state had done very little for the University, and what little had been done was in bricks and mortar," "that bricks and mortar would not command teachers, and that means to pay teachers was the great need"; "I told her," he continued, "about the monument of the young Confederate soldier who abandoned letters for arms at the call of his country—fully equipped physically, mentally, morally, in full uniform with gun, blanket, canteen, haversack, etc., but with no cartridge box—and that that young warrior of 1861 is Ed. K. Graham of the present," equipped but lacking "financial cartridges."

2. Codicil Hearing, September 4, 1917. In Jefferson County Court, Judge Alex Humphrey is questioning Stanley Sloss: "Do you recollect to have attested the two papers, one for Mrs. Bingham and one for Judge Bingham?" Sloss: "Quite distinctly. Judge Bingham and Mrs. Bingham were going to New York. I think it was the first time they went to New York after their marriage. As I recall it, they were leaving on the one o'clock train. During the course of the morning, early in the morning, quite early in the morning, Judge Bingham asked me and Miss Overman to go out to his room at the Seelbach Hotel and witness some papers and we went out and witnessed them. I never saw the contents of those papers."

3. *Louisville Courier-Journal,* June 10, 1917.

4. For example, confidential Kenan family private detective report, Ravitch's statement to the press, *New York World,* September 22, 1917.

5. Codicil Hearing, Davies testimony.

6. Confidential Kenan family private detective report.

7. *Louisville Courier-Journal,* June 20, 1917.

8. Bingham Genealogy.

9. Codicil Hearing, Davies testimony, September 4, 1917.

10. *Louisville Courier-Journal,* June 30, 1917: "Dr. M. L. Ravitch is the guest of Judge Robert Worth Bingham and Mrs. Bingham at Lincliffe, their home on the River Road."

11. Interview with Thomas S. Kenan III.

12. Kenan family sources.

13. *New York Evening Journal,* September 27, 1917.

14. American Medical Association directories. The 1916 directory lists 626 physicians. No directory was published in 1917. The 1918 directory lists 610 physicians. The decline probably was caused by doctors leaving for military service in World War I. Treatment of heart disease was well advanced by the time of Mary Lily's illness in 1917. Specialized studies of the heart began in the 17th century when the invention of the microscope and the work of William Harvey established the function of the heart, the nature of the vascular system and solved the mystery of the capillary system. The first textbook appeared in 1747 when Swiss biologist Albrecht von Haller published his work on respiration and heart function. Instruction in the care of heart disease began in America with the opening of the first medical schools here—the College of Philadelphia in 1765 and King's College of New York City in 1767. The use of the catheter was introduced 1844. The latter part of the 19th century saw rapid acceleration in the study and treatment of heart disease. Among the pioneers were Rudolph Matas of New Orleans, a vascular surgeon who devised a radically new technique for dealing with aneurysms (a ballooning of an artery due to a weakening in the wall); Harvey Cushing of The John Hopkins Medical School (1896–1912) who opened the field of neurosurgery; and Alexis Carrel who received the Nobel prize in 1912 for his work in suturing blood vessels, in blood transfusion, and in the transplantation of organs. Open heart surgery began during the 1890s when several surgeons, confronted with patients stabbed in the heart, opened the chest in desperation and sewed up the wound, thus saving the patients' lives. The study of heart function was included in the curriculum of Robert Worth Bingham himself, when he was a medical student at the University of Virginia, 1890–91.

For further history of cardiac medical training see: *Academic American Encyclopedia;* Bishop, William John, *The Early History of Surgery* (1960); Cartwright, Frederick F., *The Development of Modern Surgery* (1967); Earle, A. Scott, ed., *Surgery in America: From the Colonial Era to the Twentieth Century* (1965); *From a Surgeon's Journal, 1915–1918,* Harvey Cushing (1936).

15. Death certificate, Jefferson County public records.

16. Series of interviews with cardiologist Lawrence O'Meallie of New Orleans, February to July 1986. Dr. O'Meallie is a forensic expert on heart disease.

17. *New York Evening Journal,* September 27, 1917.

18. Ibid.

19. Interview with dermatologist John Wolf of Houston, Texas, August 1986. Dr. Wolf is an historian for the American Academy of Dermatology.

20. *Louisville Courier-Journal,* September 24, 1917.

21. Evan W. Thomas, *Syphilis: It's Course and Management* (New York: Macmillan, 1949).

22. The material on syphilis comes from a variety of standard texts including: Joseph Earle Moore, M.D., *Penicillin in Syphilis* (Springfield, Ill.: Charles C. Thomas, 1946); Thomas, *Syphilis: It's Course and Management;* Charles Clayton Dennie, M.D., *The History of Syphilis* (Springfield, Ill.: Charles C. Thomas, 1961); and *Grolier's Encyclopedia.* The discussion on morphine comes primarily from: Jerome H. Jaffe, *Morphine and Other Opium Alkaloids; Grolier's Encyclopedia; Opium from Growers to Pushers,* Peter and Betty Rose, trans. (1974); Alfred R. Lindesmith, *Addiction and Opiates* (1968); and Richard R. Lingeman, *Drugs from A to Z,* 2d ed. (New York: McGraw-Hill, 1974).

23. *Louisville Courier-Journal,* September 24, 1917.

24. Interview with dermatology historian John Wolf, August 1986.

25. Ibid.

26. Filson Club Collection: See letters dated February 21 and June 7, 1900, from Robert Worth Bingham to the respective doctors.

27. Ibid.: Letter dated July 16, 1917, from Hugh Young to Robert Worth Bingham.

28. Ibid.: Letter dated June 24, 1905, from Robert Worth Bingham to Michael Leo Ravitch.

29. *American Medical Association Journal,* March 15, 1947: Obituary of Dr. Michael Leo Ravitch.

30. As stated in the main text, Barry Bingham, Sr., takes the position that Mary Lily was an unsavable alcoholic and died because of it, while the Judge, to preserve her honor, remained silent. To prove the argument, Barry Bingham, Sr., has produced a 1933 affidavit and a 1940 letter from the papers of Hugh Young at the Alan Mason Chesney Medical Archives in the John Hopkins hospital library. According to the 1933 affidavit, in May 1917, on the eve of Young's departure for France, Bingham had written to Young saying that he had just discovered that Mary Lily was, said Young, "intermittingly a drunkard." Bingham told Young that regularly, once a month, "under some strange impulse," Mary Lily would shut herself up and drink herself into a stupor. He asked Young for help. Young interrupted his business and quickly made arrangements for Bingham to move to the Washington-Baltimore area under guise of joining the staff of Herbert Hoover, then the federal Food Conservation Commissioner in Washington. Young left for France and "was startled to hear about two months later that Mrs. Bingham had died as a result of one of those terrible sprees." Young said that upon his return from France in 1918, Bingham told him "the whole sordid story," including the rumors of morphine, poisoning, and the graveside autopsy. Young initiated an investigation and concluded there had been "no evidence of poison or foul play."

In the 1940 letter to Aleen Bingham, Young tells her that he interviewed some of the doctors who attended the graveside autopsy and that they had been duped by the Kenans into premature judgments of morphine and poisoning. Young concedes, however, that he was unable to obtain the original Bellevue autopsy report.

At first glance, the argument of Hugh Young and Barry Bingham, Sr., appears sound. But it has shaky foundations. For example, Young's hypothesis of alcoholism is based solely on what his friend Bingham told him in May 1917 when the morphine conspiracy was well underway. Furthermore, Young made extraordinary efforts in the midst of wartime to allow Bingham to move Mary Lily to the Baltimore area. But those arrangements were never followed up on by the Judge. There is no evidence that Bingham ever contemplated a move and the Hoover job was left dangling. In the meantime, Mary Lily signed the codicil and later died. Young's own 1918 investigation was confined to a minor figure in the graveside autopsy, Dr. William MacCallum, a colleague and subordinate of Young's at John Hopkins. The later investigation, in 1933, came as a consequence of Bingham's ambassadorial appointment and relied solely and vaguely on the memories of MacCallum and two other doctors. None of the three seemed to have kept notes from either the graveside autopsy or the Bellevue autopsy. Young approached Mary Lily's brother, Will Kenan, for permission to see the autopsy report and to retract the family accusations of doping and murder. Kenan refused.

The Young documents furthermore do not account for Bingham's calling in a dermatologist to treat Mary Lily's alleged heart condition, nor do they provide an answer to the heavy amount of morphine found in her system.

Young's sincerity is persuasive but his sources of information are flawed.

31. Associated Press dispatch, June 12, 1985. After spending more than $400,000 in private investigations on the case, Prince Alexander von Auersperg and Princess Annie-Laurie "Ala" Kneissl, children from Mrs. von Bulow's first marriage to an Austrian nobleman, were able to obtain prosecution of their stepfather on charges of attempted murder.

32. Ibid.

CHAPTER 17 Love

1. *Louisville Courier-Journal* and *New York Times,* December 19, 1937.
2. Letter dated May 8, 1986, from Barry Bingham, Sr., to author.
3. British guests were particularly prominent. Barry Bingham, Sr., and his wife still have a guest book the judge started. The first name in it is David Lloyd George, who had been prime minister of Great Britain. When the former King Edward VIII and his wife, the Duke and Duchess of Windsor, attended the 1951 Kentucky Derby, they stayed with their old friends the Binghams. See Joe Ward, "The Binghams: Twilight of a Tradition," *Louisville Courier-Journal* Magazine, April 20, 1986.
4. Ibid.
5. Bingham Genealogy. Robert was born on April 15, 1897. He had two marriages but no children and died in December 1965. Henrietta was born January 3, 1901, and had one marriage but no children. She died in June 1968. Barry was born February 10, 1906, and with his wife, Mary Clifford Caperton, had five children.
6. He was originally christened Robert Norwood Bingham, but his middle name was later changed to Worth.
7. Bloomsbury Square in London was the center of the group's social activities.
8. Interview with Sallie Bingham, January 1986; Alanna Nash, "The War Between the Binghams," *Working Woman,* September 1985; and Michael Kirkhorn, "The Bingham Black Sheep," *Louisville Today,* June 1979.
9. Ward, "The Binghams: Twilight of a Tradition."
10. Kirkhorn, "The Bingham Black Sheep."
11. Twice, in 1964 and 1974, *Time* magazine named the *Louisville Courier-Journal* one of the ten best daily newspapers in America during the previous decade. In 1984, however, in a stunning blow to the Binghams, it failed for the first time to make *Time's* best-ten list. During that time it was headed by Barry's son, Barry Bingham, Jr.
12. Interview with Barry Bingham, Sr., January 1986.
13. Nash, "The War Between the Binghams."
14. Ward, "The Binghams: Twilight of a Tradition."
15. Michael Wines (of the *Los Angeles Times* News Service) "A $300 Million Family Feud," *Miami Herald,* February 2, 1986; and interview with author.
16. Interview with Sallie Bingham. In 1983, after a three-year courtship, Sallie married Peters, a man who encouraged her feminist attitudes and provided discreet support in the family fight.

17. Interview with Worth Bingham's former *Chronicle* colleague, Donovan McClure, currently with the Kamber Group, Washington, D.C., August 1986.

18. Ibid.

19. Worth Bingham was one of a group of eleven businessmen who originally syndicated Cassius Clay, a young Louisville boxer who would win and rewin the heavyweight championship three times under the name of Muhammad Ali.

20. *New York Times*, January, 19, 1986. The church referred to is Episcopalian, the faith in which all the Louisville Binghams were raised.

21. Interview with Sallie Bingham, January 1986.

22. Interview with Barry Bingham, Jr., January 1986.

23. Ibid.

24. Interviews with Sallie Bingham, 1985 and 1986.

25. Ibid. Sallie Bingham has a twenty-three-year-old son, Barry, from her marriage to Ellsworth and two younger sons, William and Christopher, from her marriage to Iovenko.

26. Interview with Barry Bingham, Jr., January 1986.

27. Ibid.

28. Interview with Sallie Bingham.

29. Ibid.

30. Confidential interview, Courier-Journal building, Louisville, January 1986. The secretary asked that her name not be used.

31. Ward, "The Binghams: Twilight of a Tradition."

32. Ibid.

33. Interview with Barry Bingham, Jr., January 1986.

34. Interview with Sallie Bingham.

35. Interview with Barry Bingham, Jr., January 1986.

36. Ibid.

37. Interview with Sallie Bingham, January 1986. The managing editor reference is to Carol Sutton, who took the job in the mid-seventies. It was considered a real bold step for a paper of that size to do. Sutton went on to become ombudsman, and died in 1985.

38. Nash, "The War Between the Binghams."

39. Interview with Sallie Bingham.

40. Ibid.

41. Interview with Barry Bingham, Sr., January 1986.

42. Interview with Sallie Bingham.

43. For an example of liberal reputation: In August 1985, at the convention of the National Association of Black Journalists in Baltimore, Barry Jr. was awarded the Ida B. Wells Award for distinguished leadership in opening doors of employment opportunity for minorities in American journalism.

44. Interview with Sallie Bingham.

45. Interview with Barry Bingham, Sr., January 1986.

46. *New York Times*, January, 19, 1986.

47. Interview with Sallie Bingham.

48. Interview with Barry Bingham, Jr., January 1986.

49. Interview with Paul Janensch, January 1986.

50. Interview with Barry Bingham, Jr.

51. *Louisville Times*, January 9, 1986.

52. Congressional Record, January 15, 1986.

53. *Editor & Publisher*, May 24, 1986.

54. Interview with Sallie Bingham, July 10, 1986.

EPILOGUE

1. Noel Yancey, "The Kenan Legacy," *Spectator*, March 20, 1986.

2. Ibid.

3. Flagler Museum, Palm Beach, Florida: Ledger book F6916, pages 253 and 254.

4. Thomas S. Kenan III, *Sarah Graham Kenan Foundation* (privately published, Chapel Hill, 1984).

5. *American Weekly,* January 12, 1936.

6. *New York Times,* June 2, 1949.

7. Ibid., July 14, 1930.

8. Letter dated June 2, 1986, from Elizabeth M. Holsten, head of the Alumni Archives at the University of North Carolina, to author.

9. Michael Leo Ravitch, *The Romance of Russian Medicine* (New York: Liveright Publishing Corporation, 1937).

10. Ibid.

APPENDIX: THE COLONEL

1. William James Bingham was born April 6, 1802, and died February 19, 1866.

2. The school prospered even during the Civil War when Robert Bingham joined the Confederate army and William, prevented from entering the Confederate army because of a disability, became the dominant figure in the school's management. Late in 1863, while his brother was a prisoner of war, William officially became headmaster. A year later, in December 1864, he succeeded in obtaining a special, thirty-year charter for the school from the North Carolina General Assembly. Under its provisions, its pupils would be exempt from conscription until the age of eighteen, but would receive military training, live under military discipline, and be liable for mobilization as a separate unit in case of local emergency. Bingham himself, as headmaster, became an ex officio colonel in the state militia, and his instructors were likewise granted military commissions. By this charter, the school's curriculum was militarized for the first time, and, also for the first time, the school officially became "The Bingham School."

Meanwhile, William Bingham met with success in another quarter. During the war, he had written and published under Confederate imprint a Latin grammar (1863) and an edited translation of Caesar's Commentaries (1864). Following the war, both were used as textbooks in almost every state of the Union, and both remained in print for over twenty-five years. Bingham also produced an English grammar (1867) and a series of Latin readers. At the time of his death in 1873, less than thirty-eight years old, he was preparing a textbook on Latin prose composition.

3. Biographical sketch of William Bingham from Powell, *Dictionary of North Carolina Biography.*

4. Register's Genealogy. Thomas Steven Kenan, born February 12, 1838, graduated from the University of North Carolina in 1857, a year ahead of Robert Bingham. William Rand Kenan, born August 4, 1845, entered the university in 1860 at the age of fifteen.

5. John Milton Worth was born in 1811. His death in 1900 triggered a fierce estate fight between Bob Bingham and members of the Worth family.

6. In 1862–63, Jonathan Worth served in the legislature; he was elected state treasurer and reelected in 1864, holding the position until the state government was overthrown by the federal forces in 1865. When the provisional government was organized by President Johnson, Worth was continued in his position but resigned soon after in order to become a candidate for governor. He was elected by a large majority and continued in the executive office until July 1, 1868, when the existing state government was superseded by the one organized under the Reconstruction Act of Congress. He died at Raleigh, North Carolina, September 5, 1869.

7. The Bingham School 1921 yearbook, *Reveille to Taps;* Pack Memorial Library, Asheville, North Carolina: The fight at South Anna Bridge, June 26, 1863, was reported by Major Charles M. Stedman, the historian of the 44th Regiment.

8. "A Reminiscence" by Major Charles M. Stedman and Col. Robert Bingham in *North*

Carolina Regiments 1861–65, Vol. III, pages 24, 25, and 26, University of North Carolina archives. Hereafter referred to as Bingham Reminiscence. Bingham's hostage status derived from an 1831 Georgia state law which condemned to the gallows any abolitionist who should come into Georgia and "tamper" with the slaves. Some ten days prior to the fight at Santa Anna Bridge, Union general Straight, with 1,700 federal cavalry, had been captured by a force of 400 Confederates led by General Nathan Bedford Forrest. The state of Georgia insisted that under its law, the officers of the raiding party should be hanged. Despite the objections of Forrest and other leading Confederates, Georgia was prepared to hang Straight and his officers until the North, "very properly," says Bingham, detailed an equal number of Confederate officers to be hanged. Ultimately, the Confederate government persuaded Georgia to back down from its demands.

9. Bingham Reminiscence.

10. Ibid.

11. Ibid.

12. Register's Genealogy, page 33.

13. Shelby Foote, *The Civil War, A Narrative, Red River to Appomattox* (New York: Random House, 1974), pages 531–32.

14. Ibid., page 532.

15. Ibid.

16. Ibid., page 538.

17. Buried at the Appomattox National Monument is the famed banjo player Joe Sweeney, a native of Appomattox. He was the famed Confederate cavalry commander J. E. B. Stuart's official court musician and traveled with Stuart throughout his cavalry campaigns. Other Confederate commanders complained that Sweeney's playing and singing lured their troops to desert and join Stuart's command.

18. Bingham Reminiscence.

19. "The New South."

20. Ibid.

21. The flag was mounted on the wall of the office of the Colonel's grandson, Barry Bingham, Sr., at the time of my interview with him, January 1986.

INDEX

KENAN GENEALOGICAL TREE

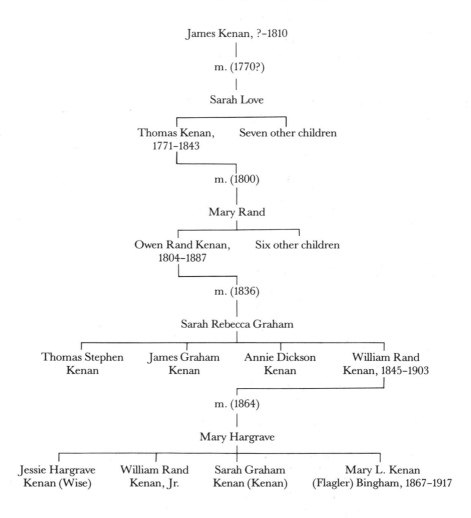

James Kenan, ?–1810

m. (1770?)

Sarah Love

Thomas Kenan,   Seven other children
1771–1843

m. (1800)

Mary Rand

Owen Rand Kenan,   Six other children
1804–1887

m. (1836)

Sarah Rebecca Graham

Thomas Stephen   James Graham   Annie Dickson   William Rand
Kenan   Kenan   Kenan   Kenan, 1845–1903

m. (1864)

Mary Hargrave

Jessie Hargrave   William Rand   Sarah Graham   Mary L. Kenan
Kenan (Wise)   Kenan, Jr.   Kenan (Kenan)   (Flagler) Bingham, 1867–1917